# Fantastic Modernity

# Fantastic Modernity

## Dialectical Readings in Romanticism and Theory

Orrin N. C. Wang

The Johns Hopkins University Press
Baltimore and London

© 1996 The Johns Hopkins University Press
All rights reserved. Published 1996
Printed in the United States of America
on acid-free paper
05 04 03 02 01 00 99 98 97 96   5 4 3 2 1

The Johns Hopkins University Press
2715 North Charles Street
Baltimore, Maryland 21218-4319
The Johns Hopkins Press Ltd., London

Library of Congress Cataloging-in-Publication Data
will be found at the end of this book.
A catalog record for this book is available from the
British Library.

ISBN 0-8018-5220-X

To the memory of the victims at
Tiananmen Square, 3 and 4 June 1989

# Contents

Acknowledgments  ix

**Introduction**
Fantastic Modernity  1

**Chapter 1**
Fantastic Reflexivities, Dialectical Transmissions  12

**Chapter 2**
Disfiguring Monuments:
History in Paul de Man and Percy Bysshe Shelley  37

**Chapter 3**
Allegories of Praxis:
Jerome McGann, Heinrich Heine, and the Ideology of
Romantic Discontent  69

**Chapter 4**
The Other Reasons:
Feminist Alterity, Feminist Romantic Studies, and
Mary Wollstonecraft   107

**Chapter 5**
American Askesis:
Harold Bloom, Ralph Waldo Emerson, and the Blinding
of America   144

**Epilogue**
Fantastic Futures, Postmodern Jacobins   182

Notes   189

Index   223

# Acknowledgments

Happily, this book owes its existence to a number of teachers, colleagues, and friends. It is my good fortune that my career has not kept these categories separate but has mixed them instead. Three individuals especially deserve my gratitude. W. J. T. Mitchell was an invaluable guide to this project from its start; he has remained a friendly and bracing inspiration who has shown me how the visionary eye and theoretical mind might meet. Neil Fraistat made several crucial interventions that brought this book to publication; he has taught me what it means to be a senior colleague in this profession. Finally, Marianne Conroy read every draft of this manuscript with a critical rigor that was as exemplary as it was unwavering; she has given me a standard of intellectual integrity that defines for me what we are about.

A number of other individuals read and commented upon various portions and versions of the book. I especially want to thank, for their intellectual generosity, James Chandler, Elizabeth Fay, Elke Frederikse, David Kaufmann, Jon Klancher, Alan Liu, Marshall Grossman, Jerome McGann, and Richard Strier. Stephen Arata, Jonathan Auerbach, Susan Lanser, Robert Levine, Elizabeth Loizeaux, Paula McDowell, John Morillo, Thomas Moser Jr., James O'Rourke, and David Wyatt all also gave me advice that was timely as it was necessary.

Parts of *Fantastic Modernity* were presented to the University of

Chicago Nineteenth-Century Workshop, the Washington Area Romanticists Group, and the Romanticism Seminar at the Center for Literary and Cultural Studies at Harvard University. I want to thank these groups, as well as my graduate students at the University of Maryland, for giving me the opportunity to clarify and explore many of the arguments of this book before receptive but demanding audiences. Also, Ann Steinecke and Elizabeth Gratch helped immensely in the preparation of the manuscript.

A Whiting Fellowship, University of Maryland Summer Grant, and American Council of Learned Societies Fellowship were all instrumental in giving me the time to complete this work. Also, parts of chapters 2, 3, and 5 have previously been published in, respectively, *Clio, ELH,* and the *Yale Journal of Criticism.*

Finally, a word about the dedication. The first version of what led to *Fantastic Modernity* was completed in early June of 1989. Motivating that version was my desire to contribute in some small way to working out the relation between theory and praxis, a relation that has been pilloried as much as exalted in North American and European universities. Those conceptual coordinates and their importance to *Fantastic Modernity,* so grimly cathected for me by the history of that late spring, have not changed. If anything, time has only made clearer how those coordinates frame the project at hand. To remember a moment beyond the North American university when the division between activism and the academy was enforced by the lives of students and others; to identify the meaning of that memory as a *theoretical* challenge—such concerns helped drive the completion of this book and defiantly attach themselves to its entrance into a larger public world.

# Fantastic Modernity

# Introduction

# Fantastic Modernity

> The time of the "learning to live," a time without tutelary present, would amount to this, to which the exordium is leading us: to learn to live *with* ghosts, in the upkeep, the conversation, the company, or the companionship, in the commerce without commerce of ghosts.
> 
> Jacques Derrida
> *Specters of Marx*

> That the world could be—or could have been—so remade, or I in it, that I could *want* it, as it would be, or I in it.
> 
> Stanley Cavell
> *In Quest of the Ordinary*

## I

This book is about the construction of knowledge, specifically the knowledge of Romanticism and postmodern literary theory. Over the past twenty-five years postmodern theory has reconfigured Romantic studies in a variety of ways. This book sets out to explore the political, cultural, and theoretical consequences of these most recent mediations of Romanticism.

Certainly, Romanticism has not been the only literary field affected by the advent of postmodern theory. In focusing on Romanticism's postmodern mediation, I join a number of critics who argue for a special relation not only between Romanticism and literary criticism but, more particularly, between Romanticism and postmodern critical theory.[1] I argue that there are two reasons for this singular relation. First, Romantic culture has to a large degree *always* been mediated. As Marilyn Butler writes, "Not until the 1860s did 'the Romantics' become an accepted collective name for Blake, Wordsworth, Coleridge, Scott, Byron, Shelley, and Keats, and an agreement begin to emerge about what an English Romantic Poet was like. . . . It was not until the twentieth century that there was analytical discussion of the abstraction 'Romanticism,' as a recognized term for theories of art, of the imagination, and of language."[2] Romanticism, then, has arguably always been a cultural invention, a historical and literary phenomenon that has always necessarily been theorized. While, moreover, other fields of literary and cultural study have also been retroactively constructed, Romanticism is distinguished by the way debates over its philosophical, aesthetic, and historical conception radically constitute its discursive force. Thus, insofar as postmodern theory argues for the mediated nature of knowledge—for its nonnatural, nontransparent state—a postmodern treatment of Romanticism displays a particularly compelling logic. As an object of study, Romanticism especially exhibits itself as a construction of knowledge; likewise, as a "general" critical disposition, postmodern theory focuses upon all knowledge as constructed. The postmodern reading of Romanticism thus vividly depicts the strategies by which Romantic knowledge has always implicitly or explicitly been known: by the transmission, revision, reception, and (mis)recognition of Romanticism's "acknowledged" authors and texts.[3]

The second reason for the singular relation between Romanticism and postmodern theory has to do with a trope that both share as a coordinate for their narrative intelligibility. For, if Romanticism is defined by its constant revisions, such revisions nevertheless consistently structure themselves around the same concept that gives contemporary theory its thematic and formal coherence: the trope of modernity, of the historical difference between the present and past. Romanticism and postmodern theory evince, however, an especially complex version of this trope. An intense dialectic informs the logic of modernity in Romanticism and postmodernism, in which the assertion of any moment as the founding origin of modernity is set against the ruthless derealization of that claim. As often as not, then, Romanticism and postmodern theory more correctly structure themselves around the trope of "fantastic modernity," in which the possibility of historical difference operates as an *aporia* of historical thought, a condition that testifies to the radical indeterminacy of historical difference as a stable form of human truth. The point of this testimony is not, however, simply to block historical thought; rather, in disputing the absolute claim of any historical event as the origin of modernity, fantastic modernity gestures toward the constitutive *mobility* of the trope of modernity, the way it *allows* various narratives of Romanticism and critical theory to prescribe implicitly or explicitly their political, literary, and epistemological interventions as eruptions of historical change. *Fantastic* refers to a phantasmic state that signals both the unrealized nature of modernity and the recalcitrance of modernity as a coding for the historical events and texts that make up Romantic and postmodern discourse.

Indeed, given the attacks by much postmodern thought upon historical categories and upon more historically particular definitions of modernity, this recalcitrance points to the way in which such attacks are still cryptonormative forms of modernity: postmodern theory, for all its challenges to historical thought, still implies, no matter how paradoxically, a break with the *epistēmē* of one retroactively conceived past.[4] Much of the singularity of the relation between Romanticism and postmodern theory derives, then, from this sense of the two as vocabularies not only on but also of the problem of modernity. They do not "solve" modernity either positively or negatively; rather, they dramatize how the dilemma of modernity incites various narratives of change, both during the late eighteenth and early nineteenth centuries and during the latter half of this century, within and beyond the confines of the North American university.

I thus employ the trope of fantastic modernity as an integral component of my own historical method and practice. If the mobility of such a trope makes one set of arguments irrelevant (whether modernity "genuinely" begins with 1789 or with Milton or with the end of a Greek antiquity), this fact asserts neither the relativism nor the interchangeability of historical events, only that those events are irreducibly open to an interrogation of the symbolic logic of their historical meaning; that their historicity, their "modernity" or "antiquity," cannot be known unless that historicity is itself made visible as part of what we can investigate tropologically and historically—two activities that necessarily interpenetrate. Likewise, if we can in fact historicize the temporal concept of modernity (as an idea in Western history which goes back to the late fifth or early sixth century or as the rise of a specifically secular historical consciousness in the eighteenth century), the trope of fantastic modernity would reject that historicization as an *absolute* condition for marking when modernity really begins.[5] Proving modernity is not what I want to do; investigating the political, epistemological, and social investments in specific figural deployments of modernity, both positive and negative, is my goal instead. I hope that the latter methodological emphasis will offer insights into a historical method that is actively sensitive to the demands of a postmodern historicism, the theoretical moment of this book's own fantastic modernity.

Both postmodern theory and Romanticism (as a body of "primary" works and as the writings of later Romanticists) are thus largely structured around the fantastic logic of modernity. In the next section I associate this logic with a short account of Romanticism's academic institutionalization and with two other ideas that organize this book: the concept of the representative figure and the notion of dialectical reading.

## II

In the literary academy the mobile troping of modernity has taken a concrete disciplinary form that, following Nietzsche, we may call a "fable" of the institutionalization of Romantic studies in the twentieth century.[6] As is well-known, this fable begins in the second decade of the twentieth century with high modernism's rejection of Romanticism, a dismissal that coincides with modernism's assertion of its own aboriginal modernity.[7] Thus, while Romanticism has been an object of professional academic scholarship as far back as the late nineteenth century, Romanticism enters the twentieth century as the negative discourse of modernism's more public, less university-bound cultural project. The next important incarnation of Romanticism occurs, however, within the boundaries of the academy, with the 1950s flourishing of academic Romantic studies in North America, signaled by such early works as Northrop Frye's *Fearful Symmetry* (1947) and M. H. Abrams's *Mirror and the Lamp* (1953) and carried on into the 1960s and beyond by Frye, Abrams, and other scholar-critics of the post–World War II generation such as René Wellek, Morse Peckham, Earl Wasserman, and the young Harold Bloom. The earlier Modernist critique had not completely effaced Romanticism from intellectual study, as the debates over Romanticism's relation to fascism and Bolshevism during the 1940s readily show. Yet, as many members of the post–World War II generation attest, there is a sense in 1950s Romantic studies of revitalizing a discourse that had earlier been relegated to the peripheries of academic and nonacademic culture.[8] This revitalization occurs, moreover, roughly during the time of two other related events: the similar installation of modernism within the university and the academic reinvention of Romanticism as the cultural origin of modernism's claims to modernity.

Beginning with Edmund Wilson's nonacademic *Axel's Castle* (1931) but continuing securely within the university through George Bornstein's *Transformations of Romanticism in Yeats, Eliot, and Stevens* (1976), a number of works argue that the Romantics are more modern than the Moderns. For the academic Romanticist this debate occasions both modernism and modern contemporaneity within Romanticism. That is, the Romantic scholar studies a modernity that begins with Romanticism, absorbs the cultural works of high modernism, and explains the "modern" moment of the Romanticist's own post–World War II era. It is within this modernity that the 1950s revitalization of Romantic studies takes place.[9] This temporal scheme is disrupted, however, by the "modernity" of postmodernism, which asserts a scission between the postmodern reading of Romanticism and the 1950s equation of Romanticism and modernism. Within this postmodern argument the temporal equivalence of Romanticism, modernism, and the "contemporary" post–World War II world suddenly becomes the antiquity not only of postmodernism but also, paradoxically, of a postmodern Romanticism.

Whereas, moreover, the 1950s revitalization of Romanticism was by and large a university-bound phenomenon, the postmodern revision of Romanticism is self-consciously attached to a dizzyingly expanded field of cultural practice. That is, in the 1960s, perhaps in the 1950s, a new cultural formation begins to be felt, what Fredric Jameson explains as the "enlargement of capitalism on a global scale."[10] While other theorists of postmodernism eschew Jameson's Marxist analysis, most agree with the sweep—the "global scale"—of his claims. Thus, like the documents of the Modernist movement over half a century earlier, the self-representations of postmodernism, for all their heterogeneous configurations, assert a modernity that occurs at a wide-ranging cultural, political, and socioeconomic level. Inside the academic confines of the university the event most obviously associated with this emerging formation—aside from, perhaps, the campus activism of the 1960s—is the theory "boom" of the '70s and '80s.[11]

Within the field of Romantic studies this wider disciplinary change coincides with a reconceptualization of Romantic knowledge carried out by a post–Vietnam War generation of scholars. In the 1970s the most visible and influential revision of Romanticism obtains in the deconstructive work of Paul de Man and other members of the loosely affiliated Yale School; the other important reinterpretation of Romanticism occurs with de Man's idiosyncratic colleague, Harold Bloom, and his theories of poetic influence and misprision. In the 1980s a new Romantic historicism emerges, informed by postmodern and poststructuralist theory; the most visible proponent of this multivaried historicism is Jerome McGann, who refunctions Romanticism through a materialist-driven ideological critique. Also gaining prominence in the mid-1980s is a feminist rereading of Romanticism, a revision powered by two different events: the reinterpretation of canonical Romanticism through theories of gender and sexual difference and the archival recovery of a number of eighteenth- and nineteenth-century female writers who lived just before, during, and after the six canonized male poets.

With the notable exception of Bloom, much of the revisionary work of the post-Vietnam generation is based on a disidentification with the Romantic modernity of the post–World War II generation. The secular humanist, archetypal, and phenomenological concerns of the '50s generation thus give way to a '70s and '80s stress on linguistic indeterminacy, historical aporias, ideological critiques, and identity politics. These changing theoretical concerns do not, however, dispute the troping of Romanticism as modernity; rather, the post–Vietnam War Romanticists largely reconfigure Romanticism's "primary" texts as the primal scene for their own postmodern theory. Complicating the immediate sense of a postmodern rupture, the post–Vietnam War generation's disavowal of the Romanticism of its '50s predecessors also coincides with this new generation's reappropriation of Romanticism as an originary site for its own postmodern modernity. This paradigm of the postmodern reconfiguration of Romanticism—a simultaneous disavowal and reappropriation of Romantic knowledge—occasions the intellectual tasks of the present book.

As its main focus, this study explores a number of key theoretical appropriations of Romanticism from the last twenty-five years. Insofar as the specific argument of each appropriation has larger implications for the study of both Romanticism and literary theory, these revisions of Romanticism evince the semiotic logic of what I call the "representative figure." This logic is itself ostensibly "Romantic," insofar as its genealogy can be traced back to Emerson's *Representative Men* (1850) and Carlyle's *On Heroes, Hero Worship and the Heroic in History* (1841), and then back further to Hazlitt's *Spirit of the Age* (1825).[12] It is this Romantic sense of equating the knowledge of a certain period or concept with a particular author which underwrites the examples of critical writings in this book. The representative figure operates at two levels: at those of the critical theorist and of the primary Romantic author being appropriated. As with my pairing of the deconstructive critic Paul de Man and the poet Percy Bysshe Shelley, the critical theorist represents a particular "school" of theoretical thought, while the Romantic writer represents a specific construction of Romanticism which advances the arguments of the theoretical school. Yet, at both levels, the way the representative figure actually operates must be qualified.

Associating each theorist with a representative logic implies, for example, a contemporary cultural and academic canonization of the theorist. For the critics I examine, however, such institutional dynamics are by no means stable. Thus, the merit of the representative figure for contemporary theory lies not in the a priori formulation of its application but, rather, in the very complication of its personifying logic, a problematic that gauges the specific conceptual and institutional situation of the various theoretical discourses being examined. The value of the representative figure lies, then, in the unevenness of its application, an asymmetry that becomes increasingly clear as the book chapters progress.

This representative logic does not actively ground the first chapter on Fredric Jameson, John Keats, A. O. Lovejoy, and Leo Spitzer, whose various works are instead acute examples of modernity's fantastic nature. The force of this logic is, rather, first seen with Paul de Man, whose status as a representative for American deconstruction—perhaps, even, for a certain postmodern identity for theory—seems the most appropriate methodological choice of the book. (Indeed, one could argue that the posthumous disclosures about de Man's wartime past have merely heightened the symbolic logic accruing to his place in the academy.) Yet even de Man's status is not simple, insofar as his essay "Shelley Disfigured" (1979) actually attacks the semiotic logic of the representative figure, what he calls the figural operation of "monumentalization" in Shelley's poem "The Triumph of Life" (1822). My next theoretical figure, Jerome McGann, represents a certain turn toward ideological and sociohistoric criticism in Romantic studies in the '80s; equally important, however, is the degree to which he does *not* represent the wide array of historically oriented criticism occurring inside and outside Romantic studies. It is this very gap that then comments upon the differences between contemporary Romantic historiography and other historical modes of inquiry, such as the Renaissance New Historicism of the 1980s. In the chapter on feminism and Romanticism no single representative figure can be found asserting, in a "definitive" manner, the relation between these two discourses. This very absence becomes a rallying point for a number of questions still facing feminist criticism today, such as the institutional relation of feminism to the rest of the American university and its genealogical relation to past intellectual traditions before the twentieth century. Finally, in the chapter on Harold Bloom the logic of the representative figure inverts itself: rather than simply representing a methodological school, the set of discourses I call "Bloomian pragmatics" work to construct a philosophy of the poetic self which coincides with the aura of Bloom's own idiosyncratic academic and literary persona. Thus, while feminist theorists resist the logic of the representative figure, Bloom is a representative figure without a recognizable constituency. This paradoxical status helps reveal one important aspect of Bloom's own inscription within the "American Sublime," his term for an American Romantic exaltation of an aboriginal vatic self. That is, Bloom's intellectual authority is based on a collective sense of history which his exaltation of the American self simultaneously signals and hides.

At the level of the primary Romantic authors being appropriated, the practice of the representative figure is complicated in two ways. The first qualification has to do with feminist Romanticists' negative appropriation of their representative figure, Mary Wollstonecraft. That is, Wollstonecraft represents one response to the Romantic tradition of masculine reason and feminine emotion which marks the *difference* between her feminist politics and those of feminist critics today. In contrast, Percy Bysshe Shelley represents a Romanticism of linguistic and historical skepticism which de Man employs positively to subvert a foundational Romanticism restored by aesthetic and literary history; likewise, the German poet and critic Heinrich Heine represents a tradition of Romantic discontent which McGann opposes to what he sees as a politically quietistic Hegelian Romanticism; and Ralph Waldo Emerson represents an American Romanticism of the self which Bloom uses to underwrite his Gnostic vision of the poetic authority of the individual life. Regardless of her negative appropriation, however, Wollstonecraft retains the same representative stature as Shelley, Heine, and Emerson. All four writers remain representative figures in the "heroically Romantic" sense, in that contemporary critics see them as championing—indeed, defining—a certain line of Romantic philosophical, literary, or political thought which critics can then use, either positively or negatively, to empower their own theoretical positions.

A second, more crucial complication lies in the way that the explicit representative roles of the Romantic writers inadequately convey the complete influence of their works upon their contemporary theoretical mediations. That is, the critical plots of de Man and the others are unable to secure completely the full historical and symbolic force of the primary Romantic narratives that they receive, revise, and reconstruct. Such contemporary critical plots cannot contain a semiotic excess in these narratives, an excess that then engages with and reconfigures the theoretical knowledge of the contemporary Romanticists and their critical schools. This fungible excess between the theorists and the Romantic writers creates an intense dialectic in which the subject and object of study— theory and Romanticism—mutually transform each other.[13] Postmodern theory's mediation of Romanticism thus occasions a series of hermeneutic instances in which the "truth" of that mediation is best approached by reading theory and Romanticism dialectically against each other. The primary analyses of *Fantastic Modernity* cohere around a number of such instances of "dialectical reading."

The critical disposition toward what I call dialectical reading most readily distinguishes this book from other works that mandate a special relation between Romanticism and literary theory. This book does not, in other words, focus upon Romanticism as simply an originary influence upon critical theory, in which a return to the *Biographia Literaria* might unproblematically explain the tenets of either New Criticism or deconstruction. Neither does this book solely view Romantic culture as a hegemonic formation that founds all the institutional and social conditions of intellectual labor that follow it. In that sense this book acknowledges the mediated nature of Romanticism as an-always-already theorized concept, yet it also insists upon the mediated state of the theoretical "metacommentary" that delivers Romanticism to us.[14] To begin to understand the social, cultural, and epistemological consequences of such metacommentary—to denaturalize and expose the commentary's own contingencies—a dialectical reading returns to the late-eighteenth- and early-nineteenth-century texts that retroactively form, though neither simply nor absolutely, Romantic discourse. Romanticism thus functions in this book as something besides either a completely mystified retroactive construction or a completely transparent, originary form of knowledge. The former is too determined, the latter too deterministic. Hence my stress on the mutually transforming dialectic that binds Romanticism and theory together. Romanticism is the transcoding of what it itself transcodes: at this moment, most visibly and forcefully, the discourse of postmodern theory. This dialectical disposition is thus as important a coordinate to my historical method as the phantasmic trope of modernity. Both mandate a human existence registered within a historical mode, even as—or precisely because—they expose the aporias and paradoxes that such an endeavor necessarily presupposes.

The overdeterminations of such historicity also tie Romanticism to postmodernism in a more specific way. Inevitably, questioning modernity's place in postmodernism means asking whether, at this historical juncture, radical historical change can carry any of the simultaneous hope and trauma of 1789, when Romanticism projected itself into the *future* as a vocabulary of modernity. To decide whether Romanticism still provides a viable vocabulary for the future is to participate in the very fantastic structure of modernity which this present study examines. Indeed, if Romanticism does appear today as merely a mystified reification of a pre-postmodern, temporally linear past, it could be argued that the era of "high" theory has also come and gone. Today in the academy, so it is claimed, we engage not in abstract theory but in cultural practice. It is exactly the unproblematic assumption of this trope of modernity, of a transparent move from theory to praxis, that many of the Romanticists and theorists in this book challenge. In doing so, their point is not to elide but, rather, to foreground the question of change in their "era," in their moment of contemporaneity. The question thus remains: as the solidity of the twentieth century's global order continues to melt into air, will both the modernity of Romanticism and literary theory exist only as Western museum pieces, or will they still somehow, dialectically, inform the world we inhabit?

Chapter 1

# Fantastic Reflexivities, Dialectical Transmissions

Elaborating the concepts of modernity and dialectical reading allows for the association of surprisingly disparate events: the contemporary Marxist wagers, for example, of Fredric Jameson's analysis of postmodernism and the historical paradoxes underwriting John Keats's simultaneous invention and acquisition of cultural capital in early-nineteenth-century England. Yet the juxtaposition of these events does not mean that they are all simply absorbed by a univocal, monolithic metacode of modernity. For, if the politics of modernity inheres in the project of effecting historical change, the modernity being effected is as heterogeneous as the contingencies of history: not only the emancipatory Romantic trajectories of 1789 or a postmodern post-1960s fin de siècle but also, as the debate between A. O. Lovejoy and Leo Spitzer demonstrates, a Romantic object of study denoted by the practice of European fascism before and during World War II. If the radical self-reflexivity of a dialectical historicism does not allow any of these events to cohere simply into a readily explainable thing-in-itself, neither does the radical aporia of this historicism's troping of modernity transcend such reflexive obstructions and reach an essential, idealized state. As the texts on Romanticism and theory in this chapter show, the historical knowledge of dialectical historicism inheres *within* such obstructions.

# Keats, Jameson, and the Postmodern Urn

> . . . to hope, till Hope creates
> From its own wreck the thing it contemplates
> Percy Bysshe Shelley
> *Prometheus Unbound*

Whether the discussion turns to Coleridge's *Biographia Literaria* or M. H. Abrams's *Mirror and the Lamp* or Jacques Derrida's and Paul de Man's contemporaneous readings of Rousseau, it can be said that our knowledge of Romanticism is largely mediated by a sense of the privileged relation between Romanticism and literary criticism. In the last twenty-five years this privileged sense has been accompanied by a set of increasingly controversial sentiments, ranging from exhilarating intimations of sublime potentialities to anxious prophecies of Western culture's forthcoming diaspora. Not coincidentally, this trajectory runs parallel to the absorption of the discipline of literary criticism by a number of increasingly polemical and ambitious terms—first *literary theory* and then just *theory,* which itself seems to exist in literature departments as both synecdoche and metaphor for our collective experience of what has come to be called the "postmodern." It might be profitable, then, to explore the current privileges, and responsibilities, of Romanticism's relation to literary theory by way of pinning down in more exacting fashion the overlapping boundaries of Romanticism and postmodernism. To do so means putting a number of other conceptual terms on the table. One key notion is how our postmodern age is informed by both a certain resistance to and retrieval of reflexivity. The other key notion risks making a general "ism" remark about the relation between Romanticism and postmodernism: that one way we can make the relation between Romanticism and postmodernism intelligible is to think of them as two vocabularies, two fields of knowledge which configure themselves around the vertiginous problem of modernity.

The only term comparable in semantic inflation to either *Romanticism* or *postmodernism,* however, is *modernity.* The relationship of Romanticism to two common uses of *modernity* demonstrates, in fact, the rather inchoate genealogical ground on which discussions of postmodernism and postmodernity take place. That is, insofar as we perceive the postmodern to be working off twentieth-century modernism, postmodernism asserts its own identity as a break with a period that represents itself as post-Romantic; on the other hand, insofar as postmodernity conceives of itself as somehow discontinuous with the Enlightenment trajectory of reason, our contemporary condition asserts its own identity as a break with an epoch that is pre-Romantic. This rather sweeping contrast could of course be enormously complicated historically, but that is exactly my point: the slippage occurring between these two uses of modernity exemplifies the unavoidable problem that modernity foregrounds even as it proposes itself as the solution to that problem. I refer to the question of historical identity and difference, which modernity structures around the possibility of a break with the past, the potentiality of a present and future defined by their exteriority to what has come before them. I use *modernity,* then, as, quoting Jürgen Habermas, the "consciousness of an epoch that relates itself to the past of antiquity, in order to view itself as the result of a transition from the old to the new," with the added proviso that antiquity need refer not only to the classical world but also to a past as mobile as the plurality of presents and futures of modernity's own asserted new moment.[1]

It is fairly easy for us to see how, as Herbert Lindenberger writes, "If theories of romanticism formulated during that time we have labeled romantic could generally be termed theories of modernity, later theories of romanticism have no less tended to concern themselves with the nature and problems of modernity."[2] Indeed, for the authors of Romanticism's "primary" texts and the generations of readers and scholars following them, the trope of Romanticism as a site of revolutionary or reactionary energies addressing a desired or lamented break with the past becomes one of the basic paradigms within the Romantic hermeneutic. I would thus venture to say that most Romanticists are comfortable with at least the proposition of Romanticism as a discourse taken up with notions of newness and historical change; this is certainly true of the Romantic scholarship of the last decade, with its own version of Romanticism cathected around the events of 1789, an investment that places our own interpretive practices within what Ernesto Laclau and Chantal Mouffe have suggestively called the "Jacobin imaginary."[3]

I would argue that postmodernism, like Romanticism, articulates the concerns of this larger sense of modernity with a particular vehemence. At its most ambitious, postmodernism employs the language of a new cultural dominant, or *epistēmē,* to posit our historical difference with the past. Of course, postmodernism also foregrounds the scandal of thought involved in asserting such a difference, as thinkers as varied as François Lyotard, Gianni Vattimo, and Francis Fukuyama identify the postmodern condition primarily by its discontinuity with history as a foundational category for human thought and action. For such thinkers the rupture implicit in postmodernism is precisely the break with an ontology based on historical progress and change. We are all familiar with the epistemological dances resulting from this paradox in the *récits* of postmodernism; we are also, however, familiar with them in the *récits* of Romanticism. That is, Romanticism's modernity is as paradoxical as postmodernism's, for, if we associate Romanticism with a certain originary historical moment, we also associate it with a discourse that exposes and demystifies the hypostatisization of that moment. From Byron and Heine to Lovejoy and de Man, from the Victorians' first use of *Romanticism* to McGann's ideological critique of the term, the assertion of Romanticism's modernity as an authentic moment of historical origination is accompanied by a discourse of skepticism and ruthless critique. Conversely, if we associate postmodernism with a radical skepticism about historical identity and change, we should also admit to the "cryptonormative" project of modernity, in Habermas's terms, which still underwrites the radical nature of this skepticism, the degree to which the decentered universe of postmodernism is still covertly oriented around avant-garde aspirations toward innovation—the shock of the "post-new," as it were.[4] Modernity's paradoxical yearnings, then, help us to see how much Romanticism is actually postmodern and how much postmodernism is still Romantic.

This formulation, of course, associates Romanticism with a teleological historicism and postmodernism with an epistemological or ontological obstruction of that historicism.[5] The trope of modernity implies more strictly a condition in which both this teleological imperative and its obstruction inform Romanticism and postmodernism simultaneously. In other words, both Romanticism and postmodernism participate in what I call a "fantastic modernity," in which it is precisely the phantom nature of modernity which at once blocks and enables our access to historical identity and difference. Fantastic modernity *is* the spirit of the Romantic and postmodern age(s), insofar as we read *spirit* not as an idealist *aufhebung* but, rather, as the ghostly sign of modernity's presence, an indeterminacy that is precisely the condition—rather than the exorcism—of the possibility of historical thought.

It is this indeterminacy that I want to link up to the question of reflexivity. Postmodernism has often been described as a condition of hyper-reflexivity, with its stress on metacritical modes of framing discourse. Yet, insofar as reflexivity predicates the possibility of critical distance and the self-consciousness of a centered being, postmodernism can also be defined as a resistance to an activity better situated within the confines of high modernism or, more distantly, the Romantic wagers of the Kantian subject. Indeed, within a certain residual but nevertheless influential formation of Romantic studies, it can be said that Romanticism is defined by the reflexive conundrum of the epistemological and ontological subject facing the objective world. The exemplary text for this formation would be Earl Wasserman's seminal essay "The Grounds of Knowledge" (1964). Wasserman's piece focuses, however, on how the Romantic writers ostensibly solve the problem of the subject-object duality. For Wasserman, Romantic poetry attempts to confirm a metaphysically discrete identity, whether through the all-absorbing Wordsworthian subject or the more complicated Shelleyan process that sidesteps the subject-object duality altogether.[6] What I want to stress, instead, is how the reflexivity of this duality actually installs a certain constitutive indeterminacy within the construction of any such identity, especially the identities that undergird the exigencies of historical periodization. It is, then, within this more radically indeterminate context that the conflicted role of reflexivity in postmodernism can best be understood as a realization of the aporia of modernity adumbrated earlier; I thus turn to two very differently canonized texts to demonstrate this relation between reflexivity and modernity's fantastic nature, with the hopes of illuminating the specific consequences this relation might have for the interpenetrating practices of Romantic studies and postmodern discourse.

My first example is Fredric Jameson's essay "Postmodernism, or The Cultural Logic of Late Capitalism" (1984); my second is John Keats's poem "Ode on a Grecian Urn" (1819). The relation between these two works is not strictly dialectical; their juxtaposition is not generated by Jameson's appropriation of either Keats's poem or the Romanticism that Keats might represent. Indeed, Jameson's relationship to Romanticism has always been tangential to his wide-ranging thought. At times Jameson defines Romanticism as Raymond Williams does, as a mystification of capital relations at the beginning of the West's industrial era. Unlike, say, Jerome McGann, however, Jameson does not see this mystification as having any real influence over our present in the way that modern and postmodern "abstractions of the sign" increasingly do.[7] At other times *Romanticism* is for Jameson simply the term that is displaced by Lukács's reading of Walter Scott's novelistic consciousness as a historical realism. Indeed, in contrast to my institutional fable, Jameson's modernism reacts to this realism much more centrally than to Romanticism per se. If anything, then, the juxtaposition of Jameson and Keats critiques the peripheral role of Romanticism in Jameson by demonstrating how "The Cultural Logic of Late Capitalism" and "Ode on a Grecian Urn" surprisingly share a conflicted reflexivity that sets up a dialectical relation *within* each work, involving each author and his respective object of study, his respective moment of modernity.

In his seminal work Jameson argues that one of postmodernism's effects is to abolish the distance between the critical subject and the critical object, creating the loss of critical self-consciousness or reflexivity.[8] Yet that essay, and the book within which it now appears, can also be seen as a work of supreme theoretical reflection, since Jameson's project is also a sustained effort to "cognitively map" the historical moment of late capitalism which allows for postmodernism, an effort that cannot escape the critical distance that enables Jameson to theorize postmodernism's elision of that very same distance. As he defiantly writes, "I have . . . meant to offer a periodizing hypothesis, and that at a moment in which the very conception of historical periodization has come to seem most problematical indeed."[9] Thus, the very epistemological giddiness of being literally lost in the Bonaventure Hotel in Los Angeles becomes for Jameson an orienting marker for a new reflection upon the mutation of postmodern space. Moreover, insofar as this postmodern space of dissolving distances and perspectives is the habitat of the postmodern critic, Jameson's project is one in which theoretical reflection is a *self*-reflection coinciding with the question of modernity. Put simply, the tension between Jameson's cognitive mapping and his postmodern loss of critical distance characterize a critical project that is trying to recognize and think through its own cultural present as a new identity— a project that is trying to recognize as its own critical object its own new self. Thus, Jameson's very apprehension of postmodernism sets into motion a critical subject trying to understand a critical object that is that very same subject; far from erasing the distance between subject and object, this motion sets itself up as a critical reflexivity that asserts the distance between critical subject and object as a metonymic and synecdochic relation obsessed with what is new: the modernity of postmodernism.

I describe this relation as "metonymic" in the sense that all the cultural events that Jameson describes—from the Bonaventure to Warhol's *Diamond Dust Shoes* to the loss of critical distance—operate as substitutes not only for the situation of the postmodern critic but also for the situation of postmodernism itself, which, even when totalized by Jameson's cognitive mapping, still operates as *only another* contiguous displacement for that which, as Jameson readily admits, cannot be fully conveyed by the realm of the symbolic. For Jameson the symbolic and the historical real have always been incommensurate. In "The Cultural Logic of Late Capitalism," however, the problem of representation appears especially charged, so much so that the essay concludes by calling for a new postmodern political art that will achieve a "breakthrough to some as yet unimaginable new mode of representing" postmodernism's "fundamental object—the world space of multinational capital."[10] The odd position of Jameson's essay, as somehow immediately before this representational "breakthrough," or *coupure,* gives his examples of postmodernism their metonymic quality, their sense of metonymically extending rather than metaphorically completing what has yet to be represented. By insisting, moreover, that "multinational capital" encodes postmodernism's cultural logic, Jameson stresses how his examples exist not discretely but, rather, contiguously in relation to that capital—a move that inadvertently exacerbates further the figural effect of metonymic displacement in the essay.

At the same time, however, Jameson's insistence on the centrality of late capitalism in his analysis causes a contrary rhetorical effect. That is, the relation between the essay's critical subject and postmodern object is *also* "synecdochic" in that Jameson's entire point is to regulate his metonymic chain precisely toward what he believes ultimately conditions the symbolic: the totalizing ground and final horizon of our contemporaneity which is the vast complex undertaking of late capitalism's present historical moment. Of course, it is exactly this reclamation of conceptual closure from a metonymic chain poised to resist any final identity (any complete semiotic suture) which distinguishes Jameson's Marxist postmodernism from the post-Marxism of, for example, Laclau and Mouffe. What has been reintroduced, then, in a particular political valence, is the question of whether Jameson's reflexivity has resolved itself into a final identity that allows us to recognize the postmodern object of study for what it is, whether his Marxist reflection does indeed secure the modernity of postmodernism as the final horizon of capital's latest purest form.

Far from answering this question, I want to make its irresolution exemplary of precisely the type of reflexive thinking connected to the problem of making both postmodernism's and Romanticism's modernity intelligible to us. If, in other words, Jameson's project does retrieve a certain critical distance, it is as a spatial figure that dramatizes the contrary demands of the metonymic and synecdochic, a radical indeterminacy that underwrites both the reflecting subject and the modernity reflected upon, a reflexivity that, far from simply consolidating the identities of the subject and its historical moment, turns both far more problematically into the ghostly, partial, *and* necessary figures of historical thought.

It is as a poem about such strange historical compulsions that I want to consider Keats's "Ode on a Grecian Urn," one of Romanticism's best-known artifacts, which, until recently, has not been given enough due as a complex meditation on how cultural artifacts convey historical difference and identity.[11] While since Cleanth Brooks the ode has usually been read as simply transcending the category of the historical, the poem's questions actually form a paradigm for the reflexive stance of the ode as a discourse of and on modernity. These questions assail a cultural artifact that is being transformed precisely into such an object by those questions, by the new interpretive attention being paid to it. As such an artifact, the urn refers not only to its past creation but also to the new historical moment that can "create" an urn on display. The speaker's questions thus replay the aesthetic and historical options that the poem's imaginary has for articulating that historical moment and its artifact; more important, those questions also replay the options of the poet as cultural critic gazing at the urn. Thus, the study of the urn by Keats's speaker is a reflexive study of the potentiality of the narrator's new relation to a new historical moment, a potentiality instanced by the poem's articulation of an emergent cultural modernity.

This articulation occurs on several different levels. First, the ode coincides with the nineteenth-century transition from private to museum collections which allows for a new consumer of a new aesthetic object—an object realized, moreover, by a new era of Anglo-European economic and military adventurism dating from the previous century. Indeed, the historical backdrop for the two acquisitions that most legitimize the British Museum in the early nineteenth century, the Egyptian collection that includes the Rosetta Stone (1802) and the Greek Elgin Marbles (1816), is Great Britain's global struggle with Napoleonic France. Coupled with this new moment in Anglo-European colonialism is also another eruption of the new which the museum sensibility of Keats's ode conveys: the complex, oftentimes contradictory responses to class formation and upheaval that orient the ode's cultural mission of aesthetic discrimination and taste. As scholars have noted, the British Museum's own collection could not have increased without the benefit of private aristocratic donations; England's neo-Hellenic revival dates at least partially back, moreover, to the Dilettanti Society, a mostly aristocratic group that undertakes a number of archival expeditions to Greece between 1734 and 1852.[12] Thus, the trajectory that allows for the movement from private to museum collections is not one of a uniform transition between two discrete identities, one aristocratic and the other populist; rather, the history of the museum in England is itself one of conflicting forces working out the class contradictions among public display, private consumption, and aristocratic privileges.[13]

These contradictions most visibly manifest themselves in the notoriously short visiting hours, perfunctory tours, and openly hostile tour guides that ordinary visitors at the British Museum endured at the turn of the century. Especially intense at the museum's inception in 1753, a fear of mob attendance guided in varying degrees the explicit policies of the museum well into Victorian times. Thus, the museum's mission of public display also announces its own resistance to the class implications of that project, a resistance that finds a special resonance, I would suggest, both in the literal physical effort that Keats requires in order to experience the visual sources of his poem's urn—through visits to the British Museum and in books belonging to the libraries of friends—and in the tenuousness of his larger class aspirations.[14] Exacerbating the class complexity that attends this conflicted nature of the museum is the point that the neo-Hellenic revival is not only for the upper and middle classes a phenomenon of architecture and art but also one of furniture and fashion, a phenomenon that confounds, in other words, the simple separation between aesthetic experience and mass consumption and the intelligible coordination of distinctions based on class and taste. The interpellation by Keats's ode of the urn as a cultural artifact asserts, then, an experience of Hellenism which is properly "aesthetic" and "historical" insofar as those categories align themselves with a certain elevation of cultural experience which opposes the "nonaesthetic" consumption of a nascent mass culture. The conceptual and literal space for this elevated cultural experience is the museum (*mouseion:* "place for the muses"), an emerging formation that in Keats's ode attempts to reconcile the contradiction between public access and aristocratic privilege by imaging the museum experience as a repetition of the experience of the individuated private collector: a repetition of a certain representation of upper-class experience—that is, the aesthetic—as the very realization of lower- and middle-class expectations paradoxically unleashed by the growing volatility of class relations.

This imaging of collective class aspiration as an individuated aesthetic experience helps to extend not only Martin Aske's remark about the privatizing character of Keats's Hellenic imagination but also Philip Fisher's characterization of "Ode on a Grecian Urn" as a museum with one work inside.[15] The oddness—and veracity—of Fisher's description is borne out in the tension between how the poem's litany of questions seems to conform to the lyrical generic expectations of a single poetic speaker and how the poem does not actually offer any real evidence of such a subject. That is, while we habitually assume the structure of the poem is that of the poet addressing the urn, the work differs radically from "Ode to a Nightingale," with its almost obsessively narcissistic grammatical relay of first-person signifiers. Indeed, aside from the possible specular logic of "Urn's" second-person hermeneutic (if there is a *thou* there must be an *I*), the only grammatical anchors for the ode's poetic voice are the rather pale first-person plural possessives—"our rhyme" and "woe / than ours"—in stanzas 1 and 5. The poem thus works through an odd, ongoing dislocation of voice which marks the dissonance between the museum as the place of a new collective access to culture and the poem's own imagined museum of the individual private collector and the individual artifact. This dissonance explains the mystified underpinnings to one interpretation of the poem's famous last line, in which *ye* refers to a human subject addressed by the urn. This reading of *ye* must be coordinated with the urn's earlier description as "a friend to man" (l. 48).[16] To read the poem's *ye* as an individuated human subject still requires us to acknowledge how *ye* participates in the larger significations of "man," a category whose representative logic refers not only to the individual but also to the human race. The poem's *ye* thus describes subjectivity through the discourse of bourgeois universalism, in which collective experience is mystified as the universal experience of an individual aesthetic consciousness. Precisely through this bourgeois tension between a privatized subjectivity and a larger collectivity, Keats's ode participates in the construction of "culture" which is, as Raymond Williams argues, the very hallmark of eighteenth- and early-nineteenth-century Europe and England—a hallmark, in other words, of their own self-reflexive modernity.[17]

The very scandals of thought which attend this construction should warn us, however, against simply conferring on that self-reflexivity the success of a self-contained closure. Such success becomes confounded when the poem's refusal to confirm either the singular or collective status of its narrative voice reappears at a number of other different levels of the poem's self-reflexive modernity. At the biographical level one might note the friable nature of Keats's own class standing, the irresolute hold he has on the access to culture which underwrites the ode's museum sensibility. The most important semiotic irresolution of the ode's specific cultural modernity occurs, however, in the urn's own relation to the challenge of literary history which both Keats and later readers of his poem confront. Insofar as the urn functions as a sign for a new neo-Hellenic revival, we can see Keats as trying to use that neo-Hellenism as a metonymic substitute for his own new poetic moment, what the Victorians will designate retroactively as Romanticism. Aske has suggestively written about the difficulties that inhere in Keats's appropriation of Greek culture for his own literary imaginary, how the temporal position of Keats "necessarily engenders a contrary sense of the alterity of Greece."[18] I would complicate Aske's point by further asserting that in "Ode on a Grecian Urn," at least, the alterity of Greece metonymically becomes the alterity of Keats's own present: the historical consciousness that allows the poem to consider its own discrete modernity is simultaneously an awareness of how fantastic such a proposition is. This proposition still structures the inquiries of our own cultural histories: we ourselves continue to work through the poem's reflexive modernity, insofar as we read Keats's cultural artifact for the same reason his poet gazes at *his* artifact. That is, as the poet's urn enables Keats to name his poetic modernity through a neo-Hellenic classicism, Keats's "Urn" enables us to name our modernity through Romanticism. We can thus see the present discussion of Keats's poem as merely the latest repetition of this reflexive hermeneutic, as it considers the metonymic relation between our fin de siècle modernity and the twin cultural artifacts—the twin "urns"—of Romanticism and postmodernism.

By reflexively invoking our own metonymic relation to Keats's poem, I am of course reintroducing the problem of the metonymic versus the synecdochic which underwrote Jameson's project, the question of whether Romanticism and postmodernism are part of an infinite chain of substitutions trying to name the phantasm of our modernity or whether either term or both together do consolidate a totalizing historical identity to which we belong. The radical irresolution of this historicizing problem is highlighted in two lines of the poem, lines usually overlooked during the typical hermeneutic frenzy that we associate with it. I refer to the unassuming transitional lines of the last stanza which follow the speaker's apostrophizing the urn as a "Cold Pastoral": "When old age shall this generation waste, / Thou shalt remain, in midst of other woe" (ll. 46–47). These words appear simply to reinforce the philosophical conundrum of aesthetic permanence versus human finitude which charges the more obviously cathected lines describing the urn's existence.

What if, however, we take the speaker seriously when he describes human finitude through the image of a generation's mortality? We might then simply ask: How do we know when a generation has passed and, conversely, when another generation—another zeitgeist, or historical moment—has been born? How do we recognize our own historical moment, so that we can recognize "other woe / than *ours*" (my emphasis)? How do we record, register, or acknowledge—how do we *read*—the historical fact that is the difference between antiquity and modernity? We do so by interpellating as an artifact objects such as the one that

Keats's ode defines precisely against the vicissitudes of history. We do so by seeing in the urn the funeral "urn" of language, the Heideggerian sense of poetry which links human mortality to history by defining language as the encrypted, entombed, and monumentalized place of absent human experience. We hollow out the urn into the endlessly deferring nonclosure of a reflexive fantastic modernity—what the ode's aestheticization of the urn paradoxically also accomplishes, insofar as the poem defines that aestheticization against a historical event, a generation's passing—which is only made intelligible through the semiotic participation of the urn, exactly what the poem withholds. It is thus the irresolution of an aesthetic and historical intelligibility which marks the place of the urn and its interrogator, whose questions demonstrate an attempted cultural self-recognition that is neither absolute nor total but, rather, precisely the reflexivity of a subject defined by the nonclosure—the fantastic status—of its asserted modernity.

Several implications can be drawn from imaging the reflexivity of modernity as first and foremost this radical nonclosure of historical identity. First, far from simply blocking our access to history, such nonclosure has in fact oriented historical studies of Romanticism for the last decade: such studies have opportunistically seized on the derealization of Romanticism as a stable identity as the starting point for their own constructions of Romanticism as a cultural artifact. The postmodern value associated with this artifact might increasingly be its exemplary artifice, the degree to which it demonstrates the nonnatural and nontransparent fact of one field of human knowledge. In that case the reflexivity of modernity might provide a sufficiently complex route for postmodern Romanticists tracking not only the two-hundred-year-old transmission and revision of Romanticism but also the critical discourses underwriting such transmission, revision, *and* tracking.

Second, I would argue that Romanticism and postmodernism transcode modernity in a particularly cathected manner, which, while certainly not essential, carries all the hegemonic force of past historical contingencies. I risk describing this cathexis as the problem of utopia, which both Jameson's and Keats's works confront in obviously different but equally urgent and brutal fashion. To confront this problem both urgently and brutally is to identify the tension that I have located in the phantasm of modernity's aporetic wagers. It is to locate that tension between a radical historical undecidability and the assertion of genuine historical change, the moral and political equivalent of what Thomas Vogler, in assigning Romanticism the status of a teleological trajectory, has called the "Romantic discourse of desire," or "our desire for a certain kind of form."[19] Such a tension lends a gravitational force to the recreation of Romanticism's texts through the languages of postmodernism, which might explain why so many Romanticists have been and are theorists. That is, for the reflexive postmodern Romanticist of the past twenty-five years, the most important candidate for the postmodern urn might be neither the Bonaventure Hotel nor video but, rather, theory itself, in metonymic and synecdochic relation to a practice in a world that is perpetually—urgently and brutally—just about to be.

Theory, then, is the privileged medium by which contemporary Romanticists know the phantasmic structure of their own postmodern modernity. When theory is also the medium for the contemporary (re)production of Romantic knowledge, *that* is when the conditions for a dialectical relation between theory and Romanticism occur. A similar situation happens with the post–World War II generation of Romanticists, in that such scholars use their methodologies to construct a Romanticism that subsumes the modernity of both modernism and of the Romanticists' own contemporaneous moment. The difference between this earlier metacritical moment and ours obtains in how the postmodern reappropriation of Romanticism simultaneously rejects this earlier subsumption—a predicament that speaks to why postmodern readings of Romanticism appear even more metacritical than the earlier generation's.

Nevertheless, the dialectical relation between Romanticism and theory is not without its precedents. Indeed, the following example of a dialectical reading of Romanticism occurs before the post–World War II generation's revitalization of Romantic studies. It concerns an explicitly politicized Romantic modernity that the '50s revitalization had in fact to "forget" in order to assert its own modern Romantic moment.[20] The success of this institutional amnesia is evinced in the uncanny affinities between debates about this earlier politicized Romanticism and about the politics of theory in the 1980s. These affinities speak to another important phenomenon: how the dialectical relation between Romanticism and theory which inheres in Romanticism's institutional transmission is often structured around a further dialectic between theory and praxis.

## Lovejoy, Spitzer, and the Reading of Romanticism and Fascism

> Every historical rupture, every advent of a new master-signifier, changes retroactively the meaning of all tradition, restructures the narration of the past, makes it readable in another, new way.
>
> Slavoj Žižek
> *The Sublime Object of Ideology*

> ... this *age,* which authors call this *critical age,* and divines this *sinful age,* and politicians this *age of revolutions* ... I choose to call it without epithet *this* age.
>
> Coleridge to Mary Evans
> 7 February 1793

Debates over the politics of theory have not stressed enough the metalepsis structuring such discussions. That is, by "politics" literary critics and historians mean either the degree to which the findings of theory will affect the structures of power within and beyond the academic institution or, conversely, the degree to which theory itself has been affected by sociohistoric practices that frame the theoretical field. In any discussion about the politics of theory it is rare to find both of these meanings given equal attention; indeed, it is more often the case that an emphasis on one meaning delimits, if not outright negates, the other. What if, however, we begin with a less broad but nonetheless exacting political responsibility? What if we first locate our political will metacritically, by considering how theory affects (and effects) praxis precisely by interrogating itself *as an effect* of sociohistoric practice?

My example of this more complicated formula is a debate that occurs between A. O. Lovejoy and Leo Spitzer during 1941–44, on the relation between German Romanticism and national socialism. In his 1941 article "The Meaning of Romanticism for the Historian of Ideas" Lovejoy argues for a continuity between a nexus of concepts—organicism, dynamism, and diversification—found in both German Romanticism and in German fascism.²¹ In his 1944 response, "*'Geistesgeschichte'* vs. History of Ideas as Applied to Hitlerism," Spitzer argues for the incompatibility between these two historical and cultural phenomena and the ideas associated with each of them.²² In examining this debate, I do not want so much to ascertain who is right or wrong as to show how their argument necessarily changes theory into praxis by transforming the institutional function of each of their articles into "performative speech acts" of the academy. This transformation is striking because, first, it demonstrates how both Lovejoy's and Spitzer's methods constitute a large part of the *object* of the debate and, second, because it shows how each method directly addresses the topic of this present analysis, the relation of theory to praxis.

It is also difficult to say what is more uncanny, the resemblance of their argument to the debate over the disclosures about the literary critic Paul de Man and his work for a collaborationist paper in Nazi-occupied Belgium in the early 1940s or the invisibility of this earlier argument in the present debate over de Man.²³ Not only are both debates structured by the historical fact of the European intellectual emigré in the American university; they also occur within apparently overlapping discursive fields, with each field interrogating the semantic, cultural, and political meaning of Romanticism and fascism.²⁴ That latter resemblance is problematic, however, since de Man's allegorical Romanticism, insofar as it underwrites the deconstructive "insights" now accused of politically suspect motives, is radically opposed to the organic Romanticism that Lovejoy associates with fascism.²⁵ The relevance of this opposition for us is that it focuses attention not on the meaning of *Romanticism* but, instead, on the negotiation of meaning for that word and others within these discursive fields. It is, moreover, precisely the metacritical negotiation over *methodology* which I want to investigate as the political effect of the dialectical relation between theory and praxis. That is, insofar as the debate over de Man is about the methodological legitimacy of reading that debate deconstructively (or nondeconstructively), that debate is conditioned by a self-reflexivity within the academic institution which makes Lovejoy's and Spitzer's exchange especially relevant for the contemporary consideration of theory's politics. That this consideration has up till now ignored the debate in which Lovejoy and Spitzer participated is a sign that the political responsibilities of such an institutional reflexivity might be more demanding than they first appear to be.

In his 1944 response to Spitzer, Lovejoy provides a useful comparison between the two theoretical methods:

> [Lovejoy's method] is "analytical" in its procedure; it regards the historic products of thought as compounds which can be better understood when they are resolved into their "elements." [Spitzer's] method treats all such products—including apparently every -ism and -ity for which language provides a general name—as "organic wholes," to which an "analytical procedure" cannot be applied, since such procedure "destroys the organic entity and makes the understanding of the whole no longer possible." The former method assumes that there can be such a thing as a history of "ideas," in the plural; the latter eschews the plural, and can be properly designated only by the "untranslatable" German compound *Geistesgeschichte*.[26]

Lovejoy's theoretical approach is chemical and atomistic; as Spitzer points out, it is derived, *"via* the immediate French models (Lanson's history of the idea of progress, etc.), from the analytical philosophy of history of the French Encyclopedists, more specifically from Voltaire's *Dictionnaire philosophique"* ("G," 201). Spitzer's method is organic and holistic; as Lovejoy points out, it "illustrates the persisting influence of certain characteristic ideas of the Romantic period" ("RS," 206). Insofar as Spitzer sees Lovejoy accusing Romantic organicism of encouraging German fascism, we can see this debate as two competing modes of historical and cultural analysis fighting over the political ramifications of the critical genealogy of one mode.[27]

We can best understand the difference between these two modes if we unpack the terms each methodology uses to describe its favored critical objects of study. For Lovejoy they are the historical products of thought he describes as the "elements" and "compounds" of the natural scientist. For Spitzer they are the holistic "climates" that refer to the complex relationships of an entire cultural period. The historian of ideas, then, generally tries to break down the compounds and larger mixtures of cultural history in order to separate and isolate the elements that make up that history. For the practitioner of *Geistesgeschichte* the tendency is the opposite, to work instead up to all the crisscrossing relationships and patterns that define the entire cultural climate. Elements, moreover, are affected by neither spatial nor temporal change, whereas climates are drastically influenced by such factors. Thus, to identify the same elements in Romanticism and Nazism is to stress the continuity between these two phenomena, whereas to image Romanticism and Nazism as climates separated by almost a century is to stress their discontinuity.

Yet Lovejoy's and Spitzer's terms also reveal the limits of both critical methodologies. In Lovejoy's case an element may combine with other elements to form a variety of compounds, but the element always stays the same; the term posits an interiority hermetically sealed from any anterior experience. As an element, Lovejoy's historical idea resists a further analysis into the material conditions of its origin; its function is to affect such conditions, not the other way around. Lovejoy does allow material conditions to affect identities at the level of the compound; this goes, however, against the basic tendency of his method, which is to analyze at the level of the elements. Spitzer ignores the fact that a climate can be made up of two climates, that there is no fundamental reason why one climate should be indifferent to an analysis that would relate it to another climate. Spitzer assumes a critical unit that is actually as hermetically sealed as Lovejoy's. Lovejoy's analysis breaks things down only to stop at the element; Spitzer's method works upward, synthesizing and identifying relations, only to stop at the climate. Both element and climate suffer, then, from a hypostatization of identity, which Lovejoy and Spitzer ably point out about each other's work ("*G,*" 194–95; "RS," 205–8).

Constantly hovering around the hypostatization of these critical identities is the theme of our present discussion, the relation of theory to praxis—or, as it appears in this debate, the relation between thought and action. In Lovejoy's case the ontological insularity of his elements inevitably leaves his method open to the charge of idealism, which is exactly part of Spitzer's attack: "Moreover, [for Lovejoy] to shift continuously from an 'idea' in the realm of thought to an 'idea' in the realm of action, and to assume their basic identity, seems to me to be based upon an illicit generalization which in our case blurs the clear lines of demarcation between thinking and action" ("*G,*" 202). Spitzer's critique of Lovejoy is accurate, and thus unfortunate, since it preempts the possibility of recovering from Lovejoy a materialist theory of thought in which thought's effect on action does not signify thought's idealist authority over action but, rather, the material reality thought and action both share.[28] Such an anti-idealist possibility exists in nascent form in Lovejoy, signaled by his use of the language of natural science—by his description of an idea as a chemical element.[29]

The situation becomes more complex, however, since Lovejoy's 1944 response to Spitzer also uses the language of the natural scientist to delimit the type of influence Lovejoy's ideas have in the "realm" of action—to depoliticize, in effect, his terms. In response to Spitzer's claim that, by arguing for the continuity of ideas in Romanticism and Nazism, Lovejoy is blaming the former for the latter, Lovejoy writes:

> To say that there is some casual relation between two events, A and B, is not to say that A is "responsible" for B, and (if B is a bad thing) that A is to be "blamed" for B; it is only to say that A is one of the antecedent conditions without which B would not have occurred in the particular way it did. To say that the German *Blitzkrieg* of 1940 could not have occurred if the internal combustion engine had not previously been invented is not to say that the invention was "responsible" for the *Blitzkrieg* or that its inventor is to be "blamed" for the horrors which his device was eventually to play a part in making possible. ("RS," 218)

In this passage, in order to deny that his analysis of Romanticism and fascism has any wider moral or political implication, Lovejoy has resorted to a rhetoric of science's intrinsic neutrality, a rhetoric that has since come under heavy critique.[30] Thus, Lovejoy's language of natural science holds out the possibility of seeing historical ideas in material terms, only to cancel out the more wide-ranging implications of that possibility.

For Spitzer historical responsibility, continuity, and causality cannot be kept apart: "if I believed, as does Prof. Lovejoy, that the main ideas of Romanticism had survived until today and that they represented the main ideas of Hitlerism, then I should *have* to believe that Romanticism has been responsible for Hitlerism" ("*G,*" 200). Thus, from its start Spitzer's attack on Lovejoy's method is *praxical* in that it represents itself as defending Romanticism against being blamed for fascism, even though in his response Lovejoy will claim that blame is beyond the scope of his analysis. Yet, in order to carry out his defense, Spitzer must deny the possibility that Lovejoy's elements are attempting, no matter how unsatisfactorily, a praxis of their own, that Lovejoy himself is trying to conceptualize how thought effects action. But, while Spitzer's idealist depiction of Lovejoy curtails any further analysis by Spitzer on how this is done, Spitzer's holistic method allows him to consider the opposite, how action, signified by historical action, effects thought: "In such enormous shifts [in the use of a concept] as this lies precisely the subject-matter which should properly concern the historian of ideas: which historical forces are responsible for the alterations? There is no driving force in any historical 'line' [of ideas] *itself*" ("*G,*" 196). If, for Spitzer, praxis is not easily or directly influenced by theory, theory is still shaped by praxis.

The shape action gives thought is at the heart of Spitzer's most telling critique of Lovejoy, that the latter has neglected exactly how and under what conditions the ideas of German Romanticism were transmitted from the past to the present:

> But it is hardly accurate [of Lovejoy] to speak of the continuous influence of these or any other Romantic ideas on the "educated and reading public." In German secondary schools and universities, the teaching of the humanities was, until the unhappy day when Hitler came to power, based upon the German *classics* of the eighteenth century. . . . In the second place—perhaps this is primary— it was precisely *not* the educated and reading public which had become conditioned for Nazism: it was from quite other ranks of society that Hitler recruited his followers. . . . Thus there is no continuity of teaching from the Schlegels to Hitler; between them there is a cultural break caused by social upheaval. ("*G,*" 200–201)

Lovejoy's response to this receptionist critique is in two parts, with one part contradicting the other. First, he claims that this discontinuity does not matter—that two elements can be the same while existing in two different periods and not be related causally. This idealist response is subverted by Lovejoy's inability to resist responding in a second manner, by flatly denying Spitzer's version of the transmission of German Romanticism and thereby tacitly admitting that the relation between the appearances of an idea in two historical periods actually does matter.

(Lovejoy's caginess is reflected by the fact that, while this two-part response concludes his article, he does not specify how his version of the transmission of Romanticism differs from Spitzer's.)

What Lovejoy—and Spitzer, for that matter—miss is that the issue of transmission is where both of their methodologies meet, in that, if an idea cannot be separated from either its production or reception, its material and sociohistoric transmission marks the space in which the realms of thought and action converge. Such a sensitivity to transmission would give Lovejoy's line of ideas the historical force Spitzer sees the line lacking. Such a sensitivity would also disrupt the a priori conceptual boundaries Spitzer constructs around his climates. The result would be that both the reified identities of Lovejoy's elements and Spitzer's climate would break down, allowing us to carry out a "history of ideas" grounded in materiality while remaining skeptical of both monumentalized periods and elementalized thoughts.

When applied to the case of Nazism, the most immediate consequence of such a sensitivity to transmission would be an enlarging of the historical field needed to satisfy such an investigation. That is, it becomes obvious that the relation between Romanticism and fascism is not exhausted solely by the immediate historic conditions of reception Spitzer adumbrates in his analysis. Thus, a broadening of such a study would lead to other ways in which German Romanticism was disseminated and reproduced as a set of signifying practices in German society in the nineteenth and twentieth centuries.[31] More important, for this analysis, is the fact that, as acts of the reception of Romanticism in the twentieth century, Lovejoy's and Spitzer's own articles become part of the cultural and political transmission of Romanticism, which their own critical positions are trying both to understand and to influence. Thus, as their attack on each other's methodology demonstrates, Lovejoy's and Spitzer's texts *dialectically constitute* part of the critical objects of their own study.

Both authors perceive their roles in such a cultural transmission differently. By denying the continuity between Romanticism and fascism, Spitzer sees himself as intervening in a transmission that would make the former responsible for the latter. In his response, at least, Lovejoy does not see that such a transmission must deal with the issue of responsibility; thus, he implies that his own part in such a transmission is also free of such responsibility, much in the same way the natural scientist is not responsible for the scientific realities he or she discovers. By taking these different stands toward what they and their respective methodologies are doing, Lovejoy and Spitzer are defining the consequences of their signifying practices and thus the material form of those practices, the academic institution.

They are saying what the institution does, by saying what they, as practitioners, of both the institution and signification, do. By arguing over what the institution has transmitted—and, more important, what it could transmit—they are also participating in that transmission and thus defining the institution's participation in it. Thus, not only does the constative function of Lovejoy's and Spitzer's words determine their performative functions; both functions also occur simultaneously. That is, Lovejoy and Spitzer are saying what they are doing, but, more important, what they are saying constitutes what "doing" means for the academic institution. This metonymic link between saying and doing marks the almost invisible moment when theory slides into praxis for Spitzer and Lovejoy, a moment, too, in which their debate enters into a dialectical relation with the academic institution—or, more precisely, the institutional forum of their debate, the *Journal of the History of Ideas*.

We can be more precise about how this debate interacts with that forum. I am referring to how Lovejoy's theoretical position changes between his initial 1941 article and his 1944 response to Spitzer. For, in contrast to his response, his 1941 article does not really appeal to the neutrality of the natural scientist. Rather, he foregrounds how the "meaning of Romanticism" can have two senses: "*viz.,* what is the word the name of, to what object or phenomenon does it point, or of what concept is it the verbal counterpart, in the usage of some person or persons; and second, the group of senses in which the word 'meaning' stands for an attribute, not of words, but of things or events, and denotes, not signification, but 'significance,' or consequence—or major consequences" ("MR," 257). Echoing his seminal essay "On the Discrimination of Romanticisms" (1923), Lovejoy argues that the first sense of Romanticism's meaning, its "signification," is unwieldy and ultimately of little use to the historian of ideas. Thus, when Lovejoy historically links Romanticism to the "tragic spectacle of Europe in 1940," he is deploying the second sense of Romanticism's meaning—that Romanticism's "significance" lies in its connection to the ideas of German national socialism. Contrary to his 1944 response to Spitzer, then, Lovejoy implies in 1941 that the job of the historian of ideas invariably leads him or her to consider not only the semantic meaning of an idea but also its contemporary political and cultural relevance. The historian of ideas becomes an active participant in the transmission of ideas, devising the "meaning" of those ideas in both senses of the word.

Moreover, since, for Lovejoy, there is no one essential semantic meaning of the term *Romanticism,* its relevant meaning—its significance—is open to the influence of differing sociohistoric conditions. Applying this axiom to Lovejoy himself, we must read his own 1941 article as a social production published roughly six months before the attack on Pearl Harbor by a leading academic who was at the same time vigorously lobbying for the intervention by the United States in the war in Europe against the Axis powers.[32] Read this way, Lovejoy's article becomes a performative speech act, making Romanticism "mean" fascism, in the sense that Lovejoy is asserting that the term *Romanticism* is relevant in 1941 insofar as it allows us to understand what in going on in Nazi Germany. For Lovejoy the meaning of *Romanticism* for the historian of ideas in 1941 is the warning about Nazi Germany which an analysis of Romanticism invokes.

In contrast to the 1941 article, the neutrality of the natural science rhetoric in Lovejoy's response to Spitzer is remarkable. Lovejoy's change in tone illustrates how much the deployment of Romanticism depends on a changing sociohistoric context. For in 1944, with the United States in the war on the side of the Allies, the meaning of *Romanticism* as a warning about German fascism is an accomplished fact. Thus, the semantic and political equation Lovejoy and Spitzer wrestle with in 1944 is not about the meaning of *Romanticism* but, rather, that of *fascism.* What is at stake in 1944 is the extent to which fascism, through the genealogies of Romanticism, informs, at the levels of ideas and methodologies, the institution in which Lovejoy and Spitzer operate. Lovejoy's retreat into the rhetoric of natural science is his own attempt to minimize that contamination. Yet Lovejoy, under different discursive circumstances, could still deploy *Romanticism* to mean *fascism*—as when he wrote, also in 1944, a position paper on Germany for the government and the army and in it reproduced his history-of-ideas methodology in order to explain German aggression.[33]

I bring up these reversals in Lovejoy's theoretical claims not to criticize him on the grounds of some ideal scholarly code but, instead, to show the extent to which the deployment of Romanticism in this debate was determined by historical conditions and a certain reflexivity within the American academic institution at that time. Indeed, the Lovejoy-Spitzer debate is representative of a number of articles published in the first half of the 1940s in which the transmission of Romanticism and fascism collided with political concerns over critical methodology and institutional influence.[34] These articles were, in turn, part of a larger trend in scholarship which took European fascism as the object of its analysis.[35] Faced with the absolute contemporaneity of its topic, this body of scholarship reflects the tension of a discourse torn between a norm of academic disinterestedness and a historical urgency that made appeals to that norm disingenuous.[36]

Adding another dimension to this urgency was the arrival in academic America of a large number of intellectual European emigrés who were both heirs to the intellectual traditions of Europe and witnesses to its recent political convulsions. Underwriting Spitzer's own argument with Lovejoy is the former's status as a recent refugee from Nazi Germany. Spitzer's scholarly attempt to separate the genealogies of Romanticism and fascism is thus contiguous with the immigrant's investment in bearing witness to the temporal and spatial dislocations that constitute the passage from the Old World to the New.[37] This metonymic link between scholarly recuperation and lived historical memory once again implicates the academic in the "real": not only is the migrant European intellectual in America the perfect analogy for the cultural historian, who, exiled to the land of present, tries to recuperate the past; the emigré is also the literal fact, the material form, of the transmission of the West's culture from past to present, and from shore to shore.[38] In 1944— and for us and for de Man today—the United States' distance from Europe stands in for the United States as a hyperpresent reality that both doubles and breaks away from a European modernity haunted by the accusation of its collusion with the catastrophe of national socialism. It is precisely the tension between this similitude and rupture which the emigré especially codifies. It is also through the emigré that this tension most clearly gains a more than literary importance. And, insofar as we as literary critics and cultural historians are also emigrés—receiving, reproducing, and retroactively deploying the knowledge of a paradoxical "country" of the past to which we belong and from which we are exiled—we would do well to consider the extraliterary ramifications that our own projects might conceal. Spitzer's identity as an emigré thus foregrounds and underwrites his vocation as a professional cultural historian. It is this dual identity of Spitzer and others which makes Spitzer's debate with Lovejoy more than just a sectarian dispute and which historically creates the institutional pressure among American intellectuals in the '40s to come to terms with the politics of Europe's critical traditions.

The question still remains, however, whether Spitzer's situation is simply a more vivid and rarified example of what should affect all our projects of literary historiography. To focus, in other words, on the political effects of institutional and scholarly self-reflexivity within the academy is not to reify the—or even to claim *a*—distance between theory's discursiveness and the historical real. Lovejoy's and Spitzer's debate is rare because its contemporaneity with its object is so obvious and immediate; the more difficult task is to see how far we can take that rarity and ruthlessly make it exemplary of all historical productions. We can begin to conceptualize a model for this task by further interrogating the degree to which Romanticism circulates within twentieth-century criticism as the reflexive catalyst for the move from theory to a certain praxis, a moment in which the critical subject takes as its object a text already theorizing, if not outright announcing, its effect on the world. Constituted by a number of texts shot through with the self-consciousness of a zeitgeist, Romanticism provides the contemporary critic with such a metacritical field, with which he or she can dialectically engage. In Lovejoy's and Spitzer's case this reflexive moment occurs less because of the self-consciousness of the German Romantics they study than because of the extent to which Spitzer's own methodology is part of the debate over Romanticism's politics. In their case it is not any particular work of Romanticism but, rather, the hypostatized identity of Romanticism itself, as a reflexive effect on the world, which dialectically transforms Lovejoy's and Spitzer's articles into part of the praxical transmission they are studying.

Lovejoy and Spitzer dramatize one important outcome of this mediation: in defining Romanticism, they cannot avoid producing its meaning in both senses of the word which Lovejoy cites. It is this twin sense of *meaning*—of signification and significance—which theory has built into the historical fact of its explanatory powers; it insures, pace Marx, the open boundary between interpretation and active change which those powers might otherwise threaten to close.

# Chapter 2

# Disfiguring Monuments

## History in Paul de Man and Percy Bysshe Shelley

> "Whence I came, partly I seem to know,
> "And how & by what paths I have been brought
>     To this dread pass, methinks even thou mayst guess;
> Why this should be my mind can compass not;
> "Whither the conqueror hurries me still less."
>     Shelley
>     "The Triumph of Life"

Such massive evidence of the failure to make the various individual readings coalesce is a somewhat melancholy spectacle. The fragmentary aspect of the whole is made more obvious still by the hypotactic manner that prevails in each of the essays taken in isolation, by the continued attempt, however ironized, to present a closed and linear argument. This apparent coherence *within* each essay is not matched by a corresponding coherence *between* them.

> Laid out diachronically in a roughly chronological sequence, they do not evolve in a manner that easily allows for dialectical progression or, ultimately, historical totalization. Rather, it seems that they always start from scratch and that their conclusions fail to add up to anything.
>
> Paul de Man
> preface to *The Rhetoric of Romanticism*

# I

In 1986 Jerome Christensen characterized a certain academic and cultural imaginary still arcing through the middle of the Reagan decade as deriving

> a specific historical gravity from the notable intersection of the heyday of campus activism in the late sixties with the first enthusiastic reception of deconstruction in America, the latter signaled by the publication in 1970 of the Johns Hopkins symposium "The Languages of Criticism and the Sciences of Man," and with the aggressive revival of romanticism by what since has become known as the Yale school, announced by Harold Bloom's landmark collection *Romanticism and Consciousness* in the same year. Both of these books were preceded by de Man's masterly essay "The Rhetoric of Temporality" in 1969. If there is such a thing as coincidence, this connection of political turmoil with deconstruction and romanticism is not it. The dominant model of our modern understanding of the relation between politics and poetry is derived from romantic experience and romantic practice.[1]

Perceptive and penetrating, these words testify now in the mid-1990s to a displaced, thwarted modernity, one that was generated in the mid-1980s by the question of deconstruction's sociohistoric identity. Christensen's sympathetic answer is to explain deconstruction's unsettling powers by way of the insurrectionary activism of New Left politics, which itself is made intelligible by the radical Jacobinism that changed Europe two centuries earlier. Underwriting and controlling the potential hyperbole of such analogies are the literal and material connections that Christensen cites, such as the shared campus locale of deconstruction and the earlier '60s activism and also the person of Paul de Man, whose deconstructive career overlaps with his growing importance as a Romantic scholar in the United States. Through such connections Christensen creates a playing field for discussions about deconstruction's politics, one whose historical logic speaks as much to the relation between deconstruction and '60s radicalism as anything else. It is, however, precisely this relation that now seems out of place during debates about deconstruction's historical and political identity; to "historicize" deconstruction today is, in other words, to gravitate toward de Man's wartime past in Nazi-occupied Belgium and his work for the collaborationist Belgian newspaper *Le Soir*. It is to see de Man's corpus as working through (and perhaps repressing) a modernity characterized not so much by the turbulence of the '60s as by the horrors of World War II.

Hence the strange displaced state of Christensen's words: they refer to a moment that has been surpassed by a set of historical concerns occurring almost half a century earlier. Yet the disjunction between 1942 and 1969 as master signifiers for deconstruction's political history might not seem as intransigent as it first appears; we can see this by returning to Christensen's essay, whose complex linkage of the New Left and Romanticism to deconstruction is underwritten by the master trope of apostasy.[2] In other words it is not simply a revolutionary imperative that binds the historical connections that Christensen makes; more important, it is the balancing of that imperative against narratives of deconstruction, '60s activism, and Romanticism which are intelligible only through a moment of betrayal or co-option, ranging from deconstruction's betrayal of stable historic and aesthetic meaning to its comfortable institutional existence within a politically conservative landscape to the larger co-option of '60s activism by the quietistic Reagan era to the even larger tales of political and cultural apostasy accruing to the British Romantic writers and their compatriots after the disappointments of the French Revolution. It is, moreover, this very trope that critics have employed in order to understand deconstruction's sociohistoric relation to de Man's writing for *Le Soir*—that de Man's mature works betray history by silencing his past, or, conversely, that such works positively betray from a leftist perspective the mystified aesthetic ideology of his youth.

My last two examples should make clear that the rhetorical similarity of these narratives does not imply an immediate coincidence in their political claims.[3] These narratives do share a political valence but one that argues against the assumption tempting much of the scholarship on de Man and *Le Soir:* that one set of historical conditions determines deconstruction's political identity and explains deconstruction's reception of all texts. A return to Christensen's displaced modernity of 1969 thus effects a historical weave that situates a de Manian Romanticism in relation to both *Le Soir* and the New Left. Such a return means recasting Christensen's trope of apostasy as a problem that appears in de Man's writings throughout his career: the difference between "thought" (or, as it appears in his prominent later works, "word") and "deed." This problem inevitably leads to de Man's perhaps most violent statement on the unreadability of historical thought and action, "Shelley Disfigured," and, as important, to the text in which de Man reads this unreadability, Shelley's poem "The Triumph of Life."[4]

The implications of this violence for deconstruction are, however, given specific form in the essay that Christensen pointedly connects to '60s activism, deconstruction, and Romanticism, "The Rhetoric of Temporality." What needs to be stressed about Paul de Man's 1969 piece is a certain institutional conflict over the transmission of Romantic studies, one that connects the problem of literary history to the political problem of the linguistic relation between word and deed. Thus, like the earlier debate between Lovejoy and Spitzer, de Man's essay connects the question of Romanticism's transmission to the relation between theory and praxis. Unlike this earlier example, however, de Man's concepts of word and deed radically complicate this relation, proleptically problematizing recent attempts to recuperate de Man's revision of Romanticism as an immediately intelligible form of political praxis.

## II

Singled out by de Man and others as a turning point in his theoretical career, "The Rhetoric of Temporality" has been used by a number of critics to create an intelligible narrative arc in de Man's mature writings

(*BI,* xii). Already encapsulated within the piece is one such arc, the transformation of de Man's earlier phenomenological concerns of time and mind into a rhetorical terminology emphasizing linguistic undecidability—the transformation, as Lindsay Waters notes, of "temporality" into the "rhetoric of temporality."[5] Such a narrative is complicated, however, insofar as its intelligibility depends on a progressive temporal linearity whose grounding ubiquity "The Rhetoric of Temporality" denies. Nowhere is this denial more crucial, and vexed, than in the role played by literary history in the essay.

The literary history present in de Man's piece is no less than the historical revision of Romanticism. I refer to what is most well-known about the essay, its argument against perceiving Romanticism as existing completely under the hegemony of the symbol, a figure of language which asserts the organic synthesis of mind and nature, signifier and signified, image and idea. Rejecting this perception and approbation of metaphysical presence, de Man insists on a more complicated history of Romanticism, one in which the celebration of the symbol in fact represses a negative linguistic knowledge, an earlier Romanticism of the allegory in which the "meaning constituted by the allegorical sign can then consist only in the *repetition* ... of a previous sign with which it can never coincide, since it is of the essence of this previous sign to be pure anteriority" (*BI,* 207). What is of special interest is the tactical description that de Man uses to shore up this argument, especially how he represents the supposed influence of the symbol in English Romanticism.

For, while de Man first turns to Coleridge, he dismisses the poet's most famous celebration of symbol over allegory in *The Statesman's Manual* as a confused distinction based on linguistic "reflection" rather than "synthesis." To locate the Anglo-American hegemony of the synthesizing symbol, de Man turns, instead, to the commentators on English Romanticism, the "English and American historians of romanticism [who have] focused on the transition that leads from eighteenth-century to romantic nature poetry" (*BI,* 193). More important, he turns to mid-twentieth-century interpreters of Romanticism, those who in 1969 would be seen as "contemporaries" of de Man's own professional and intellectual milieu: William Wimsatt, M. H. Abrams, and Earl Wasserman. In arguing with their examples of a Romantic synthesizing nature poetry, de Man attempts to show how Romantic writing actually conveys the temporal aporias of the symbol, the impossibility of the symbol's magical thinking as a sign for ontological and aesthetic stability. Thus, Wimsatt, Abrams, and Wasserman become for de Man synecdoches for a critical and poetic agency spanning the nineteenth and twentieth centuries, one that in its "symbolic conception of metaphorical language" *regresses* from "the [allegorical] truths that come to light in the last quarter of the eighteenth century" (208).

Thus, de Man couches his polemics within a literary history based on the transmission and reception of texts, in which Romanticism and the study of Romanticism—the transition from eighteenth-century to Romantic nature poetry and that transition's scholarly analysis—coincide. Without pursuing the implications of what he has wrought, de Man nevertheless gives the interpretation of Romanticism an institutional dimension, insofar as his understanding of the Romantic symbol is based primarily on a critical engagement with members of his own academic community. He makes, in nascent form, a knowledge of Romanticism a metacritical affair of sociohistoric reception, exactly the critical gesture that Tilottama Rajan has argued for as a corrective supplement to de Man's, and deconstruction's, radically linguistic priorities.[6] Three points must be made about how this critical mode of thought structures "The Rhetoric of Temporality."

First, we need to see how de Man's own allegorical Romanticism still belongs to the type of literary history implied by his explicit connection of the Romantic writers to their twentieth-century commentators. That is, even though de Man's observations turn Wimsatt's, Abrams's, and Wasserman's critical contemporaneity into the blindness of an elder generation, his own account of the Romantic allegory still structures itself within a historical scheme originating from the writing of the "last quarter of the eighteenth century." Thus, by intervening in Abrams's and Wasserman's transmission of the symbol's aesthetic mystifications, de Man does not so much repudiate as *revise* the historical transmission of Romanticism.

Second, we should observe how this historical revision has operated as a window of opportunity for various proposals concerning the politics of deconstruction *and* Romanticism. For example, the possible metonymic and metaphorical connections between de Man's institutional interventions and 1960s campus agitation underwrite the force of Christensen's historical intersections among deconstruction, Romanticism, and '60s activism.[7] This politicization of an academic argument in Romanticism is made explicit in the 1980s with Jerome McGann's leftist work *The Romantic Ideology*, which, like "The Rhetoric of Temporality," targets a tradition of Romantic organicism upheld by M. H. Abrams.[8] Making as explicit a link as McGann between academic Romanticism and the West's political tradition—and particularly emphasizing the link between de Man's historical revision and political intervention—is Christopher Norris, who argues for a growing critique in de Man's works of the "aesthetic ideology," the pervasive post-Kantian Romantic fusion of language and sense whose most mystified, totalizing forms have historically underwritten fascist and totalitarian thought. Echoed by many critics involved in the debate over de Man and *Le Soir* and structured by many of the same key terms—*organicism, Romanticism,* and *fascism*—in Lovejoy's and Spitzer's debate in the '40s, this critique of aesthetic ideology explains de Man's choice of the allegory over the symbol as a clear example of how a critical theory can operate as a political action. De Man's historical revision becomes, in other words, a form of political praxis.[9]

The third point about literary history in "The Rhetoric of Temporality" complicates this explanation, however. For historical revision is not the ultimate nor even the sole methodological framework of the essay; paralleling de Man's discussion of allegory and symbol is his later meditation on irony, in which he explicitly rejects the "dangerously satisfying" conclusion that the regressive "transition from an allegorical to a symbolic theory of poetry would find its historical equivalent in the regression from the eighteenth-century ironic novel . . . to nineteenth-century realism" (*BI,* 222). As the synchronic counterpart to allegory's diachronic experience of the disjunction between the linguistic and empirical worlds, irony is for de Man a linguistic and existential phenomenon actively hostile to historical procedures and thought: "It is a historical fact that irony becomes increasingly conscious of itself in the course of demonstrating the impossibility of our being historical" (211). De Man's response to this "fact" is to situate his approach to irony within a more self-consciously linguistic analysis. But, given de Man's description of allegory in this same section of the essay as a "successive mode capable of engendering duration as the *illusion* of a continuity that it knows to be illusionary" (226; my emphasis), the problem is not so much that history and irony are incompatible but, rather, that de Man leaves unanswered whether history itself is allegorical—whether the "historical fact" of irony's ahistoricity or symbol's and allegory's "history of an error" are examples of a "successive mode" underwritten by the "illusion of a continuity."

The question is, in part, whether the structure of "The Rhetoric of Temporality" is itself allegorical or ironic or else mimetic or even symbolic; whether the methodologies of its two sections relate linearly or exist simultaneously; and, finally, whether this succession or simultaneity—which could also be seen as either a progression or, if not a synthesis, then an imbrication—affects the intelligibility of the historical revision of Romanticism within the boundaries of the revision's own procedures. It is, of course, the very irresolution of these interpretive options which in large part gives "The Rhetoric of Temporality" its strange aporetic force. Indeed, something of the sheer undecidability of the essay's structure seems to underwrite the final vision of "literary history" which the piece offers: "The dialectical play between these two modes [allegory and irony], as well as their common interplay with mystified forms of language (such as symbolic or mimetic representation), which it is not in their power to eradicate, make up what is called literary history" (*BI,* 226).

The qualification of "what is called" is itself unsettling, since it leaves inconclusive whether there is an alternative to such a literary history. We can, however, consider de Man's inconclusiveness actually as a *condition* for historical thought by returning to and reconceiving his historical revision of Romanticism through a different set of relations between thought and deed than that found in the political argument of Norris and others, a set of relations that, like allegory and irony, also addresses the gap between language and the empirical world. De Man gestures toward such a set of relations in the decidedly phenomenological vocabulary of an earlier essay, "Wordsworth and Hölderlin," when he observes how the "poet and the historian converge . . . to the extent that they both speak of an action that precedes them, but that exists for consciousness only because of their intervention."[10] What de Man is referring to is the problem of mediation, of mediating deed by thought (and thought by deed); of mediating the actions of the empirical world by language or, more to the point, the action of Romantic literary history by the literary critic's historical revision. In relation to "The Rhetoric of Temporality," then, de Man's critical intervention paradoxically *engen-*

*ders* a history of Romanticism which precedes his revision, a history that does not, by the very fact of the intervention, exist by itself—a history that, furthermore, cannot exist except in its incommensurate relation with that intervention. Thus, if Romanticism and Romantic studies coincide, they do so in a historical identity that is ironic, a single historical act whose interiority is constitutively split, a condition that could be allegorized as the insuperable gap between the ultimately unknowable past action of Romantic literature and its present mediation by de Man's critical thought.

Thus, if historical revision exists within the aporetic structure of "The Rhetoric of Temporality," it is as a mediation that allows for a certain historical constative effect, even as the discontinuity between historical truth and language is stressed by the intervention of thought or language, an act of mediation which enacts and thus can only recede from the action—in this case, the Romantic history of allegory and symbol—which is being mediated. The power of "The Rhetoric of Temporality," then, lies in the suspension, as opposed to the simple fall or success, of this specific constative effect within the paralogical tensions of the essay, a fact that both speaks to and complicates the number of readings that equate this work solely with its history of the Romantic allegory and symbol. By "suspension" I mean the strange impossible phenomenon that inheres in the contradictory meanings of the term: as a deferral of *and* a support for the intelligibility of historicity in de Man's work. It is this suspension, this double sense of an interfering *and* enabling force, which allows the historian and poet in "Wordsworth and Hölderlin" to "speak of an action that precedes them" despite, or because of, the blockage of their own intervening presence. It is this suspension, moreover, which implicitly confronts any attempt to transform de Man's historical revision into something that could be called political use.

Such a suspension does not, in other words, allow for a simple correspondence between thought and deed, or for a method of historical reception and revision which is immediately a political intervention. What this suspension does, however, is to insist on the problem of such a correspondence and method as a necessary, constant component of the negative knowledge of language which de Man offers us. I thus want to argue that it is in the thinking through of this problem that de Man's and deconstruction's uncompromising radical skepticism paradoxically attains a startling historical and political specificity. To make this argument we must now seek rather unlikely aid from de Man's "Shelley Disfigured," an essay whose critical language of monumentalization and disfigurement reinscribes the problems of Romantic identity, the intelligibility of historical action, and historical mediation within a violently linguistic world in which the only action is the arbitrarily positing "madness of words" and historical revision is replaced by the necessarily disfiguring consequences of a blind historical reconstruction. Yet there also resides in de Man's essay another language of monumentalization and disfigurement, that of Shelley's "Triumph of Life." There exists a strong dialectical engagement between these two works and their vocabularies on monumentalization, an engagement that will show how de Man recovers from Shelley's poem its radical, epistemological skepticism but elides the reason for that skepticism: that "The Triumph of Life" offers a deconstructive critique of history and revolutionary transformation, a critique that in fact comments proleptically on the uncertainty of deconstruction's present political role. My purpose, then, is to observe the way in which history itself is constituted in its interrogation by both de Man's critical text and the text that de Man critically reads. Doing so means showing that we are in fact dealing with not only two but, rather, a number of other texts, released, as it were, through Shelley's own complicated reception of classical and post–French Revolutionary imagery (his use, I will argue, of Jean-Jacques Rousseau, Edmund Burke, Napoléon Bonaparte, and of the procession/triumph itself) and his poem's anticipation of the political problem of revolutionary identity which Karl Marx will address some thirty years later in *The Eighteenth Brumaire*.

## III

De Man's 1979 essay "Shelley Disfigured" is a sustained attack on historical thought largely underwritten for de Man by a language of historical reconstruction, by a faith in the restoration of past monuments presumably disfigured and fragmented only by the inevitable assaults of time. As de Man notes, "The Triumph of Life" has been an exemplary object of inquiry for such historical reconstruction. The poem is literally a fragment, an unfinished work cut off by the accidental death of Shelley in 1822. Its unfinished nature pertains not only to the absence of an ending but also to its status as a collection of rough manuscripts with a number of questionable lines, even in the final version approved and published by Mary Shelley.[11] The poem is also fragmentary in the sense that it is strewn with the "fragments" of a biblical, classical, and Renaissance past, numerous allusions, as Harold Bloom has pointed out, to Petrarch, Dante, and the Bible. Further, as Kenneth Neill Cameron notes, the Petrarchan allusions imply that a completed "Triumph" would still be a fragment, comparable to one of the six poems in Petrarch's own *Triumphs,* in which each poem dramatizes one aspect of existence triumphing over another.[12] In all these ways "The Triumph of Life" invites its reader to approach it as a collection of historical and textual fragments waiting to be constructed by a historical and philological effort.

The poem also invites us to see this historical effort as essential to understanding the poem's meaning, so that to reconstruct Shelley's work is also to interpret it. Aside from gleaning the poem's textual history, this is no mean feat. "The Triumph of Life" is difficult to read, given the tropological web of extended metaphors and epic similes which Shelley uses to describe the work's narrative action. This problem of interpretation is not only a formal but also a thematic obsession: Shelley punctuates his narrative with a series of questions commenting on the poem's unfolding action, questions that are ultimately left unanswered by the fragmentary nature of the work. The last question, "Then, what is Life?" is followed by several lines, with the last one cut off in midsentence. Before de Man one historically reconstructed "The Triumph of Life" by coming to terms with the unanswered question left hanging at the end of the fragment. By speculating how Shelley would have answered that question, one "completed" the poem and answered the emendatory *and* interpretive questions that haunt many of the poem's lines. To read "The Triumph of Life" critically was to be caught up in a hermeneutic that was at once literary, imaginative, historical, and philological; to unlock its code was to secure simultaneously the poem's true meaning and its true historical place.[13]

De Man begins "Shelley Disfigured" by teasing out the implications of these critical assumptions about "The Triumph of Life":

> Like several of the English romantics' major works *The Triumph of Life,* Shelley's last poem, is, as is well known, a fragment that has been unearthed, edited, reconstructed and much discussed. All this archeological labor can be considered a response to the ques-

tions that articulate one of the text's main structures.... These questions can easily be referred back to the enigmatic text they punctuate and they are characteristic of the interpretive labor associated with romanticism. In the case of this movement, they acquire an edge of urgency which is often lacking when they are addressed to earlier periods, except when these periods are themselves mediated by the neo-hellenism, the neo-medievalism or the neo-baroque of the late eighteenth and the early nineteenth century. This is not surprising, since they are precisely the archeological questions that prompt us to deduce the present from the identification of the more or less immediately anterior past, as well as from the process that leads from then to now.[14]

The question of periodization, de Man suggests, takes on a special significance when we apply it to Romanticism. "The late eighteenth and the early nineteenth century" compose our "more or less immediately anterior past"; by identifying that period as Romanticism and then saying what that Romanticism is, we say what our past was, and thus what our present is, and thereby secure our Anglo-European history. By piecing such fragments as "The Triumph of Life" together, we historically reconstruct Romanticism; through such a reconstruction we define Romanticism, name our own relation to that period, and gain access to our own historical narrative. Romanticism itself becomes a fragment of a larger whole, our own history. Or does it? Unsurprisingly, de Man believes a definition of Romanticism is more slippery than what one might think:

> What is the meaning of *The Triumph of Life,* of Shelley and of romanticism? . . . [The archeological questions we ask of Shelley, his poem, and Romanticism] allow one to conclude that *The Triumph of Life* is a fragment of something whole, or romanticism a fragment, or a moment, in a process that now includes us within its horizon. What relationship do we have to such a text that allows us to call it a fragment that we are then entitled to reconstruct, to identify and implicitly to complete? This supposes, among other things, that Shelley or romanticism are themselves entities, which, like a statue, can be broken into pieces, mutilated, or allegorized . . . after having been stiffened, frozen, erected or whatever one wants to call

the particular rigidity of statues. Is the status of a text line the status of a statue? ("SD," 40–41)

For de Man the status of a text line is the status of a statue in that the line, like the statue, invites the archeological effort of reconstruction as interpretation. But, more important for de Man, the status of a statue *is* the status of a text line in that the historical statue continually opens itself to the linguistic process of disfigurement and mutilation which defines de Man's vision of how a text works.

Thus, de Man uses the "questions of origin, of direction and identity" which punctuate Shelley's text to show how "The Triumph of Life" makes itself unreadable and, in effect, history impossible. The continual imposition on and erasure of one question by another dispel "any illusion of dialectical progress or regress." Furthermore, the imagery and syntax surrounding those questions are "tangles of meaning and of figuration" which "tie themselves into a knot which arrests the process of understanding" ("SD," 43–45). The linguistic tools with which we might reconstruct "The Triumph of Life" are themselves discontinuous, ruptured, and unreliable—or, as de Man calls them, "disfigured." For de Man the character in "The Triumph of Life" who links language and the concept of disfigurement together is Rousseau.

De Man defines disfigurement by analyzing Rousseau's first appearance in the poem:

> What I thought was an old root which grew
> To strange distortion out of the hill side . . .
> . . . . . . . . . . . . . . . . . . . . . . . . . . . . . . . . .
> And . . . the grass which methought hung so wide
>     And white, was but his thin discoloured hair,
> And . . . the holes he vainly sought to hide
>
> Were or had been eyes.
> ("TL," 182–88)

De Man reads disfigurement into these lines by arguing that they describe a reverse prosopopoeia, a loss of face: "The erasure or effacement is indeed the loss of a face, in French *figure*. Rousseau no longer, or hardly . . . has a face. Like the protagonist in the Hardy story, he is disfigured, *défiguré,* defaced" ("SD," 46).[15] By bringing in the French *figure,* de Man links Rousseau with language—the question of figure— and names the main action of that language as disfigurement, the effacement/erasure of meaning de Man sees "The Triumph of Life" enacting and which first occurs with the imposition of one question on another. For de Man, Rousseau's "defacement" occurs when Rousseau's mind is figuratively "effaced" after he drinks from the shape's cup. Just as the replacement of one question by another constitutes "a self-receding scene" that confutes rather than encourages historical narration, so too does the imprinting of "a new Vision" on Rousseau's mind also mark his metamorphosis—"My brain became as sand"—as the loss, instead of gain, of cognition.[16]

For de Man other parts of Rousseau's tale also demonstrate this loss. De Man argues, for example, that, since the language describing Rousseau's first waking moments is unstable, Rousseau awakens into a state of "glimmering" uncertainty—of a "forgetting" so radical "that we have no assurance whatever that the forgotten ever existed" ("SD," 50). Likewise, the reflective interplay of light among sun, stream, well, and shape in Rousseau's tale contains paradoxical examples of "self-contained specularity" which refute stable, self-referential, and originary meaning (55–57). The locus of this "violent . . . light" (64) is the "shape all light" ("TL," 352) gliding above the stream, whose very figure for de Man depends on the impossible suspension of language's disfiguring force.[17] For him that force is first and foremost what he calls language's arbitrary, performative power, language's ability to "posit" itself without justifying why or how it occurs.[18] This meaningless power is the payoff of de Man's essay, the cause for the shape's disfigurement, which is *not* the cause, in any linear sense, since de Man's main example of this assertive power is the imposition of the sun at the beginning of the poem, an event temporally disconnected from the events that make up the meeting between Rousseau and the shape:

> The positing power of language is both entirely arbitrary, in having a strength that cannot be reduced to necessity, and entirely inexorable in that there is no alternative to it. It stands beyond the polarities of chance and determination and can therefore not be part of a temporal sequence of events. The sequence has to be punctured by acts that cannot be made a part of it. It cannot begin . . . by telling us of

the waning of the stars under the growing impact of the sun, a natural motion which is the outcome of a mediation, but it must evoke the violent "springing forth" of a sun detached from all antecedents.... The most continuous and gradual event in nature, the subtle gradations of the dawn, is collapsed into the brusk swiftness of a single moment:

> Swift as a spirit hastening to his task
>     ... the Sun sprang forth
>     ... and the mask
>
> Of darkness fell from the awakened Earth.
> ("TL," 1–4; "SD," 62–63)

The "positing power of language," for de Man, turns history into an endless, linguistic act of "inscription" in which events are textual marks that simultaneously impose on and erase one another ("SD," 62). Because of this linguistic act, neither monument nor event can stay true to itself; both enact what Christensen names, in reference to de Man, a critical apostasy that subverts our attempt to reconstruct the monument and make sense of the event.

It is here that I want to intervene in "Shelley Disfigured" and to interrogate more fully de Man's own representation of how disfigurement and monumentalization relate. Crucial to this representation are the two contradictory ways in which language's "positing power" disfigures the "shape all light." The first way is disfiguration as a reverse prosopopoeia, the loss of face and body, the decomposition of the shape:

> "The fair shape waned in the coming light
> As veil by veil the silent splendour drops
>     From Lucifer, amid the chrysolite
>
> "Of sunrise ere it strikes the mountain tops."
> ("TL," 412–15)

De Man sees "Lucifer" as "metaphor, the bearer of light which carries over the light of the senses and of cognition from events and entities to their meaning" ("SD," 66). Whether we make this interpretive leap with de Man or not, Lucifer and "the fair shape" do lose "the contour of [their] own face or shape" ("SD," 66). Here disfiguration is an erasure of body which is then teased out to also mean a dissolution of shape. The gesture is the exact opposite of being "stiffened, frozen, erected or whatever one wants to call the particular rigidity of statues." The fair shape's and Lucifer's dissolution link the loss of this rigidity to the disfigurement of history. Language disfigures history by revealing the insubstantiality of the historical monuments we reconstruct.

But this dissolution is accompanied by an opposite gesture. According to de Man, the shape quite literally sinks from the weight of language's positing power, so "that, when we again meet the shape . . . it is no longer gliding along the river but drowned, Ophelia-like, below the surface of the water." Likewise, the rainbow which the shape first wears as a "many coloured scarf" returns, "in [Rousseau's] ensuing vision, as a rigid, stony arch said 'fiercely (to extol) the fortune' of the shape's defeat by what the poem calls 'life' " ("SD," 58).[19] Unlike the waning shape and Lucifer, the rainbow and the weighed-down shape meet a stonelike fate, in which they harden and attain the density and "particular rigidity of statues."

This movement is also disfigurement, another type of reverse prosopopoeia, since that trope is the giving of not only a face but also a body. To turn to stone is to lose one's flesh and thus one's body. In the shape's case its watery fate reveals that personification is always already disfigurement, in that the given body is always false, an inanimate simulacrum that can only stiffen, harden, and sink. Likewise, the rainbow, what de Man interprets as the organic unification of the linguistic and phenomenal worlds, is also a false body, a truth claim that exists only as a reified monument, a stone arch. The only "real" body discussed in "Shelley Disfigured" fares no better. Like the shape and the rainbow, Shelley's own drowned and disfigured body stiffens into a statue, this time because of the various interpretive and reconstructive pressures we have placed on "The Triumph of Life" and other Romantic texts: "For what we have done with the dead Shelley, and with all the other dead bodies that appear in romantic literature . . . is simply to bury them, to bury them in their own texts made into epitaphs and monumental graves. They have been made statues for the benefit of future archeologists 'digging in the grounds for the new foundations' of their own monuments. They have been transformed into historical and aesthetic objects" ("SD," 67).

Whereas Jerome McGann urges us in *The Romantic Ideology* to reach for Shelley's unburnt heart, de Man tells us any such attempt is a reconstruction of Shelley's body, which is the greatest disfigurement of all (*RI,* 13). Yet de Man's insight cannot stop this transformation: "[This monumentalization] is not avoidable, since the failure to exorcise the threat, even in the face of such evidence as the radical blockage that befalls this poem, becomes precisely the challenge to understanding that always again demands to be read. . . . No degree of knowledge can ever stop this madness, for it is the madness of words ("SD," 68). The "madness of words," the critical apostasy of de Man's own essay, is what insures monumentalization in the first place. Thus, "Shelley Disfigured" deconstructs its own assault against history, in that de Man describes for us a historical monumentalization that is a mystified state that the madness of words exposes and undoes but also *guarantees*. For de Man, of course, this guarantee is worthless, in that it only underscores the inevitability of the process of simultaneous monumentalization and disfigurement which he identifies. But this is precisely where a dialectical engagement between "Shelley Disfigured" and "The Triumph of Life" occurs. Shelley's poem, I would argue, is as obsessed with the question of monumentalization and its inevitability as de Man's essay. For "The Triumph of Life," however, this guarantee of monumentalization is the occasion for a tortured interrogation of the specificity of monuments, of what they replace, and of the politics of that replacement—in other words, of what it means to read history.

Thus, the apparent discontinuity among the questions already on the poem's surface, those of time, direction, and identity, prove for de Man the continuous imposition and erasure occurring within the poem. But de Man assumes that the only other choice for the poem besides imposition/erasure is a genetic model whereby the poem's questions propel it forward toward the possession of an ultimate answer. But what if the poem is not concerned with coming up with the right answer and is, instead, caught up with the impossibility of asking the right question? "The Triumph of Life" works, then, as an aphasia, whereby its technical and poetic virtuosity overcompensate for a conceptual stutter of which the poem is intensely aware; each question asks what it cannot hope to imagine but what nevertheless "glimmers" before us through the accretion of the questions' vocabulary and concerns. De Man's drama of imposition/erasure only signifies the rupture of the poem's horizontal movement, whereas the poem is actually occupied with its vertical effect, the accretion of questions about Life, chariot, and Rousseau which will formalize something close to the subject of its interrogation.

Standing in most obviously for that subject is Rousseau. The poet in fact asks, "Then, what is Life?" after listening to Rousseau's tale of the shape all light, which is meant to answer the poet's questions about Rousseau. And, regardless of de Man's assertion that "The Triumph of Life" thwarts its own hermeneutic impulse, "Shelley Disfigured" tells us that Rousseau is disfigurement incarnate. The knowledge of Rousseau's inevitable disfigurement goes back to de Man's 1971 essay, "The Rhetoric of Blindness: Jacques Derrida's Reading of Rousseau," in which Rousseau's texts are "literary" because they know they will be misread: "[While Rousseau's text] accounts for its own mode of writing, it states at the same time the necessity of making this statement itself in an indirect, figural way that knows it will be misunderstood by being taken literally. Accounting for the 'rhetoricity' of its own mode, the text also postulates the necessity of its own misreading. It knows and asserts that it will be misunderstood" (*BI*, 136).

At the end of "Shelley Disfigured" de Man resists making his reading a method and the disfigured Rousseau a monument. But this gesture is disingenuous in that the disfigurement of Rousseau is already a monumentalized discourse from the outset of Shelley's poem, a discourse, moreover, that Shelley inherits from Rousseau. The "misreading" and subsequent defacement of Rousseau as a private and public figure is a major theme of all of Rousseau's autobiographical works. (De Man actually acknowledges this historical fact but only to support, and thus have it circumscribed by, his linguistic argument.)[20] In the *Confessions* the threat of persecution and conspiracy plots aimed at Rousseau haunt part 2, especially after his expulsion from the Hermitage in book 9. The *Dialogues,* or *Rousseau, Judge of Jean-Jacques,* is even more intensely aware of Rousseau as a cultural monument open to defacement and misinterpretation. As Peter France relates, "The two protagonists are 'Rousseau' and 'the Frenchman'; the subject of their conversation is 'Jean-Jacques,' the strange and apparently monstrous author known to the public at large."[21] "Rousseau" defends "Jean-Jacques," just as in the *Confessions* Rousseau defends himself against the accusations of his real and imagined enemies. By his last autobiographical work, *Reveries of the Solitary Walker,* which Shelley read in 1815, Rousseau does not even attempt to rectify his public defamation; with "the desire to be better understood by men . . . extinguished in my heart," he accepts his disfigurement as his historical fate: "Very few days pass without new reflections confirming how greatly mistaken I was to count on winning back the public even in another age, since with respect to me it is led by guides who are continually renewed in the groups that have taken a dislike to me. . . . Everything is finished for me on earth."[22]

Entwined with these examples of paranoia and persecution is a powerful narcissism, an unshakable belief in the scenario that "Jean-Jacques" *is* a cultural monument at the center of the Western world. This egoism has become a cultural monument of its own, another statue that describes Rousseau and the era he inhabited. The most famous twentieth-century version of this statue is Irving Babbitt's *Rousseau and Romanticism,* which defines Romanticism as the deluded egoism of Rousseau.[23] Thus, contrary to de Man, Rousseau is actually the site from which historical statuary springs. From Rousseau comes a monumentalized discourse of Romantic egoism which Babbitt castigates and an equally monumentalized discourse of persecution which de Man exploits. Most important, from Rousseau's awareness of himself as "Jean-Jacques" comes a monumentalized discourse on monumentalization, on using a figure or statue to describe and evaluate a certain time or event. In that sense Babbitt's and de Man's use of Rousseau is explicitly "Romantic," insofar as the period between Rousseau's and Shelley's deaths is marked by attempts to periodize that era by defining the inheritance "Of what was once Rousseau" ("TL," 204), by saying what statue he actually is. The question "The Triumph of Life" tries to ask is caught up with questions about Rousseau, because who he was *was* the question people asked in order to interrogate the era they inhabited. The strategy is so conventional that it makes Shelley's interrogation of Rousseau an inquiry into the historically conventional, into how we make statues and how they underwrite the intelligibility of our social, political, and cultural lives.

The event most entwined with the identity of Rousseau is, of course, the French Revolution. When, at the end of the eighteenth century, someone asked who Rousseau was, he or she was asking what another thought of the massive changes European society had undergone and was still experiencing. As Edward Duffy puts it, "Blamed or praised for the course of modern history, Rousseau became a touchstone of allegiance in world politics."²⁴ The French Assembly first participated in this ideological monument making, when in 1790 they unanimously passed a proposal to erect a statue of Rousseau with the inscription "LA NATION FRANÇAISE LIBRE A J.-J. ROUSSEAU." In 1794 the French Assembly then installed Rousseau's ashes in the pantheon of the Revolution's heroes, making Rousseau an institutionalized figure for the assembly's own ideological and educational schemes.²⁵

To disfigure such a figure was, then, an explicitly political act aimed at France's new political institutions. Counterrevolutionaries took this act up with gusto, turning Rousseau into a monument of all the French Revolution's follies. English reactionaries characterized this Rousseau in two ways. First, Rousseau's early affiliation with Enlightenment figures was conflated with his role as "natural" man and social scientist. Out of this mix came an Enlightenment philosophe whose views on government, education, and Nature were imbedded in architectonic systems of logic and reason. But this philosophe was characterized in another way, wherein his belief in reason and clarity hid and was motivated by an overwhelming vanity and salaciousness, traits first demonstrated by Rousseau's posthumous *Confessions*. Thus, the philosophe's reason was a logic that gave way to madness and which explained all the excesses of the French Revolution.²⁶ Rousseau became the target of an anti-Jacobinist iconoclasm, which took him as an example of the false clarity and idolatry that had led to the chaos that engulfed France.

That Shelley is aware of Rousseau's many roles is made clear by his poet's first encounter with Rousseau as a wizened "old root." De Man uses the French *défiguré* to turn Rousseau's loss of face into a sign of linguistic disfigurement, but, in doing so, he elides the specific terms of diastrophism which Shelley uses to describe Rousseau, which more readily signal the various statues Rousseau becomes. For, as an old root, this image of Rousseau already contains the hardness and rigidity of a monument. More important, the image also specifies what monuments Rousseau becomes. As a root, he is both nature child and priapic figure; as a root twisted into a "strange distortion" with grass that is really "discoloured hair," he is also a parody of nature and the priapic. *Strange distortion* refers to both the publicly misunderstood figure and the perverse philosophe, "one of that deluded crew" taken in by the false clarity of the Enlightenment ("TL," 184). The absence of Rousseau's eyes further mocks the Enlightenment and French Revolutionary claims of a clear, visible system of truth. And, finally, as a root he is the Latin *radix,* the radical all Europe and England knew. Political radical, nature child, parody of the nature child, monstrous phallus, misunderstood public figure, and Enlightenment dupe—these are all various statues of Rousseau from the various ideological camps which Shelley has packed into a single image. By reading this image only as *défiguré,* de Man elides the fact that Shelley is obviously playing with the various "rhetorics of Rousseau" given to Shelley by English and European culture and that he is signaling to his audience that he is doing so.

One of these rhetorics, that of Rousseau as Enlightenment dupe, allows us to read Rousseau's encounter with the shape all light one way, as an emblem of revolutionary France's seduction by the "light" of reason.[27] Waking into the state of epistemological uncertainty which de Man describes, Rousseau encounters the shape all light which "tramples" the "embers" of his creating mind—the "fading coal" of "A Defence of Poetry"—just as Enlightenment reason extinguished all the other mental faculties of those supporting or participating in the French Revolution. Unaware of his predicament, Rousseau asks the shape who Rousseau is, just as the monstrous vanity of those in France allowed them to ask Enlightenment rationality to explain and systematize "man." The shape gives him a cup of nepenthe, the drug of forgetfulness—a fitting emblem for the new revolutionary faith that wants to create a new society, an insurrectionary modernity that will erase all past traditions of government and law. The result is the erasure of the tracks upon Rousseau's mind, which, as Edward Duffy notes, parodies "the epistemological image at the base of eighteenth-century rationalism. . . . the Lockean notion of the mind as a tabula rasa."[28] The contradictory light imagery of the entire piece becomes a parody of the logic of Enlightenment thought, as does the cartoonlike sun, a "hackneyed self-image of the Enlightenment," which begins the poem.[29]

But, if the scene with the shape can be read as a reactionary explanation of Rousseau's and France's fall from grace, it would be dangerous to conflate this explanation with any "final" understanding of the poem. Indeed, the poem invites this explanation in order to place it under critical examination. To better understand the origins of Rousseau as a vain and perverse philosophe and Enlightenment dupe means coming upon another body of monumentalized discourse which the poem exhumes, that of the conservative English writer and thinker Edmund Burke.

It is Burke who first combines the sensual egoist of the *Confessions* with the social scientist of the *Social Contract* and gives Europe and England Rousseau as the perverse philosophe, "the great professor and founder of *the philosophy of vanity* in England."[30] From Burke comes the statue of Rousseau as disfigured thinker and writer, "who has carried marks of a deranged understanding."[31] Also from Burke comes an aesthetic work that "inaugurated the Romantic critique of pictorialist poetics" and a political work that openly mocked "this new conquering empire of light and reason," "the light of which the gentlemen of France tell us they have got so abundant a share."[32] Shelley's disfigured Rousseau is thus not only a sign of the many Rousseaus of Shelley's time but also a statue of the ideology of Edmund Burke.

Like Rousseau, this statue is also explicitly about monumentalized discourse. For Burke's major attack against Rousseau, his 1791 *Letter to a Member of the National Assembly,* directly responds to the assembly's literal monumentalization of Rousseau in 1790: "To this man and this writer, as a pattern to authors and to Frenchmen, the foundries of Paris are now running for statues, with the kettles of their poor and the bells of their churches."[33] From the outset Burke's own discourse on Rousseau is beset by an awareness of canonization and the politics of that act.

There was also a revival of both Burke and Rousseau in the midteens, when Shelley began to write his major poetry.[34] It is not surprising that "The Triumph of Life," reflecting on how it formulates the subject of its interrogation, should turn to Burke and Rousseau. These two not only represent the two normalizing discourses of the period but were also intensely aware of their status as such.[35]

The poem best illustrates the dialectic between these two discourses in the way it handles its own libidinal energies. A paradigm for the sexual charge of the poem is Rousseau's description of himself "as one between desire and shame / Suspended" before the "shape all light" ("TL," 394–95). Those lines correctly describe the erotic play of Rousseau's *Confessions,* a work obsessed with the emotions surrounding secretive desires and their subsequent exposure. But Shelley's lines are also a Burkean representation of the French Revolution as an event shot through with a desire "lost to shame."[36] Thus, these lines caricature a fundamental difference between Rousseau and Burke, the former the poet of "desire" and the latter the moral voice of "shame." Likewise, the poem's crowd scenes are charged with a sensual ecstasy that then becomes a death frenzy of the species, in which the dance surrounding the chariot's procession moves from the sensual *"fête"* that inaugurates society in Rousseau's *Essay on the Origin of Languages* to the bloodthirsty mobs that gyrate through Burke's *Reflections on the Revolution in France*. Just as in the *Essay* "the original festivals developed" and "feet skipped with joy," so too in Shelley "maidens & youths fling their wild arms in air / As their feet twinkle" ("TL," 149–50).[37] But the dancers then collapse from the intensity of their passion and are replaced by "Old men, and women foully disarrayed / [who] Shake their gray hair in the insulting wind" (165–66)—gender-disturbing creatures who recall "the vilest of women" who surround the royal captives of Burke's *Reflections* with "horrid yells, and shrilling screams, and frantic dances, and infamous contumelies" (*RRF,* 85).

That famous passage from the *Reflections* is worth quoting more fully, for the other specific monument it unearths:

> The royal captives who followed the train were slowly moved along, amidst the horrid yells, and shrilling screams, and frantic dances, and infamous contumelies, and all the unutterable abominations of the furies of hell, in the abused shape of the vilest of women. After they had been made to taste, drop by drop, more than the bitterness of death, in the slow torture of a journey of twelve miles, protracted to six hours, they were, under a guard, composed of those very soldiers who had thus conducted them through this famous *triumph,* lodged in one of the old palaces of Paris, now converted into a Bastille for kings.
>
> Is this a *triumph* to be consecrated at altars? to be commemorated with grateful thanksgiving? to be offered to the divine humanity with fervent prayer and enthusiastic ejaculation? (*RRF,* 85; my emphasis)[38]

Shelley's "triumph" is thus not only a classical allusion but also part of the more immediate political vocabularies of his time. Furthermore, Burke's outcry is *itself* a direct response to the Old Jewry sermon by the ardent English supporter of the French Revolution, Dr. Richard Price, whom Burke quotes as exulting: "I am *thankful* . . . I have lived to see *Thirty Millions of People,* indignant and resolute, spurning at slavery, and demanding liberty with an irresistible voice. *Their King led in triumph and an arbitrary monarch surrendering himself to his subjects"* (*RRF*, 78). What is at stake for Burke is how anyone could view such a scene as a positive victory, a triumph, for European society and culture. He thus stresses the mistake of using the classical vocabulary of the triumph to describe a scene as bankrupt as the mob's humiliation of its royal captives in Paris. Somewhat paradoxically, he also attacks that vocabulary as part of an inherently false and illegitimate spectacle. Thus, Burke goes past the Romans to appeal to the "originators" of Western democracy, claiming that Athenian citizens would not allow the French triumph onto their stage as theater: "No theatrical audience in Athens would bear what has been borne, in the midst of the real tragedy of this triumphal day" (94). The only thing real about the "triumphal day" is its tragedy; as a simulacrum of liberty and progress, it fools no one. But, as a simulacrum, the discourse of the triumph becomes the perfect emblem of the French Revolution, as an event with no real truth or legitimacy behind the guises it steals from other centuries.

Indeed, for Burke, if Price's vision is anything, it is merely a copy of the triumphal image that was used as part of England's own revolutionary discourse in 1648. Burke's point is to argue against Price's explicit connection of this vision to the Glorious Revolution of 1688, which was commonly held to begin England's own constitutional monarchy. For, as W. J. T. Mitchell notes, "Price, like many English liberals, saw the October Days as an augury of peaceful revolution, the reconciliation of Louis XVI with the National Assembly and the French people." Thus, Price's vision "typologically fuses the triumphal procession of King Louis and the people from Versailles to Paris with Christ's entry into Jerusalem and the entry of the Israelites into the Promised Land."[39] In contrast to this vision, Burke cites from 1648 a description of the English revolutionary, Rev. Hugh Peters, whom a witness sees "riding before the king *triumphing*" (*RRF*, 79). Here Charles I is the fallen monarch, a captive of a triumphant procession that leads not to the reconciliation between a king and his people but, instead, to regicide. By imposing the 1648 usage of the triumph on Price's vision, Burke not only erases Price's christological allusion but also repudiates the liberal English politics that goes with it.[40] Instead of a Louis XVI voluntarily leading his people in triumph toward a new democratic vision, Burke gives us a Louis XVI who is a captive of the triumph and his people, a victim of a procession that for Burke is nothing more than a bloodthirsty, monstrous mob.

Burke's *Reflections* shows the "triumph" to be both a highly politicized image and a highly unstable one, whose interpretation and cultural and political affiliation are up for grabs. It is this instability that "The Triumph of Life" exploits. Coming to terms with the triumph becomes another way in which the poem exhibits how it tries to formalize the subject of its interrogation. Burke's own interrogation of Price's triumph—"Is this a triumph to be consecrated at altars?"—shows that just as "Who is Rousseau?" asks more than just the identity of Rousseau, so too do the poem's questions about the triumph ask for more than just a description of the procession's form.

When Burke attacks Price, he also ignores another reason why the revolutionaries used the triumph as a Roman allusion: because they wanted to associate their politics with a Roman republicanism of the past. But this revolutionary use of the triumph is itself an inversion, for the Roman triumphs were not so much a sign of a republican Rome as a display of foreign chieftains conquered by an imperial Rome. Shelley appears to reverse his triumph back to this imperial form:

[I] saw like clouds upon the thunder blast

    The million with fierce song and maniac dance
Ranging around; such seemed the jubilee
    As when to greet some conqueror's advance

Imperial Rome poured forth her living sea
    From senatehouse & prison & theatre
When Freedom left those who upon the free

    Had bound a yoke which soon they stooped to bear.
Nor wanted here the true similitude
    Of a triumphal pageant, for where'er

The chariot rolled a captive multitude
    Was driven.
("TL," 109–20)

Yet Shelley's "Imperial Rome" contains both totalitarian and liberational energies. Its crowds come out to meet "some conqueror's advance," ostensibly a Roman military leader returning home with the fruits of his victories. Read this way, both crowd and conqueror are part of the same imperial celebration. But those who "advance" in a Roman triumph are also the prisoners of the procession; the conqueror then becomes, like Burke's version of Price's Louis XVI and Peters's Charles I, the fallen despot, one of those "who upon the free / Had bound a yoke which soon they stooped to bear." This advance is also marked by a great sense of release within Rome itself, where those from "prison" are not only freed but also become part of a "living sea" with those from the "senatehouse" and "theatre." The wild and frantic "jubilee" around the triumph becomes not only a totalitarian mob but also a demonstration, a "riot" of democratic and populist aspirations. The captives of the triumph, moreover, are the great leaders and personages of history whom Rousseau and Shelley's poet review; they are signs of a certain way to tell history, to narrate a population's collective story through the individual careers of a handful of canonized figures. As those bound to a yoke they had freely given others, they represent history that is intrinsically totalitarian; in contrast, those "million with fierce song and maniac dance" demonstrate the artifice of that history and the possibility of moving beyond that narrative to a collective destiny. But that possibility turns in on and extinguishes itself, when, through its Roussseauist and Burkean discourses, the poem transforms its libidinal dance into a nightmarish scene of mutilation and decay.[41] Rousseau's own situation emphasizes this historical plight: standing apart from those chained to the chariot, Rousseau's personage suggests the creation of a new history after 1789, even "if it be world of agony" ("TL," 296). But, borne into the madness of the crowd, falling to the wayside exhausted and deformed, Rousseau becomes a monument to the crowd's failure to escape the monumentalized history of the chariot's captives and to create, with a vocabulary that goes beyond that monumentalized history, an as yet unspoken and unformed history of its own.

From where could such a vocabulary come? Shelley also problematizes that question, by ironically insisting on the "true similitude" of his own triumph, thereby foregrounding what Burke claims about Price, that the triumph is itself a simulacrum used to describe something that it is not. Shelley's poet's "Vision" must image its historical plight *through* a monument, a Roman triumph that divides its procession between conquered historical personages and a dancing population beyond those personages' history. To posit or imagine something new besides this history necessarily means a reliance on something old, the dancing crowd around a Roman triumph. The "millions" dancing around the chariot with their libidinal dream are then monuments in their own right, linguistic constructions open to deconstruction—to the de Manian disfigurement "Shelley Disfigured" so ably demonstrates.

To come to grips with this knowledge is not only the ascetic imperative of what Jonathan Arac has described as deconstruction's "exemplary rigor," for the consequences of disavowing this knowledge are not only linguistic but also political.[42] The fate of the poem's triumph dramatizes what happens when a revolutionary discourse forgets its own rhetoricity. For the French revolutionary triumph of both Price and Burke transforms itself in Shelley's own historical moment. The triumph crowns itself, as did Napoléon, with the "moving arch of victory" ("TL," 439) which in 1822 could not help but recall the Arc de Triomphe begun by Napoléon in 1806, the literal monument and sign of an imperial Napoleonic discourse that took over from the French Revolution such terms as *liberation, the State,* and *the people* to describe French hegemony over Europe from 1800 to 1814.[43]

We are now able to read Rousseau's encounter with the shape all light once more. Rousseau wakes into the state of radical uncertainty which de Man calls "forgetting." But, as we saw in "Shelley Disfigured," the very nature of that state means an absence of permanent erasure. History in all its aporetic force comes back to Rousseau as the shape all light and the drug nepenthe. Rousseau drinks the drug and forgets to forget, negating the negation obstructing his access to a historical consciousness. But "to forget to forget" is a highly violent form of historical awareness; the nepenthe imposes on Rousseau what has surpassed him and the French Revolution, an imperial discourse "as if from some dread war / Triumphantly returning" ("TL," 436–37). This discourse has itself forgotten its own rhetoricity, what would confute the discourse's own certainty in applying the triumph of the French Revolution to the European ambitions of Napoléon. Shelley calls the image of this discourse a "new Vision," which acknowledges the discourse's imposition on Rousseau while mocking its dependence on its "vehicle," the triumph. The catalog of horrors which ends Shelley's fragment is the devastation and oppression of Europe and England brought on by the postrevolutionary adventurism of Napoleonic France and the repressive measures of its enemies. But Shelley's poem has not forgotten its own hard lesson about disfigurement and erasure: the shadowy creatures, "numerous as the dead leaves blown" ("TL," 528) and shot through with the cold light of the chariot, stress the disfiguring textual forms this catalog of recent history must take.

"The Triumph of Life" is thus post-Enlightenment *and* post-Napoleonic. Or, more precisely, it tries to write itself past Napoléon by going back and examining all the political and linguistic lessons of monuments and discourses that lead up to his fallen figure chained to the chariot—the figure that, as de Man casually observes, is the occasion for one of Shelley's poet's most explicit meditations on the aporia between word and deed.[44] The question the poem wants to ask but cannot has as its subject something like the experience of Europe and England from the deformed Rousseau to the fallen Napoléon. That the poem cannot interrogate or form this subject except through constant substitutions of different statuary is the lesson the poem constructs out of that always receding experience.[45] Constructed in a deconstructive sense, that lesson becomes the answer de Man gives at the end of "The Resistance to Theory": "What remains impossible to decide is whether this flourishing [of theory] is a triumph or a fall."[46] What remains impossible for "The Triumph of Life" to resolve is the final form of its narration; what remains—what, indeed, is poeticized—is the limit of its historical and critical consciousness.

This lesson of uncertainty is what projects this unfinished poem past Napoléon, even as it problematizes the idea of surpassing the certainty embedded in revolutionary discourse up to and including Napoléon. By ignoring its status as a monumentalized discourse, the "arch of victory" paradoxically becomes a captive to itself, another blind historical figure. It forgets that it is, as de Man says elsewhere, one of those "texts [that] masquerade in the guise of wars or revolutions" (*BI,* 165). The most notable writer to take up this issue will be Karl Marx, whose 1851 *Eighteenth Brumaire of Louis Bonaparte* will provide a critique of revolution up to its time which will sound very familiar to readers of "The Triumph of Life" *and* Burke:

> And just when [the living] seem engaged in revolutionizing themselves and things, in creating something entirely new, precisely in such epochs of revolutionary crisis they anxiously conjure up the

spirits of the past to their service and borrow from them names, battle slogans and costumes in order to present the new scene of world history in this time-honored disguise and this borrowed language. Thus Luther donned the mask of the Apostle Paul, the Revolution of 1789 to 1814 draped itself alternately as the Roman Republic and the Roman Empire . . .[47]

Marx's project was, of course, to distinguish as radically as possible the discontinuity between the identities of bourgeois and proletarian revolutions. That this project still occupies a prominent position as a *critical problem* in leftist theoretical discourse is demonstrated in the recent statement by the post-Marxist Chantal Mouffe, that "we are undoubtedly living through the crisis of the Jacobin imaginary, which has, in diverse ways, characterized the revolutionary politics of the last two hundred years."[48] I would thus place "The Triumph of Life" and its deconstructive critique of revolutionary, and imperial, identity within a certain tradition also spanning Marx and Mouffe—that is, the recognition, thinking through, and dramatization of this "crisis of the Jacobin imaginary."

This is the tradition that de Man, through his own reception of Shelley, inherits, and which "Shelley Disfigured" and leftist critics of de Man suppress.[49] But, if "Shelley Disfigured" does elide this sociohistoric "crisis" within "The Triumph of Life," its own violent recognition of the disfiguring inevitability of monuments calls for a dialectical engagement with the object it reads, and thus for the erasure, the "forgetting," of that suppression. We can begin to intuit the implications of this double erasure into history by taking seriously Mouffe's description of this historical identity as a "crisis"—by in fact defining this identity through the sense of a constitutive semiotic fissure, one that foregrounds the degree to which the "Jacobin imaginary" is imaginary. Like de Man's historical reenvisioning of an allegorical Romanticism, then, this tradition of revolutionary politics is constitutively split between its mediation and its necessarily inauthentic self, what "Shelley Disfigured" retranslates into the arbitrary disfiguring erasure of one monument by another. But, even more clearly than in the case of de Man's historical revision, this tradition finds itself attached to the challenge of producing historical "truth," a challenge that proceeds through the aporetic relation between word and deed.

This challenge refers, moreover, not only to the general promise of carrying out a revolutionary politics but also to the more specific task of ruthlessly critiquing such politics, as Marx demanded. That is, we begin such a critique—such a recognition of the "crisis of the Jacobin imaginary"—by all too often relying on temporal schemas that unproblematically assume that words and deeds exist either in perfect correspondence or in a simple relation of cause and effect. We thus either rely on narratives in which theory, reflection, and language fall behind spontaneous action and unmediated praxis or, conversely, on narratives of a compensatory, hyperbolic mode in which words unproblematically effect change in a nonlinguistic world of action. The last part of this century has certainly added to our store of such narratives. More immediately, we have seen condensed versions of such schemes try, with varying degrees of complexity, to house either positively or negatively de Man's corpus within both leftist and collaborationist politics. We have seen such schemes attempt to conceive of deconstruction as a fallen retreat into language after the actions of either 1960s activism or 1940s fascist collaborationism or, conversely, to perceive deconstruction's deracination of aesthetic symbolism as a linguistic gesture that is immediately intelligible as an act of political demystification. Regardless of our sympathies toward such varying monuments, what a dialectical reading of de Man's works and "The Triumph of Life" exposes is how these narratives are necessarily complicated by a synchronic perception of the separation between words and deeds, one in which thought and action do not meet in a mystified synthesis but, instead, coexist simultaneously in an actively intolerable disjunction.

Such a synchronic incommensurability especially mandates against the historical construction of diachronic narratives that simply connect, and thus also differentiate, periods of predominantly pure action to, and from, those of predominantly pure reflection. Not coincidentally, much of our received knowledge of Romanticism—in either its literary biographical or world historical mode—relies on such simple constructions. Indeed, "The Triumph of Life" is arguably an exemplary "Romantic" work whose author remains one of the main candidates for such a narrative, one that would make Shelley intelligible by dividing his life into contrasting periods of action and reflection. Not coincidentally, it is this Romantic poem that mobilizes, however, a language of ever-receding statuary in order to repudiate a historical consciousness, and politics, based on the unproblematic representation of historical events. "The

Triumph of Life" already marks, in other words, a fissured historical moment that is the synchronic disjunction between Enlightenment political action and its representation.

This active semiotic incommensurability can be applied, moreover, to the other historical moments that coordinate the sociohistoric transmission and reception of de Man's writings. Thus, narratives that involve deconstruction's relation to New Left activism risk implicitly assuming the former as either a positive or a negative theoretical reflection of the latter; what is then elided is the degree to which '60s activism is its own historically and politically specific experiment with the aporia between theory and praxis.[50] Conversely, discussions about de Man and *Le Soir* need to consider the degree to which their reflections on the past rely on historical reifications that lie invisible *within* their already-acknowledged methodological mediations: the degree to which, for example, the ability to critique historically and politically Europe's fascist past is structured by an a priori concept of what signifies "fascism."[51] The point of these examples, then, is not to let such synchronic incommensurability absorb all these moments into the temporal predicament of a formalist relativism but, rather, the exact opposite: to demonstrate how detailed and thorough the "sociohistoric" can and must be in sociohistoric discussions of de Man and deconstruction and how resistant the same sociohistoric can be to such discussions.

The other side to this historical knowledge is, of course, the question of political action, which the synchronic incommensurability between words and deeds suspends much in the same way that "The Rhetoric of Temporality" suspends—that is, supports and defers—the truth claims of its historical revision. In this dialectical reading of "Shelley Disfigured" and "The Triumph of Life" it is Shelley's work that most profitably instructs those who would take political action; if Napoléon presents us with a mystified discourse that has forgotten its own rhetoricity and "Shelley Disfigured" asserts a "madness of words" which can only posit action as the disfigurement of meaning, "The Triumph of Life" presents us with a third asymmetric option, one in which politics begins with the derealization of the unproblematic correspondence of actions and their meanings. Such a derealization might propel us into a praxis whose linguistic procedures are as necessarily subtending as they are unreliable, but that is simply to return us to the semiotic *grund* of the *Eighteenth Brumaire* and Marx's opening dictum that "men make their own history, but they do not make it just as they please."[52] That is the point, I would suggest, which Shelley's Romanticism and "The Triumph of Life" proleptically make in the first place, what we can make out of de Man's own texts of nepenthe and what is called deconstruction's political future.

# Chapter 3

# Allegories of Praxis

Jerome McGann, Heinrich Heine, and the Ideology of Romantic Discontent

> A book like *The Romantic Ideology,* it has been argued, implicitly reifies this kind of romantic dynamism as a transcendent aesthetic form or set of procedures. The charge is that *The Romantic Ideology* at times simply replaces Wellek's tripartite structural representation [of imagination, nature, and symbol] with a dialectical view that is, finally, no less conceptual, for all its appeal to dynamic forms. I have come to think this criticism a just one. I also think it an important criticism, for it exposes a residual investment in a type of interpretive thought that I was explicitly trying to avoid.
>
> McGann
> "Rethinking Romanticism"

> But I beg you to take into consideration the conditions under which I an writing, the time and place.
>
> Heine
> *The Romantic School*

# I

Recently, Herbert Lindenberger offered a history of contemporary Romantic studies which intersects with our institutional fable and also provides an alternative to it:

> Those who started working on the English Romantics, above all on Wordsworth, during the mid-1950s remember the exhilaration that came from the rediscovery and reassessment of what they saw as a neglected and often maligned body of literature, one that had fallen by default into the custodial care of learned, bureaucratically entrenched antiquarians from whom they sought to wrest it away. For a considerable time romanticism served as the testing ground for such critical modes as the history of ideas, phenomenology, and, most famously, deconstruction. The publication of . . . *Deconstruction and Criticism* [in 1979] . . . celebrates the compatibility of romanticism with the methodological category in the title, yet it also, we can now see with a decade's hindsight, marks the end of the period when romanticism stood at the forefront of literary study in America.[1]

Lindenberger thus sees deconstruction's appropriation of Romanticism, emblematized by the collection that showcases de Man's "Shelley Disfigured," as the apex of a trajectory that begins with the originating modernity of mid-1950s academic Romanticism. Romanticism thus becomes the marker for a certain intellectual complexity that the Abramsian historian of ideas and the de Manian deconstructive critic implicitly share. As important, moreover, is the institutional dimension to Lindenberger's elegiac account—his point that the years between 1955 and 1979 mark a period when different Romanticists take turns representing the larger concerns and values of "literary study in

America." With the beginning of the '80s, this representative cachet is transferred for Lindenberger to scholars in the Renaissance and their critical practice of the so-called New Historicism.[2] Lindenberger is quick to add that this transfer does not impede serious historical work in Romantic studies during the decade; we might also add that New Historicism's dominating influence must be qualified by the presence in the '80s of other historicist arguments radiating out of Marxist and post-Marxist theory. Thus, if in the '80s Romanticism no longer unequivocally represents the "forefront of literary study in America," that forefront is itself marked by a methodological heterogeneity that immediately qualifies any simple generalizations about that decade's engagement with historical thought.

It is, moreover, precisely the singular, nonnormative status of Romantic studies in the '80s which allows this field to have a strong relation to the wide array of historical theories practiced during that time. As Lindenberger asserts, this is a period of intellectual ferment and controversy in Romantic studies, a time marked by a variety of critical attempts to produce a historical Romanticism that engages with the poststructuralist and postmodern claims of Continental theory. Yet most if not all of these diverse attempts respond either directly or indirectly to a certain type of ideological critique structured around the transmission and reception of Romanticism's ostensible modernity—a historical model of critical intervention which is both prefigured and problematized by de Man's historical revision in "The Rhetoric of Temporality" but which receives its most concise and stirring polemic in 1983 with Jerome McGann's *The Romantic Ideology*. This model of transmission and intervention most tellingly dramatizes the challenges facing a historical knowledge initiated by the performative desire for an "oppositional criticism," a predicament that sharply inflects literary criticism's more generalized fall into history in the '80s.[3] Its sideline status notwithstanding, the Romantic historiography of the last fifteen years allegorizes this critical will to praxis in a way that speaks directly to the question of the relevance and survival of oppositional criticism today.

## II

The engagement of literary criticism with history in the '80s and '90s could be understood by returning to the aporetic challenge to history posed by the skepticism of deconstruction which we saw apotheosized by "Shelley Disfigured." This time, however, I approach that challenge indirectly, by in fact skipping over its argument and focusing instead on the well-rehearsed critique leveled not only at the skepticism of deconstruction but also at the organic ambiguity of New Criticism: the charge that both these theoretical practices, for all their differences, dwell within the prisonhouse of language—that both deconstruction and New Criticism are merely Janus doubles of a formalism that blocks out any discussion of literature which involves social, political, and historical concerns. It is this by now familiar attack on formalism which initiates many of the various calls to history which gain prominence and legitimacy in literary studies in the early 1980s. This choice between formalism and history becomes, moreover, the site for a certain growing politicization of the academy, and, thus, while the reality and relevance of this politicization is by no means a given, its various, oftentimes contradictory claims clearly attach themselves to the promise of a criticism that will somehow be resolutely "historical" in its methodology and concerns.

What needs to be stressed, however, is how the charge of formalism becomes the very discursive gauge for the success of that promise and its attendant claims of politicization. That is, various critical modes of historical thought in the '80s find their historical and political arguments open to the same formalist critique that they themselves mobilized against the linguistic theories of the '70s.[4] One version of this critique is to call attention to the academic setting of sociohistoric criticism in the '80s and thus to dismiss the oppositional self-representation of such writings as a mystification of an inevitably formalist endeavor surrounded by the brute reality of institutional and professional limitations. Such a notion of "formalist politics" arguably underwrites many of the charges of co-option directed even, or especially, toward the academic Marxism and post-Marxism of that decade. There is also the more specific charge that it is not only the institutional context but the very theory of certain historical criticism which is in actuality another version of formalism. New Historicism and Renaissance studies—Lindenberger's successors to deconstruction and Romanticism—have been increasingly targeted as fields in which Foucaultian-inspired theories of genealogy and power legitimate a historicism that is at once quietistic and formalist.[5] Thus, one could argue that the '80s end with the New Historicism uncomfortably, if not uncannily, repeating the institutional fate of its supposedly displaced predecessor, American deconstruction. Unlike the Romanticism of Lovejoy and Spitzer, which represents a European intellectual modernity oftentimes too threateningly close to U.S. shores, deconstruction and New Historicism signify an attenuation by the American academy of the ostensibly genuine, disruptive power of Continental—first Derridean and then Foucaultian—theory. Within the American academy the self-reflexive signifier for this attenuation is the charge, and countercharge, of formalist thought.

We could, of course, complicate this institutional overview with a number of subplots, such as the various pre–*Le Soir* arguments for deconstruction's relation to Marxism and politics which continue through most of '80s.[6] What I want to concentrate on, however, is the specific commentary that Romantic studies in the '80s can make about the charge of formalism in New Historicist readings of the Renaissance. I take as my point of departure Jon Klancher's recent suggestions about why Romantic studies seem to resist the New Historicist gestures of "subversion" and "containment" which operate so brilliantly in Renaissance studies. One reason that Klancher gives is the difference between the two historical objects under examination: whereas the New Historicist oscillation between subversion and containment finds its perfect homology in the representation of a Renaissance in which "politics and literature were still undifferentiated realms," such a troping of politics discovers in English Romanticism a historical problematic that assumes "neither a new historicist's identification of power and culture, nor their Romantic opposition."[7] As Klancher later elaborates:

> The diversity of method and strategy in [recent Romanticist historicist work] suggest that—contrary to the assumption of an absolutist state in Renaissance new historicism—there is no single material or political framework against which to read Romantic texts. English Romantic writings were staged within an unstable ensemble of older institutions in crisis (state and church) and emerging institutional events which pressured any act of cultural reproduction—the marketplace and its industrializing, the new media and their reading audiences, the alternative institutions of radical dissent, shifting

modes of social hierarchy. Reading Romantic texts historically will therefore often mean trying to position those texts among institutional pressures and possibilities.[8]

Thus, for Klancher, Romanticism as a historical period presents a set of uneven, asymmetric relations among and within the economic, cultural, and political spheres, relations that discourage the homologies of power between state and literature which characterize Renaissance New Historicism. Such homologies have been the very targets of the charges that Renaissance New Historicism invites a formalism in which the oscillation between subversion and containment repeats itself between, among, and within all levels of Renaissance "society," either at the Royal courts of the Old World or the trading and military posts of the New. It is, moreover, the temporal extension of one such homology which occasions Klancher's other reason for why contemporary Romantic historiography differs from Renaissance New Historicism: the way Renaissance New Historicists implicitly identify "a Renaissance culture saturated with power with a postmodern culture powerless to resist."[9]

Klancher thus also argues that the popularity of New Historicism is based in part on a perceived similarity between the Renaissance and one version of our contemporary postmodernism. For Klancher this similarity threatens to conflate the two periods of time into a sociohistoric monad saturated by a neo-Foucaultian technology of power, an ongoing spectacle of subversion and containment which risks "making historical criticism a transhistorical echo of the present."[10] In contrast, Klancher identifies in Romantic studies a tendency opposed to this convergence of the past and present, one in which the point is to disrupt any unproblematic identification between the two. Thus, Romantic studies in the '80s distinguishes itself from Renaissance New Historicism at two levels: first, through its reinvention as a historical object of study marked by inchoateness and material asymmetries and, second, through the realization of a historical subject—the contemporary Romantic critic—characterized by a commitment to "disengage" the present from the reifications of a Romantic past. These two levels are, of course, connected, since such reifications are in fact the ideological representations of a Romanticism that is produced and reproduced by the "original" Romantic writers and their later (especially mid-twentieth-century) interpreters, the totalizing representations of aesthetic and imaginative transcendence that the '80s "reinvention" of that period is supposed to contest. This double action of reinvention and disengagement marks Romanticism in the '80s as a metacritical field of knowledge, whose realization depends heavily on the transmission, reception, and rejection of its various aesthetic, philosophic, and political premises. Following Klancher, I would thus argue that this self-reflexive sense of the '80s Romantic historicist's own participation in the (re)production of Romantic knowledge particularly distinguishes the historical project of Romantic studies from the paradigmatic operations of Renaissance New Historicism.

We can begin to understand what this difference means by considering another critique of Renaissance New Historicism. Whereas Klancher and others warn that such studies risk conflating the Renaissance with a politically retrograde postmodern present, Louis Montrose distinguishes American work in the Renaissance from its British "materialist" counterpart by arguing that American scholars are on the whole unconcerned with applying their New Historicist versions of the past to the present.[11] These apparently contradictory observations actually express the same insight: both Klancher and Montrose point to the relative lack of reflexivity which characterizes the New Historical work as a vehicle and product of cultural transmission—in which the very unconcern for the use of the past by the present allows for the conflation of the two.

Insofar as both Klancher and Montrose charge that New Historicism largely fails to interrogate the relation between the past and the present, we could argue that Renaissance New Historicism actually resembles in this instance the Romantic scholarship of the post–World War II generation, a scholarship characterized by the apparently unproblematic continuity it posits between Romanticism and its mid-twentieth-century interlocutors. I would add, however, that for the latter, *unproblematic* does not necessarily mean unreflexive, insofar as this continuity is part of the explicit argument that the post–World War II generation makes in order to overcome the High Modernist critique of Romanticism. This continuity is "unproblematic," then, only in the sense that Abrams, Frye, and others set out to discover and affirm it as a solution to this critique. This celebration of Romanticism as the transmission of Romantic knowledge both structures and antagonizes the "new wave" of "interventionist" Romantic studies which begins in the late 1960s with Paul de Man's rereading of the Romantic symbol and which continues in the 1980s with Jerome McGann's *Romantic Ideology,* to cite the most prominent work among a number of historical projects. It is thus no small accident that the one prominent Romanticist study to employ Foucaultian theories of power in the '80s—Clifford Siskin's *The Historicity of Romantic Discourse* (1988)—does so by structuring its own version of subversion and containment around a model of transmission, one that responds directly to both de Man's and McGann's attempted historical revisions. It is also no coincidence that two of the scholars most notably linked early on to a New Historicist approach in Romanticism, Alan Liu and Marjorie Levinson, carry out their own metacritiques of this methodology, critiques that in their different ways foreground each critic's own part in reproducing and transmitting what they have set out to study historically.[12]

We are now in a position to consider a provisional conclusion. While both Renaissance and Romantic studies invoke history in the 1980s, the latter's invocations of history actually proleptically critique the former's, insofar as the interventionist arguments in Romantic studies in the early '80s against the post–World War II generation of Romanticism prefigure the charges of formalism leveled against Renaissance New Historicism in the late '80s. That is, despite their many striking differences, both New Historicism and post–World War II Romanticism are equally disinclined to interrogate how our notions of the past and present are subtended through the necessary acts of transmitting and (re)producing the historical past. Such disinterest preempts historically inclined critics from engaging with the process of transmission in an explicitly skeptical manner; in contrast, many '80s Romanticists embrace with particular intransigence the stance of the oppositional, interventionist critic who self-consciously interrogates such a transmission. Thus, while in a less prominent position than other forms of historiography, the study of Romanticism vividly demonstrates in condensed form how differing methodological issues inform the differing ways history and politics interpenetrate in the academy during the '80s. And, insofar as the interventionist critique of post–World War II Romanticism does coincide with the charge of formalism against Renaissance New Historicism, contemporary Romantic studies presents us with an alternative to the ostensible political cul-de-sac of New Historicism's infinitely expanding weave of subversion and containment. Thus, through its very nature as the proposition, and denial, of a modernity that might still include us "within its horizon" ("SD," 40), Romanticism and its historiography assert the wagers of a historical knowledge that, contrary to the neo-Foucaultian claims of New Historical power, is defiantly emancipatory in its final goals and forms.

While perhaps extremely satisfying, this conclusion is also highly problematic. We could, of course, first note how such a conclusion necessarily simplifies a more diverse and conflicted representation of New Historicism in and beyond Renaissance studies, one that would relate Renaissance New Historicism to both its more recognizably activist British counterpart and to the volatile field of American literature, in which a more "properly" New Historical approach exists alongside an equally aggressive historical revisionism.[13] For Romantic historicism, however, the more immediate danger lies in prematurely conferring onto its critical disposition an unreflected, revolutionary "Titanism" similar to what Christopher Norris sees de Man critiquing in Wordsworth's fellow travelers in *The Prelude*.[14] Thus, while the issue of metacritical transmission does indeed distinguish Romantic historical work in the '80s, we cannot stop and confuse this observation with the rhetorical closure of a political solution. Indeed, such a confusion would be symptomatic of the theoretical problematic that a more deliberate consideration of the politics of this transmission unearths.

If, then, historical criticism in the '80s discovers that it is still too formalist, the metacriticism of Romantic historicism needs to ask whether it is reflexive enough. To ask such a question is not, moreover, simply to test the good critical faith that most Romanticists already possess, insofar as few Romanticists actively confuse themselves with Titans in their writing lives. It is, instead, to use the distinctive structure of Romantic historicism to show how the formalist problems of New Historicism reappear in the antinomies between theory and praxis, description and prescription, critique and prophecy, which both motivate and block the more unabashedly oppositional literary historicism of the '80s, chiefly the leftist criticism radiating out of Marxist and post-Marxist thought.

We can begin to make these connections by first clarifying more fully what problems confront Romantic historicism and its metacritical model of historical revision. Most important are the implications of situating that model within a certain act of repetition, one in which every revisionary intervention asserts the possibility of freeing itself from the "Romantic" history it interrogates while simultaneously demonstrating its connections, overt and covert, to either that history or a new Romanticism produced by that intervention. Romanticists have either used or been used by this double movement in many ways. There is, for example, the reabsorption of the interventionist critic into a prior Romanticism, an event that underwrites Clifford Siskin's claims about a ubiquitous Romantic discourse of "self-development" and Frances Ferguson's similar argument about the Kantian sublime.[15] There is also the explicit use of the "representative figure" in the counter-genealogies of the revisionist readings themselves, such as de Man's appropriation of Rousseau, Wordsworth, and Shelley and McGann's use of the German poet Heinrich Heine in *The Romantic Ideology*. What interests me here, however, is a less explicit transmission and reproduction of Romanticism, one that relates to the revisionist historical Romanticism of the '80s in an elliptical but telling manner. I refer to the transmission of English Romanticism in twentieth-century criticism not as Wellek's transcendent triad of imagination, nature, and symbol but, rather, as the ongoing promise of Enlightenment revolutionary politics.[16]

We could trace this transmission back to Crane Brinton's *The Political Ideas of the English Romanticists* (1926) and in this half century to David Erdman's *Blake: Prophet against Empire* (1954), Carl Woodring's *Politics in English Romantic Poetry* (1970), and Kenneth Neill Cameron's *Shelley: The Golden Years* (1974). As Brinton described his subject, "it is seldom . . . that a whole generation devotes itself to politics as feverently as did that of 1800 in England."[17] Thus, in contrast to the "Romantic opposition" between politics and culture which Klancher sees recent Romantic historiography disputing, there has in the past existed, perhaps in a minor key, a Romanticism that resembles the New Historicist Renaissance in its correlation of culture and power. Unlike this latter conflation, however, the politics of this Romanticism takes its cue not from the exigencies of the Royal court but, instead, from the polemics of the West's radically "new" bourgeois democracies. I would distinguish this line of Romanticism—especially its 1970s version—in two main ways. First, while perhaps equally affected by the campus politics of the late '60s as the postmodern Romanticism that we have been tracking, the work of Woodring, Erdman, and Cameron is generated out of an Anglo-American tradition of intellectual biography more at home with the methodologies of the post–World War II Romanticist than with those of the theoretically engaged Romantic historicist of the '80s and '90s. Second, in contrast to both the post–World War II generation and this latter historicism, this line of Romantic study believes its subject to be best understood as neither a transcendence nor a betrayal but, rather, as an advancement of the politics generated by the social convulsions that rock the last half of the eighteenth century in England, Europe, and the United States.

The relation of contemporary Romantic historicism to this earlier line is one of both explicit acknowledgment and implicit elision. Certainly, contemporary Romantic scholars have cited their debt to this earlier line in public fashion. Indeed, McGann's political use of his own career-long engagement with Byron in *The Romantic Ideology* echoes the critical relations that Erdman and Cameron develop with their politically Romantic representative figures, Blake and Shelley.[18] McGann's intellectual genealogy comes not only from such explicitly acknowledged figures as Raymond Williams, Theodor Adorno, and Mikhail Bakhtin but also from this earlier American tradition of Romantic scholarship. McGann would, then, be one of the first figures of this tradition to combine such scholarship with the critical momentum of postmodern theory. At this point, however, a certain slippage occurs, where the coincidence of McGann's project with this earlier tradition *hides* a confusion between two different models of historicism: where the earlier line of Romantic historicism transmits the ostensibly progressive modernity of Romanticism's politics, McGann and other '80s Romanticists intervene in the transmission of the supposedly retrograde modernity of Romanticism's politically transcending aesthetics.

This is not to say that this earlier line of Romantic historicism is unable to recognize the limits of its English poets' politics or that recent Romantic revisionary historicism simply envisions a monolithic Romanticism of aesthetic transcendence which the oppositional critic can then cavalierly dismiss. It is, however, to insist on a crucial difference between the roles of the critic in each of these models: the earlier historicist tendency is to stress a continuity between the assumed political ideals of an emancipatory Romanticism and the present, whereas the more recent historicist tendency is to assert a discontinuity between that present and an assumed Romantic ideology of aesthetic quietism. The implications of this difference become clearer when we consider how the contemporary structure of historical intervention and revision relates to the identity of the oppositional critic, a relation that, while perhaps simply metonymic, oftentimes carries the uninterrogated vocational force of a metaphoric sublimation.

Thus, if, as Gerald Graff suggests, terms such as *opposition* and *subversion* carry too inflationary a weight in literary studies today, I would venture that a large part of this effect is the consequence of assuming at this historical juncture an inherent relation between a revisionary methodology and an oppositional politics—in which the methodology implicitly proves the presence of such a politics.[19] Indeed, one could in fact see such an idealized metaphorical identity underwriting the relation between the postmodern Romanticists' revision of the post–World War II generation and the former's varied claims for a more large and resonant modernity. More specifically, such a metaphorical identity suggests why Wordsworth studies continue to occupy a central place throughout the Romantic historical revisionism of the '80s: in auto-apotheosizing a life of politically changing allegiances, Wordsworth creates a poetics of rationalized apostasy which the oppositional critic can challenge at the levels of both "original" production and "supplementary" transmission.[20] Moreover, such a challenge allows the critic to press for our discontinuity from Wordsworth's Romanticism while simultaneously recovering the urgency of the poet's rejected Jacobinism for our own time. Thus, while debates over Shelley's and Blake's supposed retreats into idealism do make up part of our current store of Romantic knowledge, such arguments cannot so cogently structure their recovery of a certain insurrectionary Romanticism around a revisionist moment of self-reflexive intervention. Instead, precisely because of the earlier Romanticist line of Erdman, Cameron, and others, such debates necessarily reveal that we have yet to consider the degree to which the emancipatory politics of historical revisionism overlap with the emancipatory politics of a Romanticism that is realized through a model of *unproblematic* transmission—an imbrication that the interventionary identity of oppositional critics itself resists.

My point here is not simply to dismiss this identity, as if, as some have argued, ideological criticism is somehow trumped by the profound discovery of the ideological nature of its own interventions. Critiques within the field of such criticism—as varied as those of de Man, Eagleton, Jameson, and Žižek—have long since extended and complicated the wishful profundity of this elementary insight. I want nonetheless to suggest that contemporary Romantic historicism all too often risks assuming that oppositional criticism simply opposes a certain received past and, in doing so, confers to such opposition an emancipatory aura that then substitutes for an intelligible oppositional politics of the present. Romantic historicism is particularly susceptible to such a danger because of the strong form of its metacritical revision and the emancipatory Romanticism that covertly subtends that form. That is, insofar as that revision disengages Romantic studies from a certain mystified past, the temporal nature of its critical object—history, in short—implies a future distinguished by its demystified potential. Again, it is not simply that the implication is wrong, unattainable, or silly or that it is proof of the revision's own ideological containment. The point is how that implication is encouraged by what it then continues: an Enlightenment-inflected Romanticism of progressive futurity which then deflects any further investigation into the possible political character of present Romantic historiography.[21]

For McGann, at least, the argument for this political character comes largely from an explicit engagement with British and European Marxism—an engagement that further complicates his historicism in a telling manner. On the one hand, his covert emancipatory Romanticism, which erupts in parts of *The Romantic Ideology,* such as in McGann's assault on the academic "priests and clerics" (*RI,* 1), reproduces a rhetoric of radical bourgeois humanism which the method and politics of *The Eighteenth Brumaire* and *The German Ideology* ruthlessly critique. On the other hand, the futurity of McGann's Romanticism reproduces the *vexed* nature of this critique by foregrounding the question about whether Marx's own categories represent an actual dialectical break with or a simple continuation of this Romanticism of Enlightenment social progress. It is not so much that McGann does or does not answer this latter question as that his own ideological critique of Romanticism allows this question to coexist too easily with the uninterrogated Enlightenment Romantic imaginary of 1789.

Thus, as an emblem of a dominant strain of Romantic historicism in the '80s and '90s, McGann demonstrates in condensed form the larger challenge facing leftist oppositional criticism during this time: the challenge of working through the mixed messages that occur when we confuse what we study with what we should do, when we allow the asymmetries of methodology, prescription, and historical object to cohere into the symmetry of the oppositional interventionist critic, a symmetry ironically defined by its political rejection of the formalism of other linguistic and historical methods.[22] And, while the purpose of this symmetry is to construct political intervention and prescription as stable and intelligible practices—we should intervene *here* and thus oppose *this*—the possibility arises that such a symmetry is actually itself a decisive blind that hides an ever-expanding historical complexity that resists such self-satisfied oppositional agencies as much as it does the homologies of New Historicism. We can begin to appreciate this dilemma by considering how McGann's uneasy blend of Marxist and emancipatory Romantic thought is reenacted in the contrast between two texts, one by Raymond Williams and another by McGann, which underwrite one of the most promising consequences of revisionist critical insight into Romanticism's historical transmission: the presence of an aggressively materialist disposition in Romantic studies today.

## III

Oftentimes invoked as a key term in the historical project of the present study, *materialism* orients much of the methodology and theory of recent Romantic historiography. Three related issues particularly explain the term's increasing ubiquity. First, insofar as critics have recently defined Romanticism as the philosophical and aesthetic evasion of a material world of social practices, Romantic historiography can be said to be motivated by a certain binary—materialism versus idealism—which makes the thematic recuperation of the former term a major goal in the reinterpretation of Romantic literature. Second, as Klancher notes, the technology, industry, and culture of bookmaking, reading, and selling expand exponentially during the late eighteenth and early nineteenth centuries; the consequence of this growth is a wide array of cultural artifacts and formations—differing editions and differing reading publics—whose study invites what has come to be called a materialist approach. Third, insofar as an oppositional Romantic historicism is defined by the reflexive question of Romanticism's transmission, such a historicism gravitates toward the various vehicles of that transmission, vehicles that in their physical and institutional reality once again invite the categories and questions of a materialist analysis.

Materialism, then, operates as a hegemonic discourse within Romantic studies which links a set of signifiers ranging from Romanticism's own ideological preoccupations to the historical "meaning" of the period's industrial revolutions to the metacritical question of how Romanticism is transmitted and (re)produced. The fact that for the oppositional critic this "metacritical" question is also political speaks to a fourth, more inchoate reason for the connection between materialism and recent Romantic historicism, a reason that transmutes the metonymic links among materialism's various semiotic functions into a metaphoric solidarity. Materialism functions as a historical and political *value* that implicitly distinguishes such a historicism from the idealist and formalist approaches to literature and history which supposedly underwrite fields as diverse as post–World War II Romantic studies, American deconstruction, and Renaissance New Historicism.

Indeed, one can in fact see McGann's fifteen-year-long development of a theory of textual materiality as the "positive" reading of literature which should "follow" the negative critique that *The Romantic Ideology* carries out against Romanticism's idealist mystifications.[23] Not only does such a theory deny such mystifications when it emphasizes Romantic literature as a body of "works" produced under and characterized by specific physical conditions; a materialist disposition also replaces such mystifications with these conditions as the values and insights realized by a literary hermeneutic—the values and insights that then *justify* the practice of that hermeneutic in the first place. That such a justification dovetails nicely with the wide-ranging use of a materialist ethos in Marxist theory would seem only to buttress the coincidence of contemporary Romantic historicism with a serious and genuine political criticism. Yet this cohesion simply links Marxist theory metonymically to a theoretical inchoateness that operates at the more particular level of materialism's presence in Romantic historiography. While, in other words, materialism is increasingly invoked as a certain defense against the apolitical pitfalls of formalism and idealism, the specific ways in which this defense operates oftentimes radically contradict one another. Thus, in his most explicit engagement with the Yale School, the book *Social Values and Poetic Acts* (1988), McGann distinguishes his project from deconstruction's negative critique by invoking in effect a materialism that marks the "fault line" between his focus on the "socio-historical dimensions of literary work" and deconstruction's preoccupation with a "purely linguistic . . . structure of relations"—relations that consign literary works to a Coleridgean "Life-in-Death" of ghostly political alienation. Yet, for Terry Eagleton and others, materialism marks the spot at which deconstruction and ideological criticism coincide, insofar as materiality is the brute excess of the "real," a semiotic excess that always reveals the limits of any signifying system attempting to reconcile, and thus dominate, the phenomenal and linguistic worlds.[24] Thus, in one argument materialism functions as the proof of history's *readability,* whereas in the other it functions as a sign of the world's irreducible *unreadability.* Thus, the question remains: Does materialism actually "solve" the imperatives of a political criticism, or does it actually provide cover for a number of theoretical operations that are better understood, like Blake's adverse wheels, to be turning against one another? The second scenario certainly complicates the possibility of materialism as a political "answer" to formalism, as can be seen in the contrast between two seminal essays that stand behind recent Romantic historicism: Raymond Williams's "The Romantic Artist," in *Culture and Society* (1958), and McGann's "Keats and the Historical Method in Literary Criticism," in *The Beauty of Inflections* (1985).

In contrast to the difference between McGann's and Eagleton's uses of materialism, the difference between McGann's and Williams's pieces is subtle to the point of invisibility. Indeed, the two essays seem highly compatible: first published in 1979, "Keats and the Historical Method" inaugurates McGann's turn toward a sociohistoric method that in many ways extends the materialist view of literature and culture which Williams develops in *Culture and Society* and elsewhere, most notably *Marxism and Literature* (1977). In *Culture and Society* Williams confers onto Romanticism a key historical role in the elision of materialist thinking about culture: he sees the Romantic poets as creating an idealist aesthetics that, while criticizing the new economic and social relations of England, also ghettoizes British literature by separating the poetic imagination from those relations. Much of the Romantic historicism of the '80s has sought to change this de facto ghettoization of the Romantic genius, and, indeed, this critique appears to structure McGann's early essay on Keats. Based on a series of ever-expanding readings of Keats's poetry, McGann's piece ends with an analysis of "To Autumn" (1819) which strongly echoes Williams's earlier argument: for McGann, Keats's poem dramatizes the impossible desire for a self-sufficient world of the imagination, independent from Keats's own historical proximity to such events as the Peterloo Massacre of 1819. McGann's argument, moreover, is based on an analysis of the *textual history* of "To Autumn"; indeed, the temporal composition of the poem and the historical circumstances of its first edition are as crucial to McGann as any "internal" reading of the work.[25] Thus, McGann's interpretation does not only reveal in Keats's poem an idealist dynamic similar to Williams's historical overview of the Romantic period. As important, McGann achieves this interpretation by restoring to Keats's work its material history—by carrying out in his methodology what he and Williams both appear to focus on in theory.

Thus, in theory and in practice McGann's essay appears to participate in the same trajectory as Williams's earlier work on materialism and Romanticism. Yet this convergence hides an almost imperceptible conceptual fissure best approached through the contrasting rhetorical structures of the essays. Whereas McGann's piece steadily exfoliates into an ever-increasing field of social, material, and political relations, Williams's work begins with such a field by echoing Crane Brinton with the opening line, "Than the poets from Blake and Wordsworth to Shelley and Keats there have been few generations of creative writers more deeply interested and involved in study and criticism of the society of their day."[26] This rhetorical divergence signals larger theoretical and historical differences. Writing at a moment when the American academy was just beginning to cast around for new approaches to literature, McGann's essay narrates through its examples the *recovery* of historicism as a model for literary studies in North America. In contrast, Williams's work assumes that Romanticism and Romantic studies operate in a field that can be discussed immediately in political and social terms.[27] The point of such an initial acknowledgment is thus to distinguish among the different levels of historical analysis which construct Romanticism as a field of knowledge. In other words, rather than initiate within Romantic studies a methodological discourse that sutures together the "social," "historical," and "political," Williams's observation of the political character of Romanticism separates such categories:

> In every case [of the Romantic poets], however, the political criticism is now less interesting than the wider social criticism: those first apprehensions of the essential significance of the Industrial Revolution, which all felt and none revoked. Beyond this, again, is a different kind of response, which is a main root of the idea of

culture. At this very time of political, social and economic change there is a radical change also in ideas of art, of the artist, and of their place in society. It is this significant change that I wish to adduce.[28]

This "change" is the self-privileging of the Romantic artist which allows art to critique society only from art's self-imposed transcendent isolation from the rest of the world. In *Marxism and Literature* Williams will in effect fight the influence of this change in Marx's own thought, insofar as that work attempts to overcome the scission between the material and the ideal, ostensibly initiated by the "notorious" Marxist legacy of the concept of base and superstructure.[29] Yet it is this very legacy that—rhetorically, at least—underwrites the priorities of "The Romantic Artist" and which allows Williams to focus on how the role of the Romantic artist in society changes and to read that change in terms of the historical separation of the material from the ideal. "Beyond" the political and social dimensions of the Romantics' writings lies, in other words, an object of study which perhaps eschews the clumsy delimitation of the "economic base" but which nevertheless links Williams's own subject of history to the economic in the last instance, the change in the mode of production in which the Romantic artist participates as both cause and effect. Thus, the materialism of "The Romantic Artist" is the materialism of a Marxist narrative that not only asserts the conditions of production as the conditions of materiality but which also invests such conditions with a certain epistemological intelligibility—the intelligibility of a *dialectical* materialism that then enframes all emancipatory agendas and their differing moments in history.

It is the relation of McGann's historical method to Williams's dialectical materialism which is in question. One could argue that McGann's reading of "To Autumn" converges nicely with such a materialism, insofar as he asserts that the poem's construction of a universal autumn is an ideological defense against the historically specific seasonal changes that underpin the work's actual creation, changes that are crucially marked by Keats's late-summer and early-fall stay at Winchester, where he wrote the poem and avoided the social turmoil that followed the Peterloo Massacre. Thus, we could see McGann's reading as specifying hermeneutically what Williams theorizes more broadly, in that McGann demonstrates how one particular text responds to events that refer to the violent advent of a new moment in capitalism.

It is, then, in reference to such a moment that the "truth" effect of one of McGann's final assertions can be understood: "[Keats's poem]—like all human works—is true only in the context of its field of social relations."[30] The problem, however, is that McGann's "field of social relations" need not refer to such a moment; that is, as the ultimate referent of the Peterloo Massacre, such a field might signify "nothing" more than events such as the massacre. Sidmouth's state terrorism and the English workers' agitation for economic reform, like the revolutions of 1776 and 1789, could be part of the sweeping narrative of dialectical materialism; on the other hand, they need not be, in the sense that their historical invocation does not immediately imply their place within such a *grand récit*. It is therefore no coincidence that McGann compares "To Autumn" to Shelley's explicitly political responses to the massacre; in doing so, McGann in effect retrieves from the aesthetically retiring pose of Keats's poem a sociopolitical response of the type that Williams initially acknowledges only in order to move beyond, to his own focus on the changing role of the Romantic artist. This discontinuity between the levels of history in McGann's and Williams's inquiries supports the sense of irresolution which haunts the ultimate referent of McGann's "field of social relations"—the question of whether its materiality signifies a more properly Marxist narrative of production or a more politically "immanent" set of social antagonisms. And this irresolution then inevitably affects whether materialism provides a stable political answer to historical formalism, insofar as such an answer cannot evade Marx's own point, that the differing resolutions to this predicament make for severe differences in analyses, categories, and, at some point, politics—politics that could conceivably belong to the Enlightenment's projections of futurity rather than Marx's own.

It is true that McGann cites both Bakhtin's linguistic theories and Marx's "sense of the pastness of the past" in his argument. Yet such leftist affiliations simply show how much the political question of McGann's materialism actually runs through a vast spectrum of leftist and Marxist thought and through all the differing cries for a social and political criticism of literature which gain visibility in the academy in the '80s. Indeed, within Marxism one version of this question appears as the Scylla and Charybdis of spontaneism and a priori totalization. From the perspective of a critique of Marxism's totalizing tendencies, then, the possible discontinuity between McGann's field of social relations and dialectical materialism might not necessarily be a bad thing, given the number of recent arguments, Marxist and non-Marxist, which have been leveled against Marxism's dependence on its grand metanarratives. The point still remains that contemporary materialist historiography must own up to its use of dialectical materialism as, in Barthes's term, an *alibi* for the phantom presence of its own political prescriptions.[31] In doing so, moreover, such a historiography must then face a larger issue: the degree to which the ghostly structure of this alibi is not an aberration but, rather, a condition of the attempt to realize historical thought.

That is, the question then becomes whether the semiotic irresolution of dialectical materialism's referents—the semiotic oscillation of McGann's field of social relations away from and toward Marx's narrative of dialectical materialism—is actually a rarified example of a historical predicament that impinges not only on Marxism but on all forms of historical thought. I refer to the problem of historical identity—the degree to which we define history as in fact the semiotic dissolution and nonclosure of all such forms of historical thinking, the radical blockage of historical representation, knowledge, and praxis which simultaneously enables those very categories. This problem of historical identity is the very one that de Man and Shelley confront in their own engagements with the demands of the "Jacobin imaginary"; it also structures the metacritical questions of method and value which presently underwrite the paradoxical occupation of materialism in Romantic historiography by a number of contradictory signifiers. This problem also radically affects the particular identity of the oppositional critic, as McGann's interventionary project in *The Romantic Ideology* forcefully shows.

McGann's reading in that work of the German poet and critic Heinrich Heine is fitting, in that the former's methodologically ambivalent relation to Marxism reproduces the latter's own 1843–44 relation to Marx, which because of its contemporaneity cannot be simply categorized in either genetic or teleological terms. Yet what is most crucial about McGann's analysis of Heine's critical study *The Romantic School* (1833) is how it structures his own model of historical revisionism around Heine's past critical actions, actions that are themselves self-reflexive and retroactive interventions in the transmission of German Romanticism. A dialectical excess occurs, however, when McGann misrecognizes himself in Heine's project. This misrecognition fissures rather than unifies their twin readings and thus discloses a bifurcating set of politics and aesthetics which complicates the assumed stability of recent Romantic historicism as an oppositional criticism. What is so compelling about this bifurcation is the way in which the identity of the oppositional critic splits into what can only be called its mirror opposite, a predicament so acute as to call forth the eruption of a formalism within a historicism ostensibly defined by the negation of that term.

## IV

Examining how McGann's text reorders and reinterprets a number of Heine's remarks on the German poet Ludwig Uhland reveals the chiasmic nature of McGann's political, theoretical, and literary insights. Thus, McGann sees Heine's revision of German Romanticism as a literary recuperation of Uhland, whereas Heine actually rejects such a recuperation; McGann sees Heine identifying within Uhland's poetry a self-critical, progressive futurity, whereas Heine actually shows how Uhland's neo-medieval, neo-Catholic Romanticism presages a future German imperialism; and, finally, McGann sees Heine interpreting both Uhland's poems and his retirement from poetry as literary and biographical signs of this progressive futurity, whereas Heine employs such literary and historical events as either ironic commentary on Germany's present Protestant modernity or grim prophecy of Germany's military future. Through these reversals Heine's *Romantic School* dialectically challenges the stability of the historical knowledge presumed in the interventionary revisionism of McGann's *Romantic Ideology*. Before proceeding, then, it might be helpful to consider more fully how the example of Heine relates theoretically to the rest of the argument in McGann's 1983 book.

McGann's use of Heine has never been the focus of the numerous critical responses to the short but widely influential polemic of *The Romantic Ideology*. Understandably, both McGann and his audience are primarily concerned with the reception of British Romanticism in the American academy; within that context it makes sense to concentrate on

McGann's general theoretical arguments and how they relate to his specific critiques of contemporary Romanticists such as (most notably) M. H. Abrams and of the British Romantic poets themselves—Byron, Wordsworth, Coleridge, and company.[32] Nevertheless, it is McGann's exegesis of Heine's critical evaluation of Uhland which is the linchpin to the historicist argument in McGann's book.

This linchpin coincides with McGann's notion of the "past-present dialectic," his argument for the brute fact of historical difference and for the unavoidability of thinking through how the past shapes the present by transmitting itself to the present and, conversely, how the present receives and reshapes the past. Indeed, for McGann, the "Romantic ideology" is generated by an erasure of the past-present dialectic—the erasure that many twentieth-century Romantic scholars accomplish when they selectively interpret English writing from the late eighteenth and early nineteenth centuries in order to create and teach an ahistorical, universalizing Romanticism that is characterized by its apolitical mystifications of mind and nature. The existence of this mystified Romanticism becomes an axiom in Romantic historiography during the '80s, as does McGann's polemical intervention into the transmission and reification of this totalizing Romanticism, exemplified in *The Romantic Ideology* by M. H. Abrams's *Natural Supernaturalism.*

In this particular critical plot, however, neither McGann nor Abrams greatly embodies the difference between the "past" and the "present" by himself. By contrast, in McGann's exegesis on Heine, the past-present dialectic acts vividly within Heine's own identity as a critic, in that Heine's critical and historical consciousness is structured around his distinctly different reactions to Uhland's poetry in 1803 and 1833. Thus, Heine does not simply practice a historically oriented criticism that McGann wants to appropriate. Heine also exemplifies that criticism, in that his critical voice is defined by the contrast between its present and past historical experiences.

McGann tries to locate his own critical agency within this constitutive split between Heine's past and present experiences. This attempt dovetails with how McGann interprets Heine's project as an explicit recuperation of Uhland's poetry. In McGann's view Heine sees Uhland's work as an ongoing literary and political force in Heine's 1833 present. I will argue, however, that Heine's piece actually argues against such a recuperation and that such a resistance dialectically bespeaks a larger theoretical disidentification between McGann and Heine and between McGann and himself. Heine's critical practice is actually what McGann's interventionary analysis could be, except for the misrecognition of Heine which McGann projects onto Heine and which McGann imposes on himself.

Underwriting this misrecognition of Heine is McGann's sense of an actively self-critical progressive futurity that Heine attributes to Uhland's poems, thus allowing them to remain "alive" in 1833. Punctuating McGann's reading in key moments, this futurity is a specific example of the Enlightenment-inflected Romanticism that explicitly and implicitly contributes to the identity of the oppositional, interventionary Romanticist. Despite the Enlightenment-inflected character of *his* political and literary reputation, however, Heine rejects the totalizing explanatory force of this progressive revisionism for a more grim assessment of Uhland's present literary reputation and Germany's future military adventures. In doing so, Heine's historical argument dialectically reworks McGann's reading, highlighting how this progressive futurity is the interpretive tool that causes McGann's analysis to diverge markedly from Heine's own critical claims.

Given the complicated interpretive relations among McGann, Heine, and Uhland, a summary of McGann's general argument about Heine might be helpful. Heine's essay on Uhland appears perfect for McGann: the entire piece revolves around Heine's conscious recognition of the difference between 1813, when Heine first reads the poet, and 1833, the year of his present appraisal. Like McGann's own historical revisionism, then, Heine's criticism bases its self-reflexivity on the disrupting impositions of temporal change. Thus, the passage of time dramatically transforms Heine's feeling toward his past reception of Uhland in 1813:

> But I beg you to take into consideration the conditions under which I am writing, the time and place. Twenty years ago—I was a boy—yes, then, with what abounding enthusiasm I could have celebrated the excellent Uhland! Then I felt his excellence perhaps better than now; he was closer to me in thought and feelings. But since then so much has happened! What seemed to me so splendid, that chivalrous, Catholic world, those knights who cut and thrust at each other in aristocratic tournaments, those gentle squires and well-bred no-

ble ladies, those Nordic heroes and Minnesingers, those monks and nuns, those ancestral vaults and awesome shudders, those pallid sentiments of renunciation to the accompaniment of bellringing, and the everlasting melancholy wailing—how bitterly it has been spoiled for me since then![33]

In McGann's exegesis this passage is followed by a second quotation that appears to be an immediate elaboration of the first:

I hold this same volume [of Uhland's poetry] in my hands once more, but twenty years have passed since then, I have heard and seen much in the meantime, a very great deal, I no longer believe there are people without heads, and the old spectral show no longer has any effect on my feelings. The house in which I am sitting and reading is on the Boulevard Montmartre; here the wildest waves of the times break; here screech the loudest voices of the modern age; there is laughing, roaring, and beating of drums; the National Guard marches past in double-quick time; and everyone in speaking French.—Is this the place to read Uhland's poems? (*HH,* 261)

McGann's response to, and for, Heine is immediate and direct: "The answer to this question is 'yes.' Heine writes a lengthy and generous commentary on Uhland here, and he quotes in full—himself re-reads and forces us to read—two of Uhland's old Romantic poems; the one a Romantic literary ballad of the past ('Der Schäfer'), the other an anti-Napoleonic marching song ('Vorwärts!')" (*RI,* 50–51). McGann thus retrieves from Heine's criticism a narrative that is based on familiar Romantic topoi, the acknowledgment and transcendence of temporal change. Yet McGann sees Heine putting a decidedly "non-Romantic" spin on this narrative, insofar as Heine's hermeneutics actually assert a historical consciousness fiercely based on temporal difference.

Thus, central to McGann's thesis about Heine's "generous commentary" is McGann's argument that Uhland's "Der Schäfer" anticipates Heine's rereading of it in 1833. That is, Heine is still able to read Uhland's ballad not because it preserves the aura of Heine's initial 1813 reading experience but, rather, because the poem actually predicts its own alienation from that experience. For McGann, Heine recovers Uhland's poem because it reinforces rather than abolishes the differences between 1813 and 1833. Thus, McGann quotes Heine's description of his 1813 reading experience of "Der Schäfer" as a moment in magical thinking actively structured by the poem's own proleptic demystification of that moment:

> Sitting amid the ruins of the old castles and reciting this poem, I sometimes heard the nymphs in the Rhine, which flows by there, imitating my words, and from the water came a sighing and a moaning with a comical pathos:
>
> Down came a muffled, ghostly tone,
> "Farewell, O shepherd mine!"
>
> But I ignored the chaffing of the nymphs, even when they giggled ironically at the most beautiful passages in Uhland's poems. (*HH*, 260)

McGann reads this passage thus:

> Heine's brilliant commentary reminds us of two important facts about all poetic interpretations. First . . . Heine shows that when he read [the ballad] in 1813 his reading was . . . a Romantic reading fully in sympathy with the ballad's own thematized narrative. Second, Heine's commentary shows that Uhland's ballad—once again, not the poem itself—passes an ironical judgment upon this Romantic reading. In 1813 Heine was himself vaguely aware of this irony but he chose to ignore it and to follow the impulse of his Romantic enthusiasm. With the passage of twenty years, however, he sees very clearly what he was only able to intuit in a vague way in 1813. (*RI*, 52–53)

By apparently anticipating Heine's own retroactive disavowal of his 1813 reading, Uhland's ballad becomes a model for McGann's own practice of historical revision, a practice that dismisses an ideologically mystified past while simultaneously recovering a past that engenders its own ideological self-critique. Through Heine, McGann attacks the reifications of history under the banner of historical thought; history is revised yet also, and as important, rehabilitated as the stable ground for McGann's own practice and critique.

It is possible, however, to come away with a much more grim representation of history in Heine, one that dramatically rejects this summary of historical revisionism as a narrative of historical recovery. This rejection becomes clear when we use Heine to show dialectically how McGann's exegesis actually reorders the narrative structure of Heine's essay. That is, Heine does not answer his question "Is this the place to read Uhland's poems?" by rereading "Der Schäfer" as a work that in 1813 anticipates its own ideological self-critique in 1833. McGann has in fact scrambled Heine's order of response, the latter's narrative structure of cause and effect. Heine's reading of "Der Schäfer" with the giggling ironic nymphs engenders his question about reading Uhland in 1833, with the ballad's reading coming in between the two passages that McGann cites—"But I beg you . . ." and "I hold this same . . ."—and thus before the key line, "Is this the place to read Uhland's poems?" The force of this arrangement is much more pessimistic than the one McGann's exegesis dramatizes: Heine's reading of "Der Schäfer" is not a positive reply to the question of whether it can be read in the present of 1833; rather, the question is a rhetorical one that summarizes the frustration of trying to carry out that very hermeneutic, and historical, act. The "chaffing nymphs" refer to an "ironical judgment" more ruthless than the one McGann depicts, a judgment of "Der Schäfer" as a ballad that does not foretell "the passing of its own dreams" but, rather, the passing of its own self out of Heine's world of 1833.

Heine's account emits, morever, a radically opposite tale not only of Uhland's reputation but also of the politics of cultural transmission which McGann finds in Heine's futurity. A key moment in this further bifurcation occurs when McGann interprets Heine's statement that "We love and honor [Uhland] now perhaps all the more because we are about to part from him forever" as a proclamation that Uhland's poetry is aware of its "historical particularity" and commitment to the future. Once again McGann sustains his argument by rearranging the structure of Heine's essay. McGann's support for his interpretation of "We love and honor . . ." consists of two passages that occur before that line:

> And we can readily understand that our excellent Uhland's ballads and romances found the greatest favor not simply among the patriots of 1813, among upright youths and lovely maidens, but also

among many persons endowed with greater powers and among many modern thinkers.

I have added the year 1813 to the word "patriots" in order to distinguish them from present-day patriots who no longer live off the memories of the so-called War of Liberation. Those older patriots must derive the sweetest pleasure from Uhland's muse, since most of his poems are completely impregnated with the spirit of their time, a time when they themselves were reveling in youthful emotions and proud hopes. They passed on the preference for Uhland's poems to their disciples. (*HH*, 264)

Presented as elaborations of "We love and honor . . . ," these passages apparently argue that Uhland's poetry has a progressive imperative that influences not only the "Romantically" inclined of past generations ("upright youths and lovely maidens") but also those "persons endowed with greater powers" and "many modern thinkers." This positive influence has, moreover, been transmitted from the generation of 1813 to that of 1833: "They [the elders of 1813] passed on the preference for Uhland's poems to their disciples." Thus, Uhland's historical reflexivity not only honors historical difference; it also underwrites its own model of historical transmission and continuity as well.

Yet we can also attach these passages to another more complicated model of transmission in Heine's piece, one that—unlike McGann's version—links Uhland's function in the rest of Heine's essay to more historically specific tendencies in Germany in 1833. Thus, just before the two passages that McGann cites, Heine comments on the specific consequences of Uhland's Romantic voice:

And indeed, when observed closely, the women in Uhland's poems are merely lovely phantoms, moonlight personified, with milk in their veins and sweet tears in their eyes, that is, tears without salt. If we compare Uhland's knights with the knights of the ancient songs, they seem to consist of tin armor with nothing but flowers beneath it instead of flesh and bones. . . .

But this is not meant as criticism. Mr. Uhland had no intention of producing a faithful copy of the German past, he perhaps meant to delight us merely by its image, and he created a pleasant reflection of it from the dusky surface of his spirit. . . . Portraits of the past exercise their magic even in the palest evocation. Even men who espouse the modern age always retain a secret fondness for the traditions of olden times; even the weakest echo of these ghostly voices moves us strangely. (*HH*, 263–64)

In this passage Heine identifies a process of reification uncannily similar to the one that McGann sees occurring with the "contemporary" Abramsian academic reception of the British Romantics, a process in which Germany uncritically accepts Uhland's singular representation of its medieval past.[34] This is the phenomenon to which the passages beginning "And we can readily understand . . ." and "I have added the year 1813 . . ." actually refer; in this scenario the "youths and lovely maidens" and "modern thinkers" of 1813 are all seduced by a poetry that produces the "weakest echo" of the past," "milk in [the lovely phantoms'] veins," and "tears without salt." Thus, Uhland's poems do not anticipate the futurity of 1833's modernity; instead, Uhland's ideological refashioning of Germany's past is so strong that his poetry seduces the adherents to the "modern age" in both 1813 and 1833. The "preference for Uhland's poems" which those readers in 1813 pass on to those in 1833 has nothing to do with a self-conscious commitment toward future change; rather, it has to do with how Uhland's neo-Catholic Romanticism contains a McGannian Romantic opiate, "tin armor with nothing but flowers beneath it instead of flesh and bones"—a literary drug that comes from how Uhland "soft-boil[s] . . . in his sentimentality the robust strains of the heroic saga and the folksong [in order] to make them palatable to the modern public [of 1813]" (263).

Heine specifies, moreover, who the "disciples" of 1833 are. They are not simply those individuals who receive the "preference for Uhland's poems" from the "patriots of 1813"; they are also, more specifically, those "boys on the athletic grounds [who were] given credit for patriotism if they bought Uhland's poems" (*HH,* 264). Heine's original French stresses what this fact about Uhland's 1833 audience means: "Pour les jeunes gens qui s'adonnait aux exercises gymnastiques fondés alors par le gallophobe Jaher *(Jahn)* pour régénérer le physique de la nation allemande [For the young people who threw themselves into the gymnastic clubs founded, then, by the anti-French *Jahn* in order to revive the physique of the German nation]" (my translation).[35] Commenting on these clubs, Heine's American translator, Charles Godfrey Leland, notes from his vantage point of 1891 that "the gymnastic clubs or *Turner Verein,* have been of incalculable benefit to Germany, and were a prominent cause of the superiority of the German soldiers in the last war with France."[36] Thus, writing *The Romantic School* in Paris in self-imposed exile from Germany, Heine in 1833 fashions a critique of Uhland which finds its futurity not in the latter's poetry but, rather, in the grim prophecy of the former's own critical imagination. Heine critiques Uhland at least in part to warn his audience—to expose them to a reification of German Romantic values directly related to the rise of German imperialism.[37]

This misrecognition of Heine's essay's futurity, in terms of both its location and grim tenor, causes McGann to misread—literally to reverse—a number of other political and literary points that underpin the piece's estimation of Uhland. McGann twice stresses, for example, what he considers to be Heine's simple, positive comments about the "War of Liberation," the European struggle of 1805–15 against Napoléon—how the patriots of 1813 simultaneously "live off the memories of the so-called War of Liberation" and "derive the sweetest pleasure from Uhland's muse." Buoyed by those quotes, McGann claims that Heine sees Uhland's "Vorwärts" as a poem that both "celebrates the 'War of Liberation' as it was being waged in the 1813 struggles against Napoleon" and urges "in 1833 a new message of progress and self-criticism" (*RI,* 54). For McGann "Uhland's poetry is part of—will always be part of—what Heine calls the 'War of Liberation' " (53), a commitment to political praxis and progressive struggle.

The historical consequences of the War of Liberation were not, however, simply progressive. Napoléon represented himself, not entirely perversely, as the bearer of the French Revolution and thus the enemy of the feudal monarchies. His defeat in Germany after the War of Liberation was a blow to both the possibility of a representative government and the rights of, among others, the German Jewish people. Frederick William III's restored monarchy was a Prussia of repression, university censorship, and anti-Semitic pogroms; as Frederic Ewen writes, "It seemed as if the Middle Ages had returned."[38] As a German Jew who later converted to Protestantism, Heine would have at least been aware of these consequences of the War of Liberation. Such a historical convergence is, however, erased by McGann's more uniform sense of Heine's and Uhland's progressive futurity. What is lost, then, is the tension between Uhland's neo-medieval poetry and an account of early-nineteenth-century Continental history which is not simply sincere in its progressive sentiment but also mediated by a critique—Heine's—which is conflicted, ironic, ruthless, perhaps even parodic. What is lost is a vocabulary in Heine of German patriotism—"the *so-called* Wars of Liberation"—which connects German populism to German nationalism, anti-Semitism, and antidemocratic sentiment.

This loss of politically ironic tension also structures McGann's account of how Heine explains Uhland's retirement from verse. McGann stresses how Heine "points out that Uhland forsook his poetry in the latter part of his career in order to become 'an ardent representative of the rights of the people in the Würtemberg Diet,' and a 'bold speaker for civic equality and freedom of thought' " (*RI,* 53). For McGann it is Uhland's "self-critical and progressive character" that makes him give up his poetry and commit himself to a political life. As McGann quotes Heine, "precisely because [Uhland's] intentions toward the modern age were so honorable, he could no longer keep on singing the old song about ancient times with his old enthusiasm" (*HH,* 262). Yet such a seemingly transparent reception of Heine's opinion hides a more complex and ironic estimation by the critic of Germany's "modern age." This evaluation comes through in the full passage from which McGann selects his quotes:

> I explain Uhland's silence by the contradiction between the inclinations of his muse and the demands of his political position. The elegiac poet who was able to celebrate the Catholic feudal past in such beautiful ballads and romances . . . has since become an ardent representative of the rights of people in the Würtemberg Diet, a bold speaker for civic equality and freedom of thought. Mr. Uhland proved that these democratic and Protestant views of his are genuine and pure by the great personal sacrifices that he has made for them. Having once won a poet's laurels, he now also won the oak wreath of civic virtue. But precisely because his intentions toward the modern age were so honorable, he could no longer keep on singing the old song about ancient times with his old enthusiasm. And since his Pegasus was only a knight's steed that liked to trot

back into the past but immediately became balky when it was supposed to go ahead into modern life, good Uhland dismounted with a smile, and calmly had the intractable beast unsaddled and led to the stable. There he has remained until the present day, and like his colleague, the steed Bayard, he has all kinds of virtues and only a single defect—he is dead. (262–63)

Contrary to McGann's overriding thesis, Uhland's role in this passage as a "bold speaker for civic equality and freedom of thought" does not simply extend the progressive self-critique of his poetry's ostensible futurity; rather, that role is based on the "contradiction" between Uhland's past poetic "muse" and the present "demands of his political position." Heine apparently does describe this historical contradiction in glowing terms, invoking both the "poet's laurels" and the "oak wreath of the civic virtue," yet those celebratory terms and Uhland's "personal sacrifices"—his steps toward converting vocationally from a literary Catholicism to a political Protestantism—are immediately placed in an ironic tension with Heine's next image of Uhland's poetry as a "knight's steed" of the past who is "balky" in "modern life" and who is willingly led by its smiling rider, Uhland, to its stable and a quiet death.[39]

Heine expands this conceit into an image that once again tears at the progressive logic that McGann imparts to Heine and Uhland: "Sharper eyes than mine claim to have perceived that the tall knightly steed with the gay-colored armorial trappings and proud plumes of feathers never really suited his middle-class rider, who wore on his feet instead of boots with golden spurs only shoes and silk stockings, and on his head, instead of a helmet, only a Tübingen doctoral cap" (*HH,* 263).[40] Thus, Uhland does participate in a narrative of modernity, but one whose hyperbolic discontinuities stress a present marked not only by a liberal activism of "civic virtue" but also by a bourgeois attenuation of life, registered in a tone that is paradoxically both elegiac and satirical. This indeterminacy of tone is symptomatic of the entire piece's ambivalent evaluation of a Protestant modernity that is both disengaged from and held in thrall by Uhland's neo-medieval Catholicism. What is clear about this evaluation is that it does not cohere, either semantically or structurally, around Uhland's poetry as a self-critical, progressive imperative that unites the asserted differences of past and present into an ongoing dialectic of the future. Instead, the one projection of Uhland into 1833 and beyond—the grim reification of a mystified German past for the "disciples" of the *Turner Verein*—conjoins asymmetrically with the hyperbolic imagery of Uhland's retirement from verse to produce an overwhelming sense of the anachronistic relation of Uhland's poetry to Germany's modern times.

We can now return to Heine's conclusion and the meaning of his key sentence, "We love and honor [Uhland] now perhaps all the more because we are about to part from him forever." The future *is* referred to here, but not in the fashion that McGann's reading avers and not with the same political and cultural resonances that his reading attributes to Heine, Uhland, Germany, and France. Heine ends the essay by apparently citing several lines from Uhland's "Vorwärts!" McGann asserts that this citation works in the same way that the mocking nymphs of "Der Schäfer" do, as Heine's acknowledgment of the self-critical and progressive spirit of Uhland's poetry, as Heine seeing within such work "a voice whose full contemporaneity is only achieved through a vision of the future, a sense of the imperatives which drive what is present toward what must come" (*RI,* 55). This final passage is the one that follows the key sentence, "We love and honor [Uhland] . . . ." Together these lines read:

> We love and honor [Uhland] now perhaps all the more because we are to lose him forever.
> 
> Oh, not from a frivolous whim, but obeying the law of necessity, Germany is stirring—Pious, peaceful Germany!—It casts a melancholy glance at the past it leaves behind, once more it bends tenderly over the ancient era which gazes at us, so deathly pale, from Uhland's poems, and it bids farewell with a kiss. And another kiss, even a tear, for all I care! But let us tarry no longer in idle compassion.—
> 
> Forward, forward, one and all!
> France now sounds the valiant call:
>     Forward!
> 
> (*HH,* 268)

One point should immediately be made: the lines "Forward, forward, one and all! / France now sounds the valiant call: / Forward!" are not from "Vorwärts!" That poem is a marching song against Napoléon, while these lines are the result of Heine's own wit, a syntactical pun on the actual lines of "Vorwärts!" which transforms the poem's celebration of Germany into a panegyric for the political and cultural destiny of *France*. If, then, there is anything like McGann's progressive futurity in Heine's essay, it is actually located here, in the implied example of Paris's social and aesthetic experiments, in the idea that France is still pursuing in 1833 the political and cultural horizons created by the July Revolution of 1830.

Heine undermines, moreover, the idea that the German nation might find its future in the rarified reifications of its own past cultural imaginary. Thus, Heine's explicit enthusiasm for France's putative destiny is less important than the implicit sense of foreboding which haunts his words on Germany, words that imply a German future resistant to Heine's own francophile version of "Vorwärts!" With his own historical position mediated by the Franco-Prussian War in 1870, Leland offers an interpretation of such a foreboding: "Only a true *vates* or poet-prophet, could have clearly understood or foreseen, as Heine did when he wrote [on Uhland], that Germany had really taken leave of its romantic past and was about to enter on a new and more practical career."[41] I take that "practical career" to mean the rise of German imperialism in the latter part of the century, an event that retroactively transforms Heine's words—"Germany is stirring—Pious, peaceful Germany"—into a prophecy that is at once ominous, sarcastic, and true.[42]

The occasion for this prophecy is indeed Heine's final judgment of Uhland, but it is a judgment that is the reverse of McGann's progressive, self-critical futurity. Instead, Heine's forecasts are underwritten by the doubly anachronistic effect of Uhland's poetry—the break between Uhland's dreamy Catholic medievalism and Germany's 1833 Protestant modernity as well as the militant reifying recuperation of that medievalism by that modernity. In both cases the effect of Uhland's poetry in the present is seen by Heine as predicated on that poetry's absence from the present, a point underscored by Heine's French version of his key phrase, "We love and honor . . .": "Et nous le vénérons et l'aimons peut-être d'autant plus qu'il entre pour nous dans le domaine du passé."[43] For Heine, Uhland's presence in 1833 is based on the fact that he is elsewhere, literally in the "domain of the past." Thus, contrary to McGann's recuperation of Uhland and its attendant sociopolitical narrative, Heine's recognition of history is based on the departure of Uhland from the political and cultural imaginary of 1833 and beyond. It is precisely this departure, moreover, which organizes and grounds Heine's opinions about the politics and literature of Germany and France. These opinions become in McGann's account of Heine their own symmetrical opposites, the points that undergird the reversal of Heine's announcement of Uhland's departure, the recuperation of Uhland by McGann.

Thus, in retrieving from the past a model for his own interventionist revisions of the past, McGann conjures up a mirror opposite not only of a section of *The Romantic School* but also of his own project, insofar as his recuperation of Uhland elides the potential compatibility between his past-present dialectic and the temporal consciousness that subtends Heine's grim musings on the transmission and reification of German Catholic medievalism and its relation to Germany's military future. We could argue, however, that *The Romantic Ideology* is itself constitutively split between its ruthless critique of Romanticism and its unwillingness to signal the departure of the British Romantics from, once again, a twentieth-century critical modernity. From that perspective McGann's rehabilitation of Uhland semiotically adheres McGann's ideological critique to, paradoxically, the preservationary trajectory of his book's text-centered readings of the self-critical potential of the British Romantics.[44] McGann's remarkable reversals of Heine's literary and political comments becomes intelligible, then, as the former's own inevitable fall into an ideological structure worthy of the symmetries of Marx's camera obscura.

We can, however, go further and see that ideological structure and its mirror doublings as constituting an event more akin to Paul de Man's notion of literary blindness and insight, insofar as we broaden the political consequences of McGann's doublings and reversals into a lesson of what de Man always described as textuality but what I will call history. That is, as an emblem of the '80s Romanticist as historical revisionist and oppositional critic, McGann turns to Heine in order to ground that emblematic status in the critical insights of a prior Romantic revisionist; what McGann accomplishes, however, is a set of political and literary insights that blind him to the reverse set of insights in Heine—meanings that actually subtend McGann's own relation to Heine. McGann's insights blind him, as it were, to himself; they blind McGann to Heine *as* McGann. The insight that this blindness gives us is the cautionary tale of the historicist's own doubling away from history (itself a historical event), of the revisionist oppositional critic's own moment of estrangement from him- or herself, even as that interventionary agency is mobilized as the occasion for a certain historical knowledge and political practice.

Perhaps the most startling moment of this estrangement errupts in McGann's case at the level of what we have called the material, precisely what McGann's critical practices have most forcefully come to represent. For Heine does not simply imply France's progressive futurity over Germany by parodying a stanza of Uhland's "Vorwärts!"; he explicitly announces that situation by underlining France—"*France* now sounds the valiant call"—in a way that various German and English editions represent through bold or italicized print. The translation that McGann employs does not relay this stress nor the fact that the entire concluding paragraph to this section of *The Romantic School*—what begins with "Oh, not from a frivolous whim" and what I have argued is a prophetic critique of German imperialism—was suppressed by German censors, a prominent reason for the notoriously corrupt state of Heine's manuscripts.[45] Thus, the very "solution" to Romanticism's ideologies, a materialist historiography, is at once present and elided in McGann's literal and figural refashioning of Heine's words. A discontinuity in material transmission lies, then, at the heart of the interpretive argument that will set the groundwork for, perhaps even the possibility of, a materially oriented historicism in, and beyond, Romantic studies in the '80s and '90s. Far from existing outside the historical and linguistic dilemma of McGann's historicist misrecognitions, the material shows itself to be part of the relentless bifurcations of literature, history, and politics which McGann's reading of Heine evinces.

Indeed, this relentless bifurcation of meaning appears to characterize the "textual condition" that underwrites McGann's materialist theories on editing and anthologizing: "Every text has variants of itself screaming to get out, or antithetical texts waiting to make themselves known. These variants and antitheses appear (and multiply) over time, as the hidden features of the textual media are developed and made explicit."[46] These lines could very well describe the process by which McGann's reading of Heine ultimately—that is, historically—yields up its own counternarrative. More so than McGann's insistence on the social nature of texts, this semiotic indeterminacy might actually be

McGann's larger contribution to the political question of how texts, the social world, and historical knowledge relate. Indeed, the tension between McGann's textual materialism and a more strictly dialectical materialism would be symptomatic of this larger sense of bifurcating meaning. This semiotic indeterminacy would then engage with more deterministic, Left-inflected readings of the social world. In that sense McGann's fifteen-year-long work on textual materialism both explicitly theorizes and implicitly dramatizes what the Heine section of *The Romantic Ideology* confronts in 1983.

I would thus argue for a stronger link between the critical practices of *The Romantic Ideology* and McGann's work on the materiality of the text. In many ways the short fierce polemic of McGann's 1983 book might seem overtaken, surpassed by the rich amount of work that McGann has done on the textual condition of literature's material makeup. Indeed, in a recent essay, "Rethinking Romanticism," McGann acknowledges the conceptual, idealized level of argument in *The Romantic Ideology,* a "residual investment in a type of interpretive thought" which his focus on editing and anthologizing attempts to correct.[47] As the first epigraph to this chapter demonstrates, however, this acknowledgment resembles nothing less than the self-critical, progressive futurity that provides the semiotic *grund* for so many of the diverging meanings in McGann's reading of Heine. This observation does not negate how McGann's 1992 self-revision both acknowledges and bridges the gap between *The Romantic Ideology* and his other critical practices. Rather, McGann's self-revision illustrates the volatility and ubiquity of the trope of progressive futurity in and beyond *The Romantic Ideology.* The importance of this 1983 book lies in its dramatic engagement with one series of consequences of this trope, as they are played out within the political, epistemological, and institutional polemics of a new radical form of oppositional historicism.

That is, McGann's and Heine's dialectical critical relationship provides us with a vividly singular example of a radically unstable condition in historical revisionism, one that in its uncanny reproduction of symmetrically opposite insights emits a challenge to leftist criticism which is as acutely formalist as those leveled at the neo-Foucaultian cul-de-sacs of New Historical power in the late '80s. It is in the open-ended question of the pervasiveness of this condition that McGann's use of Heine takes on, to paraphrase de Man once again, the sublimity of a historical error that underwrites historical knowledge, as opposed to a critical mistake that we can simply isolate from our ongoing intellectual tasks. Within the relatively narrow field of contemporary Romantic historiography, the question then becomes to what degree the interventionary Romanticist is as volatile an identity as the Romanticism being revised—to what degree will the critical identity of the revisionist be shot through, outpaced, or split by the demands of history, including those generated by the very participation of the Romanticist in the revision of Romanticism. To what degree can that identity be split by the very tactics designed to acknowledge, shore up, and control such scissions of a presumed contemporary critical consciousness—by, as in McGann's case, the valorization of a self-critical progressiveness that would at once admit to, exploit, and heal the trauma of historical difference within and beyond the critical subject? And to what degree will history ironically configure that subject and his or her object of inquiry to produce, as also in the case of McGann, allegories of praxis immediately stalked, indeed defined, by their doppelgänger narratives?

Currently, these questions have reappeared at and now dominate another more broad and ambitious level of historical knowledge and praxis, in the sense that the revisionary oppositional Romanticist can still be seen as merely one local metonym for Marxism's own attempt to participate in and master history. McGann's own ambivalent relation to Marxism becomes an appropriate context for our present inquiry into this endeavor, in that the Heine section of *The Romantic Ideology* can either be described as an aporetic condition of history which problematizes Marxism or as a Left-inflected historicism that demonstrates the blockages of all history. Both descriptions actually pertain to the particular contours of the current impasse facing Marxism and the world today. I do not refer to the banal and uncritical equation between the fall of the Soviet empire and the demise of Marxism. Rather, I mean the dark promise that actually follows our acceptance of how thoroughly bankrupt and mystified *capitalism's* own explanations of and promises for our post–cold war fin-de-siècle are and, thus, how Marxism, as capitalism's most rigorous science of critique, will merely provide us with the most "genuine"—the most global, complex, paradoxical, and contradictory—explanation for the world's atrophy and decline. I refer to the grim prospect that in Marxism's rigors we will merely find the most authentic legitimation for the pessimism of our age.

It is here that the problematic of oppositional agency defiantly resurfaces, with all its attendant questions of affiliation, solidarity, consequence, and, as McGann and Heine especially highlight, representation and intelligibility. It is as a response to Marxism's contemporary impasse that the specific oppositional agency of Enlightenment Romanticism takes on another identity besides those that already structure McGann's *Romantic Ideology* as a vocational influence, an uninterrogated ideological blind, and as the progressive self-critical futurity that is McGann's own strategy for managing the temporal doubling of the oppositional critic. This other identity partakes of the thought of Ernest Bloch, an earlier fellow traveler also invested, like McGann, in the wagers of the past and their transmission. Unlike Heine's, and McGann's, stress on the past as a simultaneous point of departure and reification and McGann's further refunctioning of the past as a self-critical recuperation of itself and the enlightened present, Bloch conceives of the past as a failed promise, a past potentiality estranged from the present by historical contingencies whose ontological fact we now habitually project onto the present and future.[48] As such a previously blocked reserve, Enlightenment Romanticism thus becomes a possible position *toward* which we can struggle, one that will then engage proleptically with Marxism's current crisis and inspire the post-Marxisms of a postmodern Left. Of course, to begin even to think of such a position is to posit a historical position beyond our own impasse, at which the "final" mystification breached is that of the de Manian allegory of praxis which enshrines its own exhaustion. It is into that breach that McGann's and other projects of 1980s Romantic historiography now still throw themselves and where the Romanticist as the postmodern Jacobin defiantly continues the aporetic challenge of ruthless critique.

**Chapter 4**

# The Other Reasons

## Feminist Alterity, Feminist Romantic Studies, and Mary Wollstonecraft

Further, it is no longer clear that feminist theory ought to try to settle the questions of primary identity in order to get on with the task of politics. Instead, we ought to ask, what political possibilities are the consequence of a radical critique of the categories of identity? What new shape of politics emerges when identity as a common ground no longer constrains the discourse on feminist politics?
    Judith Butler
    *Gender Trouble*

It is not, I assert, a bold attempt to emulate masculine virtues; it is not the enchantment of literary pursuits, or the steady investigation of scientific subjects, that leads women astray from duty.
    Mary Wollstonecraft
    *A Vindication of the Rights of Woman*

# I

Meditating on the relation of gender to the teaching and studying of Romantic knowledge, Mary Jacobus has recently written:

> This is what the great teachers offer, especially to students of high Romanticism—not critical practice, still less literary theory, but what one might call leadings from above. . . . Like the Leech Gatherer, these critics are simply there ("not stood, not sat, but *'was'* ") in the sublime landscape of Wordsworth studies. . . .
>
> I want to ask: to what extent does installing oneself in this tradition also mean constituting oneself as looking like Wordsworth, Bloom, or Hartman—i.e. masculine? . . . What does it mean to confront the model of pedagogical autobiography advanced by Wordsworth if one happens to be a woman student, or a feminist critic, or even an autobiographical women poet?[1]

Jacobus narrates a parable of Romantic transmission that strikingly echoes the one that we saw galvanize the critical projects of de Man and McGann in the previous chapters. Like the symbol-oriented, organic Romanticism that de Man and McGann react to in their differing ways, the "high Romanticism" that Jacobus finds in the "sublime landscape of Wordsworth studies" is defined by a model of transmission which recognizes its own success in terms of its ability to reproduce, reconvey, and revalidate the values of an assumed originary poetic source. And, as we saw implicitly in de Man and explicitly in McGann, Jacobus's model is characterized by its academic and institutional dimensions. Thus, as Jacobus's reference to the "great teachers" makes clear, high Romanticism is further defined by the act, and the trope, of pedagogy. Unlike de Man and McGann, however, Jacobus does not focus her parable upon any of the "great teachers" of post–World War II Romanticism, such as M. H. Abrams or René Wellek; instead, she connects Wordsworth to Abrams's student Harold Bloom and to Bloom's former Yale School compatriot Geoffrey Hartman.[2] Thus, Jacobus's gender-inflected question at the end of the passage at once appropriates, extends, and transforms the narrative of Romantic transmission and its convergence with postmodern theory—in a highly condensed but nonetheless fitting allegory, as it were, for feminism's own profitably disorienting interventions into the theoretical debates of the last twenty-five years.

Pursuing Jacobus's question involves considering both what a feminist reading of Romanticism means for Romanticism as well as what it means institutionally, theoretically, and politically for that reading itself. That is, the opportunistic hermeneutic crystallized by Jacobus's pointed question comments not only on the nearly two-hundred-year-old patriarchal formations of a learned (in both senses of the word) Romanticism but also on the opportunities and impasses that characterize the current feminist study of Romanticism. Describing this "current" situation is, of course, a risky proposition at best, since no other field in Romantic studies is expanding so quickly, with new critical work on female writers from the late eighteenth and early nineteenth centuries occurring at an exponential rate. Clarifying the meaning of this work might, however, be a constant, built-in component of this scholarship, especially since the volatility and furious pace of the field could very well be symptomatic of a deeper condition that the theorization of Romanticism and gender together effects. Jacobus's words help us begin to make sense of this condition by allowing us to connect the field not simply to the archival recovery of women authors but also to the larger conceptual framework of the teaching and studying—the transmission—of Romanticism.

If, moreover, feminist Romantic studies reconceptualizes Romanticism's transmission through issues of gender, the criticism underwriting such studies is structured by yet another question of intellectual legacy: the pre-twentieth-century origins of feminist Romanticists' own theories of gender. My intervention into both of these problems of intellectual transmission will involve a reading of Mary Wollstonecraft's *Vindication of the Rights of Woman* (1792), a work whose vehemently nonessentialist politics has yet to be fully recognized by current scholars of Wollstonecraft, Romanticism, and gender, even as its polemics anticipate many of the theoretical aporias facing feminists and feminist Romanticists today. Recovering the legacy of those antinomies in Wollstonecraft reveals how she proleptically accomplishes what the theorization of Romanticism and gender together effects, insofar as her writing derealizes the categories of Romanticism and gender even as it demonstrates their intimate and crucial relations. Further, the problematic reputation of this great activist for education dialectically reassembles a space for her contemporary reception which comments on the complex politics of desiring "great teachers" of feminist theory from and before the late twentieth century. The transmission of Wollstonecraft's own reputation in and by feminist Romantic studies thus has broad implications not only for the study of Romanticism and gender but also for the place of feminist theory's own modernity in the postmodern "era." First, however, we must work through in more detail the feminist implications of the particular model of Romantic transmission which Jacobus identifies and see how the questions of a feminist nonessentialism and a feminist historiography of Romanticism are underwritten by the overlapping binaries of nature and culture, language and culture, and language and biology.

## II

Today it is hard to imagine the study of gender without considering a wider theoretical discursive field, one that many now identify through and as the problem of "identity politics." Central to this problem is the opposition between nature and culture, a binary that arguably subtends any discussion of subjectivity in feminist, race, or gay studies. Indeed, as a category considered by itself or in relation to other categories, gender foregrounds a constitutive split between nature and culture.[3] Appropriately enough, this split gains an especially powerful momentum in the intellectual imaginary of the eighteenth century, so much so that we continue routinely to resort to it in order to help define what "Romanticism" was and is. I say appropriately, since this binary and its attendant aporias also continue to condition the relation between feminist theory and Romanticism at a number of complicated levels—some of which are overtly enabling in their support for an interventionary feminist critique and some of which are potentially enabling because they complicate that critique in ways that have yet to be fully explored by a nonessentialist feminist critical practice.

First, it is important to see how this binary underwrites the model of Romantic transmission which Jacobus both identifies and critiques: how, in other words, the split between nature and culture occasions in Jacobus's thought a feminist version of the reigning trope in Romantic historiography today, the trope of intervention. Jacobus's emblem for the pedagogical Romantic transmission in which she herself intervenes is the institution of Wordsworth studies, a particularly apt choice when one considers how, especially after the reifying consolidation of Romantic studies around the works of the six major male Romantic poets in the 1950s and 1960s, to study British Romanticism is arguably to understand Wordsworth—to *be* Wordsworth insofar as one aspired to participate in a Wordsworthian imaginary of poetic, philosophic, and ethical values. No doubt this pedagogical imperative goes a long way in explaining further the revisionary power of 1980s ideological critiques of Wordsworth. Following Jacobus, we can further observe how the ideological ramifications of "being Wordsworth" necessarily overlap with questions of how intellectual and aesthetic traditions relate to issues of gender, questions that the poet himself addresses in a sublimely detailed and self-reflexive manner.

An especially vivid and condensed version of these dynamics is Wordsworth's "Michael" (1800), a poem explicitly about transmission and inheritance. As has often been noted, Wordsworth gives these themes a tellingly poetic and aesthetic dimension, when at the beginning of the work the poet explains how he will tell the story of Michael:

> For the delight of a few natural hearts;
> And, with yet fonder feeling, for the sake
> Of youthful Poets, who among these hills
> Will be my second self when I am gone.
> (36–39)[4]

If Wordsworth studies in the latter half of this century become a sublime institution in English literature, that power largely rests on the degree to which such studies succeed in achieving these "Wordsworthian" sentiments—how they reduplicate the pedagogical structure of these lines, which *is* the structure of reduplication, of teaching and learning as best we can how to be the poet's "second self." In "Michael," of course, this parable of poetic transmission is attached to the story of another hoped-for reduplication between the "Son and Father," Luke and Michael. Luke, however, is not able to overcome the burden of debt which Michael's nephew has placed on Michael and his property, and so the hoped-for transmission of the sheepfold from father to son is thwarted. The poem elegizes this disruption of an inheritance, of the failure of Luke to become, like Michael, the shepherd of their land. In doing so, however, the poem restores the line of transmission and the shepherd's second self, insofar as Michael inspires, indeed becomes, "Michael," a work that recreates the mechanics of Michael's bequest in terms of the inheritance of poetic insight that the poet draws from the shepherd and, in turn, bestows on his "youthful Poets."[5]

What "Michael" thus naturalizes—and, by extension, what Wordsworth studies for most of the latter part of this century internalizes—is a poetic authority based on a model of patrimony, itself a naturalization of specific social, gender, and economic relations to which, conversely, Wordsworth's poem actively contributes. This blurring of nature and culture, moreover, allows the study of Wordsworth, and by extension the study of Romanticism, to perform a sublime prestidigitation, whereby the sources of Romanticism's pedagogical and aesthetic legitimacy are simultaneously displayed and hidden. That is, teachers and students of Wordsworth, like the poet of "Michael," resort to images of masculine inheritance in order to legitimate their own genealogy; conversely, precisely because such images are "merely" tropes for a poetic transmission, they preempt the exposure of the cultural and social contingencies that irreducibly inform the "natural" authority of biological gender difference which makes the concept of a "legitimate" genealogy—of masculine transmission—intelligible. It is precisely the dependence of this intelligibility on an idealized biological difference in gender which Jacobus's question explicitly reveals.

Jacobus calls the semiotic bluff, as it were, of these tropes, revealing how the authority of patrilineal metaphors necessarily smuggle in their own logic of exclusion. She pushes this logic to its extreme by revealing the assumption of biological difference in patrimony's referential field, so that we may ask: If the pedagogy of Wordsworth studies models itself on a line of patrilineal inheritance, to what degree does that model affect a female poet or female reader of Wordsworth aspiring to the poetic knowledge of Wordsworth's second self? To what degree does that model covertly and overtly demand from such a subject a virtual poetics of cross-dressing? And how do the exigencies of such a cross-dressing then comment on the stability of Wordsworth's, and Romanticism's, established lines of transmission, on a pedagogy that was for a large part of this century the earning of an inheritance from Wordsworth?[6]

Such derealizing questions demonstrate how a feminist study of Romanticism implicitly carries out its own gender-inflected critique of the transmission and reception of Romanticism. Yet the implications of such a critique are far from simple. While, for example, such a critique might mandate a new focus on female writers from the Romantic era, the relation between these two scholarly activities rapidly becomes complicated. For, if the exposure of an idealized biological difference enables an intervention in Romantic studies, biological difference by itself certainly cannnot manage all the ramifications for Romantic, feminist Romantic, *and* feminist studies which its foregrounding initiates. That is, while biological difference can bracingly expose the cultural mystifications of Romantic patrimony, it cannot simply by itself replace that mystification as the object of a feminist revision of Romanticism. Crudely put, a study of women does not immediately insure either a feminist or a feminist Romanticist methodology. To ask, then, what the latter methodology, especially, means is to recuperate the category of culture as a necessary axis along which the female subject of the late eighteenth and early nineteenth centuries and Romanticism are to be understood. Moreover, the notion of such an axis is necessary precisely because it implies that this feminine subjectivity and Romanticism are to be understood together dialectically. These are no simple tasks.

We can begin to appreciate the formidable nature of these demands by considering our own reception of one of the first female readers of William Wordsworth, Dorothy Wordsworth. The feminist recuperation of Dorothy can be described succinctly as the attempt to provide her with a discursive space other than the pedagogical interpellation she receives in "Tintern Abbey" as another of William's second selves.[7] The oppressive power of that pedagogical relation rests on the overwhelming interpenetration of its metaphoric and metonymic qualities. That is, William recognizes himself in Dorothy because she is both a metonym and a metaphor for him, because of her close proximity to her brother and because of the ease with which his narrative is able to make her person signify his own life expericnces, the maturing of "wild ecstasies" into a "sober pleasure" that becomes itself a hallmark for a certain reception of William and Romanticism. To read Dorothy against the grain of this reception is thus first to make visible again the seam that divides these metonymic and metaphoric qualities and then to critique ruthlessly the metaphoric dissolution of Dorothy into simply another signifier for William's Romantic *lebenswelt*. Such a critical move occasions, however, the scandalous possibility that, like Dorothy's relation to William, her relation to Romantic studies is merely metonymic, a contingency authorized not by any metaphoric system but, rather, by an arbitrary dependence on the proximity of a bloodline—the metonymic Other, as it were, to the metaphoric reduplication of William's poetic patrimony.[8]

This is not to say that compelling work has not been and cannot be done on Dorothy's literary and cultural value independent from and as a commentary on William's own Romantic self-representations.[9] The point is to recover, instead, the scandal of thought which subtends the originating reason for the institutional recovery of Dorothy as an object of study in Romanticism—because she is simply *there,* next to William and other members of the Lake School. To do so is, of course, to work immediately on transforming the metonymic relation between Dorothy and William into a metaphor for something other than William, to coordinate Dorothy's biological difference from William with a larger cultural, literary, historical, or social formation. These strategies may or may not have anything crucial to do with defining Romanticism, or, more precisely, defining Romanticism through the category of gender. A certain arbitrariness thus returns to the conceptualization of a feminist study of Dorothy, which is not simply an abstract issue, since it is this very arbitrariness that continues to influence the critical responses of feminist Romanticist studies in the '80s and '90s.

In other words, the predicament of Dorothy Wordsworth's reception and study allegorizes a metonymic relation to Romanticism which at least partially underwrites feminist Romantic studies since their inception in the early to mid-1980s after the dominating influences of deconstructive and ideological readings of Romanticism begin to relax.[10] As Anne Mellor notes, the works that most notably define this inception are Mary Poovey's *The Proper Lady and the Woman Writer* (1984), Mary Jacobus's *Reading Woman* (1986), and Margaret Homans's *Women Writers and Poetic Identity* (1980) and *Bearing the Word* (1987).[11] If these feminist works intersect with Romantic studies, it is mostly because Poovey's, Jacobus's, and Homans's objects of study—Mary Wollstonecraft, Mary Shelley, and Jane Austen, among others—are largely, like Dorothy Wordsworth, writers who are already part of the outer orbit of Romantic studies who in the past have been made intelligible largely by their temporal, physical, or figurative proximity to the more "central" male authors of the Romantic canon.[12] These critical works reveal new and exciting ways to read these female authors from the eighteenth and nineteenth centuries. Still, a certain logic of metonymy at least partially structures the disciplinary recognition of Poovey's, Jacobus's, and Homans's works as "feminist Romanticist" criticism: all such works employ a recognizably gender-oriented approach—either historically, linguistically, or psychoanalytically based—in order to read a number of female writers largely associated with Romanticism; *feminist* and *Romanticist* thus converge in a manner that forestalls any full interrogation into the possibly contingent nature of their relation. This is not to say that these influential works do not resort to Romanticism as a methodological category in their gender-oriented reading; only that the question of the necessity of theorizing feminism and Romanticism together, of considering what this project might mean, does not play a central role in the institutionalization of feminist approaches to Romanticism in the '80s.[13]

The implications of this still largely unacknowledged, self-reflexive question might actually enable us to understand the current complex predicament of feminist Romantic studies in the '90s, a situation in which two different impulses define such critical work. I refer, first, to the exhilarating archival recovery of a host of female writers whose present institutionalized links to the male Romantic canon are much less vivid than those of Dorothy Wordsworth and the other subjects of Poovey, Jacobus, and Homans and, second, to the revising of canonical Romanticism as a cultural formation that can be best understood through the troping of gender.[14]

To juxtapose the archival recovery of Romantic female writers with the reconceptualization of canonical Romanticism through the category of gender is to highlight, no matter how crudely, a difference in methodological focus initiated by the opposition between biology and culture. As with the complementary distinction between archival research and theoretical conceptualization, however, this binary's greatest effect is to dismantle the very illusion of its stability. To add to or recover from the Romantic canon a number of female writers is, in other words, to beg the question of what a Romantic female writer is—to beg the question of what Romanticism as a cultural and historical category signifies in that identity. Simultaneously, to refunction canonical Romanticism through the troping of gender is to risk reifying a certain a priori essentialist historical identity dependent on biology—the autonomous domain of the six male poets—which, among other things, precludes the participation of female writers in a larger, more complex historical dynamic.[15] As these problems imply, moreover, the instability of the opposition between biology and culture does not mean that a conceptual resolution simply lies in the equation of female writers with a culture of feminine Romanticism or of male writers with a masculine Romanticism. Rather, these methodological problems indicate how biology and culture constantly transform the categories of investigation underwriting these two critical impulses and how such transformations challenge in a number of diverse, asymmetric ways the need to theorize feminism and Romanticism together.

With regards to the ongoing recovery of such female authors as Mary Robinson, Helen Maria Williams, Charlotte Smith, Joanna Baillie, and Felicia Hemans, this challenge is most visibly cathected in the question of whether this recuperation is simply a recovery of a number of writers most obviously connected to one another by their biological gender or whether it represents a more thorough reordering of our literary history which will use these writers to reinstate one or more hitherto forgotten categories of literary, cultural, and social activity. Perhaps I overstate the starkness of this contrast, but I do so in order to press the question of the compatibility of these writers with the present disciplinary site of their recovery, Romanticism and Romantic studies.

There is, first of all, the question of periodization: whether the implicit historical specificity of British Romanticism adequately makes intelligible the recovery of what is in effect several generations of female writers, "beginning" with the bluestocking circle in the 1770s and "concluding" with such individuals as Joanna Baillie (1762–1851), Mary Betham (1776–1852), and Margaret Hodson (1778–1852). Given the complex and lengthy chronology of these writers, it is uncertain whether terms such as *early Romantic* or *late Romantic*—drawn from the chronology of the six male poets—realize in a historically satisfactory manner what is being studied when we read such female authors. Obviously enough, then, the feminine Romanticism associated with their recovery must imply a further aesthetic, philosophic, or social category, such as Stuart Curran's suggestion that a number of the writers' works engage with either the topic of everyday life or that of alienated sensibility.[16] A new problem then arises, however, in that such concepts as Curran's are immediately recognizable as part of the very topoi that are employed by various thinkers to understand "mainstream" British Romanticism.[17] One could, of course, argue that it is in the very difference between the use of such concepts in canonical Romanticism and their use in feminine

Romanticism that the latter realizes its identity. We might then wonder whether the stress on such a difference makes the *Romanticism* in feminine Romanticism an irrelevant totalizing constraint on the eighteenth- and nineteenth-century writers being recovered, a contingent disciplinary reification whose residual, compulsive presence at once impinges on and confuses whatever is being used to categorize the writers' works beyond that of the "individual author."[18] Conversely, we might also wonder whether the circulation of the topics of everyday life and alienated sensibility between a "normative" and a feminine Romanticism intimates a potentially more unstable movement of signs than that gendered binary affords. Such an instability might then be the reoccurring lesson of Romanticism's own ontological and epistemological *self*-incompatibility. This lesson—that of, among others, Lovejoy and de Man—would thus find its latest dramatization in the methodological and categorical contradictions that underwrite the recovery of "more" Romantic female writers. The aporias of such a recovery would then simply be part of the latest example of a general predicament within literary history itself, a constitutive self-resistance that the fantastic project of Romanticism and Romantic studies enacts again and again in the dialectical interplay between its ontological self-assertions and autocritiques.

As my earlier usage of *fantastic* implies, however, the point of such an observation would not be to paralyze the specific project of literary history at hand; rather, the question would be how a more explicit sense of this aporetic predicament might be internalized as *part* of the literary and cultural history of eighteenth- and nineteenth-century female writers being recovered. To begin even to answer that question means considering the other primary critical impulse of feminist Romanticist studies: the locating of questions of gender not simply in the biology of rediscovered female writers but also in the cultural and literary formations that are used to define the very *ism*, or *ism*s, of Romanticism. This emphasis on the cultural trope of gender would speak both to the question of a feminine Romanticism of female writers and to the possibility of a masculine poetics of the canonized male authors. Given the monolithic (re)presentations of canonical Romanticism in deconstructive and ideological criticism, it is not surprising that the possibility of a patriarchal Romanticism should underwrite a forceful interventionary scholarship that includes not only Jacobus's recent work on Wordsworth but also Anne

Mellor's *Romanticism and Gender* (1993), Marlon Ross's *The Contours of Masculine Desire* (1989), and Homans's earlier *Bearing the Word*.[19] From either a historical or a linguistic perspective, these works identify a masculinist literary culture in the late eighteenth and early nineteenth centuries which finds an intimate and particular realization in high Romanticism's writings. As empowering as such an identification is, however, it is not without its risks. For, if the archival recovery of biological female writers immediately demonstrates the imbrication of such a project with further cultural theorizations, the cultural troping of gender necessarily carries within itself the residue of a semantic overdetermination that is the idealization of biological difference. While, in other words, biology constantly reveals the (cultural) nonclosure of its meanings, culture constantly risks treating its own categories as if they had achieved the (biological) closure of meaning.[20]

This is not to say that any of these revisionary readings of an androcentric Romanticism are simply essentialist in their diagnoses. Indeed, Mellor and Ross, because of their focus on both male and female writers, seem especially aware of the reifying dangers inherent in a methodology based on categorizing Romanticism through gender. Still, in using gender to orient the intelligibility of its assertions, such a methodology risks hypostatizing the very effects of the socially and linguistically constructed differences in gender which the methodology simultaneously exposes.[21] I take Jacobus to be speaking to the particular dynamics of this danger in her prescient essay on *Villette* from 1979. Jacobus first identifies in Brontë's novel a "feminization of the Romantic imagination" in which woman, writing, passion, and Romanticism all serve as subversive, repressed, and conflicted signs for fissures within the nineteenth-century patriarchal imaginary. But, while that very "feminization . . . is a triumph, it runs the attendant risk of creating a feminine ghetto. The annexing of special powers of feeling and intuition to women and its consequences (their relegation to incompetent dependency) has an equally strong Romantic tradition; women, idiots and children, like the debased version of the Romantic poet, become at once privileged and (legally) irresponsible."[22]

Jacobus's dual reaction to Brontë's feminized, Gothic Romanticism can also be applied to the topic of high Romanticism's masculine identity, so that, complicating my own extension of Jacobus's interventionary questioning of Wordsworth studies, we might wonder whether the exposure of high Romanticism's tropological gender not only liberates but also constricts the reading of gender difference in Romanticism. That is, while canonical Romanticism might have an ideology or self-representation of organic totality, this does not mean that it is an organic totality; similarly, an ideology of masculine Romanticism does not imply a high Romanticism absolutely fixed by a masculine gender. As Anne Mellor writes, the "construction of British literary Romanticism as a rigid binary opposition based on gender does not do justice to the critical complexity of many of the literary texts produced in England between 1780 and 1830. . . . Any writer, male or female, could occupy the 'masculine' or the 'feminine' ideological or subject position, even within the same work."[23] Thus, the particular attempts to define Romanticism through gender especially gain in semantic significance when they are read dialogically together, as in the linking of Jacobus's positive feminization of Brontë's emotional Romanticism to Irving Babbitt's modernist negative feminization of canonical Romanticism or as in Alan Richardson's refunctioning of Ross's argument, so that Romanticism is primarily defined not as the romance of masculine poetic desire but, instead, as the masculine colonization of previously feminized social and literary traits.[24] In the various ways these different arguments intervene in, contest, and qualify one another, one can see a surplus of signification which is the result of theorizing Romanticism's "gender." It is such a surplus of signs, I would contend, which should explicitly subtend the feminist intervention of gender in Romantic studies; which should, in effect, be the self-reflexive response to the question of theorizing Romanticism and feminism together.[25]

We have, in fact, used such a surplus and its fierce circulation to structure the critical narrative just told about the constant oscillation between the changing roles of biology and culture in feminist Romantic studies. To summarize, we have seen how the masculine troping of high Romantic—that is, Wordsworthian—entailment is exposed by the interventionary presence of that trope's referent, an idealized biological gender. On the one hand, the interventionary reflexivity of biological difference orients a new focus on female writers; on the other, because of the conceptual limits of biological difference, this same reflexivity dialectically demands a cultural categorization beyond biology. In turn, that categorization might or might not depend on Romanticism or gender. Moreover, insofar as Romanticism and gender are culturally defined together, the recognition of either a masculine or feminine Romanticism finds itself risking the same reifying predicament as biological difference. That these various scenarios seem to reenact as many impasses as opportunities for feminist Romantic studies speaks, I think, not so much to the failure of any one discrete scenario as to the repetition of certain constitutive aporias as the discursive playing field for feminist Romanticist studies, a condition particularly exacerbated by the open-ended semiotic nature of both "gender" and "Romanticism." That is, to define Romanticism by gender, or gender by Romanticism, means defining two terms that are marked not so much by the centrifugal pull of any one meaning but, rather, by the centripetal force of their circulation among a number of diverse, oftentimes contradictory signs. This circulation of signs, then, must be recognized as the starting point for any feminist literary history of Romanticism or, for that matter, any specific use of such a history for feminist theory's ongoing, defiantly millennial claims.[26]

We are now almost finally in a position to turn to Mary Wollstonecraft and her assuredly defiant *A Vindication of the Rights of Woman*, which is, in effect, a proleptic allegory for the circulation of signs in feminist Romantic studies. Like the present institution of feminist studies, Wollstonecraft's project is to make intelligible a particular history and politics of gender; like the strategy of many today in that institution, her argument depends on a nonessentialist view of gender and of the binaries—between and among the biological and the cultural—which structure gender difference. Moreover, both Wollstonecraft's works and her literary reputation shed a special light on the possible conjoining of feminism and Romanticism. Four interrelated issues, especially, stand out.

First, while Wollstonecraft does belong to the "outer" orbit of canonized Romantic writers, that disciplinary affiliation is actually problematic, insofar as one can argue that Wollstonecraft is an Enlightenment writer with an intensely conflicted relation to Romanticism. This latter view is, moreover, gendered, insofar as the Enlightenment is associated with a masculine reason at odds with a feminized Romanticism of emotion and sensibility. The history of Wollstonecraft scholarship is characterized by an uncritical assumption of this gendered opposition, so much so that the scholarship can be said to signify that opposition. Wollstonecraft's own writing argues, however, against the easy assumption of this binary and thus intervenes in the problematic practice of one of the most visible, and oldest, uses of gender in Romanticism *and* Romantic studies. Second, Wollstonecraft herself apparently employs gender in order to define Romanticism when, in *A Vindication of the Rights of Man* (1790), she attacks the unseemly emotional sensibility of Edmund Burke. Unlike, however, the gendered contrast between reason and feeling which undergirds Wollstonecraft criticism, Wollstonecraft's definition of Romantic sensibility is a local strategy that is caught up in a dialectical interplay with a number of other changing terms that also define masculinity, femininity, reason, and feeling. Thus, Wollstonecraft's own discursive strategies provide us with a self-reflexive model of theorizing gender which does not so much reify Romanticism's gendered identity as dramatize the problem, and politics, of identity in Romanticism's various discourses. Third, Wollstonecraft provides us with a "new" perspective on our own contemporary critical scene, insofar as that scene has been recently associated with a renewed interest in Romantic feeling and sensibility, an interest that is fueled at least in part by the contested ideological signification of the emotions as either a masculine or feminine activity.[27] *The Rights of Woman* turns this debate inside out by disrupting the gendered identity of reason as a masculine identity defined by its difference from an emotional feminine alterity. In doing so, Wollstonecraft's text extends, complements, and complicates the topoi of our own contemporary critical investigations. Fourth, and finally, in a perhaps scandalously obvious manner *The Rights of Woman* is a politically didactic manifesto; it thus forcefully links together Romanticism and feminism as two projects of modernity, of historical praxis and change. Such millennial investments actively structure Wollstonecraft's nonessentialist argument and provide a healthy reminder about its basic wager: that the circulation of signs inherent in Wollstonecraft's project does not obviate but, rather, exposes the uneven relations of power in the political and social worlds, the relations that make the thinking through of gender the difference between life and death. Wollstonecraft's project thus asserts a continuity between theory and praxis which is the activist appropriation of Romanticism's and feminism's fantastic modernity, the fantastic performative space of historical difference as programmatic, historical change.

To invoke this final conjoining of feminism and Romanticism in Wollstonecraft is, moreover, to consider how she further impinges on the question of feminist theory's own late-twentieth-century modernity. For, unlike de Man's appropriation of Shelley and Rousseau or McGann's use of Marx and Heine, feminist scholars have not really appropriated Wollstonecraft as anything closely resembling the "initiator of [the] discursive practices" that are used to read either Wollstonecraft or Romanticism.[28] Unlike the critical positions of de Man and McGann, then, the modernity of the feminist study of Romanticism is characterized by how it has not appropriated any representative Romantic figure in order to empower its own theoretical position—how its relation to such objects of study has not first and foremost been a dialectical one. The lack of Wollstonecraft's theoretical influence upon Wollstonecraft's Romanticist readers, both admiring and negative, can thus stand in for a larger critical plot: how feminist literary and cultural theory, unlike deconstruction or Marxism, is really a twentieth-century proposition; how, aside from a complicated relation to Freud and perhaps Marx, feminist theory's genealogy does not explicitly depend on eighteenth- or nineteenth-century precursors the way it does on Simone de Beauvoir, Kate Millett, the North American historiography of *Madwoman in the Attic,* and the post-Lacanian incursions of the various new French feminisms. The question of Wollstonecraft's intellectual legacy and transmission therefore effects a singular resonance within and beyond feminist studies, one that installs gender difference within the very possibility of an intellectual history for a discursive or disciplinary field.[29]

## III

It is uncannily fitting that Mary Shelley should dedicate her famous Romantic novel, *Frankenstein,* to her father, William Godwin, and not to her mother, Mary Wollstonecraft. The literal, and literary, gap between mother and daughter is an appropriate emblem for the discontinuity between Wollstonecraft's theoretical writing and the work of contemporary feminist literary critics.[30] This discontinuity is largely due to a public monumentalization and disfigurement of Wollstonecraft by her contemporaries which is similar, I would suggest, to the posthumous process that afflicted the writer she both admired and criticized, Jean-Jacques Rousseau.[31] Much of the initial hostility toward both figures was associated with English horror at the French Revolution. Just as counterrevolutionaries viewed Rousseau's social thought and the politics of the French Revolution as one and the same, so too did many people view Wollstonecraft's Protestant bourgeois radicalism as an irrevocable contamination of her feminist position.[32] In both cases conservative critics saw the Reign of Terror as an inevitable consequence of each thinker's writing. A second, more important similarity is the extent to which late-eighteenth- and early-nineteenth-century readers connected each thinker's theory with his or her biography.[33] In each case a theory associated with Enlightenment reason was subverted by a life of unrestrained passion and immoral activity. For such readers of Wollstonecraft and Rousseau this subversion of theory by biography allegorized again what was occurring in France: a rational agenda of emancipation overcome by the uncontrollable demands of an irrational Reign of Terror. It is this early-nineteenth-century monument of Wollstonecraft, as an individual aspiring to rational discourse while hopelessly repressing irrational emotion, which we have inherited and who has haunted even the most sympathetic perceptions of her by contemporary feminist critics.

This is not to say that this reputation has remained completely the same since its inception. One change in this monument has been what exactly constitutes the "proof" of Wollstonecraft's unstable personal life. In its incarnation at the turn of the nineteenth century Wollstonecraft's emotional instability was signified by every aspect of her lifestyle: her various love affairs, her illegitimate child, the "unconventional" form of her relationship to Godwin, and her attempted suicides. Today only Wollstonecraft's attempted suicides can carry any of the same biographical weight. But, just as the signs for her personal emotional life have changed, so too has the evaluation of those signs. Instead of seeing that life as a set of negative traits, a mark of Wollstonecraft's hypocrisy and limitations, most contemporary feminists see her private life as an emotional resource that Wollstonecraft heeded too little. For contemporary feminists the emotional traces of Wollstonecraft's life are unstable but in a positive sense; they represent needs and desires that have the potential to subvert patriarchal norms as much as Wollstonecraft's "reasoned" Enlightenment agenda. Indeed, they have become needs and desires tragically or inevitably hampered by that agenda.

Two things concerning Wollstonecraft's reputation, moreover, have remained relatively constant over the last two centuries. The first is the basic duality underwriting that reputation, reason versus imagination;

the second, the genders assigned to the terms of that duality. No one has argued, in other words, with Mary Jacobus's description of the rational side of that duality as "the predominantly male discourse of Enlightenment Reason, or 'sense.' "[34] Opposing this discourse is the Otherness of Wollstonecraft's writing and biography, a chain of signifiers which links together such terms as *femininity, imagination, irrationality, sensibility,* and *passion*. In even the most sympathetic readings of Wollstonecraft, contemporary critics such as Cora Kaplan, Mary Poovey, and Mary Jacobus have portrayed her as trapped by this duality—at best, as reproducing the problems of this trap for our contemporary edification.[35] In all cases Wollstonecraft remains an individual experiencing an identity crisis; if she is no longer as the nineteenth century represented her, an unstable woman whose life proves her error, she remains an individual reacting to the interpellating textual and personal effects of two opposing discourses, male reason and female imagination.

Associated with this perception of Wollstonecraft's identity is a literary history that narrativizes her texts in terms of a progress from her critical work, *The Rights of Woman,* to her unfinished novel, *The Wrongs of Woman; or Maria*. The basic form of this narrative is one in which Wollstonecraft is more able, in her later works, to face the Otherness of her life—whether that be female desire or the "imaginative and linguistic excess" of female writing—which she represses or attacks in favor of male reason in *The Rights of Woman*.[36] It is a mistake, however, to view *The Rights of Woman* as a text that is somehow blind to the insights of Wollstonecraft's other works. *The Rights of Woman* is a much more complex work about repression, reason, imagination, and gender than the present monument of Wollstonecraft allows. My reading of Wollstonecraft differs from that expressed by the present monument in three ways. First, rather than seeing Wollstonecraft as being caught between the gender demands of male reason and female imagination, I see her text actively trying to disrupt that duality's assignation of gender, by strategically associating "woman" with a variety of local, contradictory identities.[37] The second difference is that I also see Wollstonecraft's text preempting that very duality by destabilizing the opposition between reason and the host of terms the text contrasts with reason. The complicated relationships between reason and those terms underwrite not only Wollstonecraft's critique of the "feminine" imagination but also her critique of that imagination's structure of repression. Those complex relationships also underwrite the very semantic and stylistic tensions of her text which contemporary critics have only been able to recognize as a repression of female Otherness by male reason. Finally, the third difference is that I see these textual tensions also pointing to a certain reflexivity within Wollstonecraft's work, a reflexivity for which *The Rights of Woman* is given too little credit. Far from being a text blind to the limits of its own political and didactic discourse, *The Rights of Woman* carries out an ideological critique of its own teleological and millennial aspirations, precisely through its dissolution of the semantic identities that separate reason from passion.

I want to take up first the issue of what *woman* means in *The Rights of Woman*. Wollstonecraft is most famous for equating *woman* with *human,* that beneficiary of both Enlightenment and post-Enlightenment theories of democratic principles. It is in that spirit of a humanistic, democratic discourse that Wollstonecraft addresses the beginning of her book to M. Talleyrand-Périgord, the influential member of the new Republic of France, the nation most strongly associated with those democratic, antimonarchist ideals. It is also in the spirit of that same discourse that Wollstonecraft chastises Talleyrand for not extending, in a government pamphlet, the human rights of education to women as well as to men: "I wish, Sir, to set some investigations of this kind afloat in France, and should they lead to a confirmation of my principles, when your constitution is revised the Rights of Woman may be respected, if it be fully proved that reason calls for this respect, and loudly demands JUSTICE for one half of the human race."[38]

As Wollstonecraft's words imply, the discourse she wants to enter primarily associates the human with the other half of the race, man. This fact has been turned against her, in that critics have accused Wollstonecraft of being blind to what happens to the feminine within such a discourse.[39] Such a critique argues that a universal term such as *human* hides inequality and sexual difference; by equating *woman* with *human,* which equates with *man,* Wollstonecraft can only reproduce that elision. But this critique ignores the possibility of a metaleptic effect caused by Wollstonecraft's incursion—that she is in fact introducing the alterity of sexual difference into this supposedly universal discourse and thus enabling, as Ernesto Laclau and Chantal Mouffe claim, "the birth of feminism through the use made of it in the democratic discourse, which was thus displaced from the field of political equality to the field of equality between the sexes."[40]

Nor does *woman* signify only democratic humanism in *The Rights of Woman*. Wollstonecraft associates the feminine with a variety of oftentimes contradictory qualities and positions. Because of these other significations, the equivalence between the feminine and democratic humanism does not reach the critical mass of an essential equation. Rather, this equivalence and the other instances of gender assignment operate as localized semantic moments, dependent on the situational strategy of a fluid political polemic.

These local moments in *The Rights of Woman* constitute an argument by analogy, a strategy whose ubiquity must then be taken into account when we wish to determine the ontological status of those analogies. Yet, while the very number and variety of these analogies make them nonessentialist, they are not arbitrary. That is, all of Wollstonecraft's analogies are determined by the same theme; each analogy links women to a role of power—or powerlessness—at a different position within the sociohistoric world of late-eighteenth-century England. But, while the theme of power thus structures Wollstonecraft's analogies, power itself is denied any essential signification. That is, in each example of women's empowerment or victimization, power is constituted by a different combination of codes of age, class, and gender. The result is a concrete depiction of the condition of women in the late eighteenth century which simultaneously repudiates the idea that there is any essential character to its catalog of women's empowered and victimized identities.

In repudiating such a character, Wollstonecraft employs a linguistic method that denies what Laclau and Mouffe call "a fully sutured space" to both the patriarchy and the women it oppresses. Such a space posits an identity so sealed from outside signification that the identity achieves the "transparency of a closed symbolic order."[41] It is precisely this symbolic closure that the variety of Wollstonecraft's analogies denies. Yet, simultaneously, because of their role in articulating the position of women within eighteenth-century patriarchy, these analogies still deal with the brute fact of power and oppression.

Thus, while Wollstonecraft's polemic for women's rights utilizes the equation between woman and the human race, her critique of women's present condition associates women with the Others of democratic discourse: Eastern princes, Roman emperors, monarchs, and the aristocratic class. Here *woman* signifies a power that is not based on self-determination but, rather, on the analogy between the unearned, arbitrary trappings of despotic privilege and the equally capricious influence of physical beauty. Hence, we have Wollstonecraft's rejection of such sexual influence in her famous reply to Rousseau: "I do not wish [women] to have power over men; but over themselves" (62; chap. 4).[42] But the tyrant's/woman's power over the people/man is also a powerlessness that must be constituted through other analogies, in which the fact of women's limited opportunities and helplessness is signified by children and the lower class. Thus, women are slaves oppressed by men who are tyrants, whose power is actually like that of women limited like children and the poor. Women are oppressed, but it is by a master-slave dialectic that resists any easy condensation of gender or class identities.

One might object that, while women have been either "slaves or despots," *The Rights of Woman* still associates the utopian democratic ideal with the "manly." That opposition certainly does operate in Wollstonecraft's text. Yet that duality becomes a fundamentally reified part of Wollstonecraft's thought only when we ignore the other positions and roles of gender which crisscross that duality, such as the fact that the discourse of the monarch rests on examples of male despotism—for example, Louis XIV—and that the politically progressive concept of modesty is chiefly associated with the feminine. Likewise, Wollstonecraft disparages Lord Chesterfield's worldly letters to his son as "unmanly"—that is, effeminate—for their libertine exploitation of women (106; chap. 5), while at the same time she begins her attack on Mrs. Piozzi's statement, that "all [women's] arts are employed to gain and keep the heart of man," by calling Piozzi's ideas "truly masculine sentiments" (102; chap. 5). Certainly, Wollstonecraft does not want Piozzi to be less masculine in the way Chesterfield is, nor does she want Chesterfield to be more manly in the way Piozzi is. "Unmanly" and "truly masculine" do not constitute the intrinsic identities of gendered subjects, nor is Wollstonecraft downgrading them as such; rather, they are each a sign of a particular position within eighteenth-century English patriarchy, a position whose deadly denotative force Wollstonecraft dramatizes through the semantics, and politics, of gender.

By having the feminine and the masculine occupy, at different strategic moments, the key position of both her negative critique and utopian polemic, Wollstonecraft is, in effect, deconstructing the intrinsic identity of a gendered subject. Just as important, Wollstonecraft sees this deconstruction taking place within the context of an English androcentric society demanding the opposite of this deconstruction from its female population, so that "a virtuous man may have a choleric or a sanguine constitution, be gay or grave, unreproved; be firm till he is almost overbearing, or, weakly submissive, have no will or opinion of his own; but all women are to be levelled, by meekness and docility, into one character of yielding softness and gentle compliance" (95; chap. 5). It is in this spirit, of an attack on the "one character," that we should read Wollstonecraft's famous dictum that boys and girls should study together in order to produce "modesty without those sexual distinctions that taint the mind" (165; chap. 12). Wollstonecraft is not trying to efface sexual difference here; instead, she is attempting to disrupt the imprisoning codification of sexual identity as constructed in invidious social distinctions. Similarly, when Wollstonecraft criticizes the French educative system by saying, "[young girls] were treated like women [i.e., coquettes] almost from their very birth," she is not consigning "women" to an eternal identification with "coquetry" (81; chap. 5). Rather, she is trying to break up that singular identity imposed on those girls, by exposing the identity's dependence upon linguistic and pedagogical structures: "they were treated *like* women almost from their very birth."

This strategy of gender *dis*identification is clear in one footnote in which Wollstonecraft comments upon how men behave differently in front of women, depending upon the degree to which women stress their own "feminine" identity: "Men are not always men in the company of women, nor would women always remember that they are women, if they were allowed to acquire more understanding" (123; chap. 7). On which term, *men* or *women,* should we confer originary status, to start this sentence's chain of signification? And who is the second "they"? The meaning of the first clause and its relation to the rest of the sentence change, depending on which, and how many, of the gender terms are placed in italics. This syntactical and grammatical indeterminacy succinctly dramatizes the dizzying spiral of signification that structures the absolute necessity and irreducible problem of sexual identity in *The Rights of Woman.* It is the text's consciousness of this indeterminacy which redirects the rage of sentences, such as the following one, away from an essential "woman" and toward the host of social, psychological, and linguistic forces that work to shore up the ontology of that identity: "This desire of being always women, is the very consciousness that degrades the sex" (99; chap. 5).[43]

By thus attacking the concept of a single feminine identity, *The Rights of Woman* escapes being located only within a duality of male reason and female imagination. It is precisely the hegemonic force of that duality which Wollstonecraft disrupts, by deploying the feminine in a host of contradictory roles. But Wollstonecraft also disrupts this duality by subverting the unitary identities of imagination and reason. She emplots gender, repression, reason, and imagination in a narrative that is more complicated than the one that the duality of male reason and female imagination implies.

There are two exemplary moments in *The Rights of Woman* in which Wollstonecraft appears explicitly to repress the female imagination in order to preserve male reason. One moment occurs when Wollstonecraft asserts that young children of the same sex should not be housed or educated together, so that they will not learn from one another the "vices, which render the body weak," specifically, masturbation (164; chap. 12).[44] Here one can image the female imagination as a feminine interest in sexuality and pleasure, an interest that Wollstonecraft must repress in the name of a disembodied male rationality. The other moment occurs during Wollstonecraft's introductory remarks on style, when she promises not "to cull my phrases or polish my style . . . for, wishing rather to persuade by the force of my arguments, than dazzle by the elegance of my language, I shall not waste my time in rounding periods, or in fabricating the turgid bombast of artificial feelings" (10; introd.). Here the female imagination can be reinscribed within a feminine discourse of sensual and emotional rhetoric which Wollstonecraft also dismisses in favor of a more masculine type of writing and style of reason. Thus, one could argue that, through these two instances in the text, *The Rights of Woman* attempts both thematically and formally to repress a feminine alterity in favor of a masculine ontology of Enlightenment reason. Seemingly disparate, Wollstonecraft's view of writing and her prohibition against masturbation are connected, but not by the apparent, simple model of a male reason repressing a female imagination.[45]

First, let us consider Wollstonecraft's words against masturbation. Her interdiction comes as part of a broader polemic, against the "wearisome confinement" women experience at school together, which is even worse than what young men suffer. In a passage just before the one on masturbation, Wollstonecraft describes the negative effect of this confinement in vivid terms.

> The pure animal spirits, which make both mind and body shoot out, and unfold the tender blossoms of hope, are turned sour, and vented in vain wishes or pert repinings, that contract the faculties and spoil the temper; else they mount to the brain, and sharpening the understanding before it gains proportionable strength, produce that pitiful cunning which disgracefully characterizes the female mind—and I fear will ever characterize it whilst women remain the slaves of power! (164; chap. 12)

We notice immediately that Wollstonecraft has, as she often does, characterized the female in negative terms. But more important is the specific way in which she characterizes the female as negative. In this passage the "female mind" is the consequence of the "souring" of the "pure animal spirits"—"spirits" charged by a sensual articulation, verging on the explicitly sexual for both the male ("shoot out") and female ("tender blossoms") organs. How do we reconcile Wollstonecraft's positive evaluation of these terms with her admonitions against masturbation? I would argue that, instead of a simultaneous acknowledgment and repression of sexuality, this passage is a parable that warns against the repression of sexuality, the "animal spirits." More precisely, Wollstonecraft's sexual language provides a biological metaphor for the process of social growth which Wollstonecraft opposes to the deforming and stunting socializing process women had to undergo under England's educational system. The product of this system is woman, the female mind, whose essential consignment to this gender identity is undercut not only by Wollstonecraft's visionary cry ("whilst women remain . . .") but also by the male configuration of masturbation and loss which structures the entire procedure ("animal spirits . . . turned sour"), which itself is undercut, in turn, by the biological gender of Wollstonecraft's subjects: ghettoized young girls who are "obliged to pace with steady deportment stupidly backwards and forwards . . . instead of bounding . . . in the various attitudes so conducive to health" (164; chap. 12).

These young girls, moreover, are not the sole victims of this oppressive system of single-sex confinement. For in the next paragraph Wollstonecraft shifts her attention from the girls to the "boys [who] infallibly lose that decent bashfulness" in the setting of a single-sex school (164; chap. 12). Thus, while it is the confined group of girls whose animal spirits metaphorically "turn sour," it is the equally segregated group of boys who actually learn the "vices, which render the body weak."

Thus, masturbation functions as a sign for this whole pedagogical system of "souring" and also as the final figurative and literal consequence of this system: the vice that girls and boys will experience because of their isolation from one another.[46] By attacking that final consequence, Wollstonecraft is weighing in against the entire system, in which masturbation functions as a repression of the potential of mind and body. As such, the passage on masturbation exemplifies one particular target of Wollstonecraft's polemic, the repression of women's full emotional life by the schizophrenic identity men impose on them: both coy mistress and chaste wife. (The fact that schoolboys specifically fall prey to masturbation stresses, for Wollstonecraft, how both sexes suffer the consequences of this repression.) Wollstonecraft's critique of this identity underscores the reason why she distinguishes between modesty and the desire for a good reputation. Modesty is the state of life one achieves after experiencing passion and the vicissitudes of life, whereas the desire for a good reputation is the hypocritical, deforming state that passes ignorance off as innocence and whose end result is a titillation caused by the repression of desire. Thus, Wollstonecraft does not repress passion in favor of a repressive reason; instead, she attacks passion when it has been repressed, when it is not allowed to become part of a lived experience, but is exploited instead as the fuel for what amounts to a solipsistic, masturbatory imagination.[47]

This is Wollstonecraft's critique of a certain type of "feminized" and "Romantic" imagination. By looking at this sensibility in *The Rights of Woman* more closely, we can understand more fully the implications of her introductory attack on a writing style of supposed sensuality and feeling. Her emblem for this imagination is none other than Jean-Jacques Rousseau, who, as the writer of *Emile,* lays out in his education of Sophie the most specific blueprint for this particular kind of "feminization" of the female subject. But Rousseau is also the chief example of someone who indulges in this type of imagination:

> Even [Rousseau's] virtues also led him astray; for, born with warm constitution and lively fancy, nature carried him toward the other sex with such eager fondness, that he soon became lascivious. *Had he given away to these desires,* the fire would have extinguished itself in a natural manner; but virtue and a romantic kind of delicacy, made him practice self-denial; yet when fear, delicacy, or virtue, restrained him, he debauched his imagination, and reflecting on the sensations to which fancy gave force, he traced them in the most glowing colours, and sunk them deep into his soul. (91; chap. 5; my emphasis)

If Rousseau had given into his lasciviousness, if he had actually met, rather than just gone toward, the other sex, his animal spirits would not have gone "sour," and his imagination would not have been "debauched."[48] Here *virtue* and *self-denial* are not continous with *modesty* and *reason;* rather, the former terms are part of the moral ideology that is also responsible for the isolation of young girls in education and the specific type of female mind which is the result of such an isolation. Moreover, that literal isolation reminds us that the effects of feminine delicacy and virtue differ for Rousseau and for the women defined by this same code. For Wollstonecraft, Rousseau's Romantic imagination underwrites the identities of both women and men, but it assigns them to asymmetrical positions of power.

It is true that, for his contemporaries and later critics, Rousseau signified a sensibility that was always figured pejoratively in feminine terms.[49] Thus, we might be tempted to see Wollstonecraft's critique of Rousseau's imagination as merely reproducing the hierarchy of gender values which she is trying to attack. Our analysis of the circulation of gender in Wollstonecraft—especially in her interdiction against masturbation—should warn us against that temptation. But Wollstonecraft also subverts the temptation by assigning that sensibility to the premier patriarch of her day, Edmund Burke. Her association between Burke and this sensibility goes back to *A Vindication of the Rights of Men* (1790), which portrays Burke's *Reflections on the Revolution in France* (1790) as the reaction of an individual overcome by an unreasonable and emotional sensibility.[50] This emotional sensibility, like Rousseau's, victimizes women with a particular type of feminization, even as it exemplifies that feminization.[51] In much the same way *The Rights of Woman* attacks the tautological reasoning of Burke's valorization of prejudice in the *Reflections* by likening that type of argument to "what is vulgarly termed a woman's reason" (113; chap. 5). Wollstonecraft's point is not that women essentially reason through prejudice but, rather, that Burke reasons in a way that patriarchy has "vulgarly" associated with the feminine.[52]

By identifying Burke and Rousseau with a "sensibility" that they and others have imposed on women, Wollstonecraft has, in effect, deconstructed their sexual politics, foregrounding the contradictions of their own logic of gender and identity. This is the context of Wollstonecraft's attack on a writing style full of the "turgid bombast of artificial feeling." That is, Wollstonecraft and her contemporaries attacked Burke's *Reflections* on the very issue of a contradictory style, on how he described the French Revolution as a hysterical event, even though hysteria more aptly described his own emotional, oftentimes lurid style. This sensational style of Burke's is the target of Tom Paine's treatise *The Rights of Man* (1791, 1792) and Wollstonecraft's own *Rights of Men*.[53] By thus condemning a style of "sickly delicacy" and "false sentiments" at the beginning of *The Rights of Woman,* Wollstonecraft is not so much repressing a feminine style in favor of a male rationality as devaluing that style and disrupting its gender by associating it with one of the leading English fathers of the day.

One could still argue that, because of Wollstonecraft's own rambling and passionate style, she merely reproduces the irrational emotion she finds in Burke, even as she makes claims for the rational nature of her own work.[54] That argument would carry more force if the duality operating in Wollstonecraft's passage really was between reason and emotion. Yet she dismisses the "turgid bombast of artificial feeling" because it comes "from the head" and "never reach[es] the heart" (10; introd.). In fact, the duality dominating this passage is one between "*false* sentiments" and "*natural* emotions of the heart" (10; introd.; my emphasis). Without the experience of such "natural emotions" one cannot become a "rational and immortal being"; instead, like the confined school girls, one's life—and writing—is stunted by the titillating "sickly delicacy" exemplified by the inflamed imagination of Rousseau. I would also stress that, for Wollstonecraft, these natural emotions must be experienced. Indeed, false sentiments are "false" only because they have not been experienced, since the purpose of the natural emotions is in fact to lead one to reason through error. Elsewhere Wollstonecraft is explicit about how the experiential negativity of the passions is fundamentally involved in this dialectical progress toward reason and how that progress has, in Wollstonecraft's time, been gender coded:

> I must therefore venture to doubt whether what has been thought an axiom in morals may not have been a dogmatical assertion made by men who have coolly seen mankind through the medium of books, and say, in direct contradiction to them, that the regulation of the passions is not, always, wisdom—On the contrary, it should seem, that one reason why men have superior judgment, and more fortitude then women, is undoubtedly this, that they give a freer scope to the grand passions, and by more frequently going astray enlarge their minds. If then by the exercise of their own reason they fix on some stable principle, they have probably to thank the force of their passions, nourished by *false* views of life, and permitted to overleap the boundary that secures content. (110; chap. 5)

Thus, "superior judgment and . . . fortitude" depend on a prior experience of emotions which allows us to learn through our mistakes and our incorrect beliefs. One might argue, however, that such a schema accepts the passions as a fundamental part of life, only to relegate them still to a secondary role in relation to the final goal of this entire process, reason; that is, the passions are important only insofar as their negativity paves the way to our final attainment of reason. This critique is valid, in that it refers to one major aspect of *The Rights of Woman,* the utopian teleological impulse of the book, which images society and the individual as progressing toward the realization of their full potential, figured through the twin goals of God and reason. This Enlightenment diachronicity underwrites much of Wollstonecraft's polemic: she opposes it to a "propensity to enjoy the present moment" which is imposed on and internalized by women and which stunts their political and social potential as much as their literal confinement in school (52; chap. 4). Yet this diachronicity and its politics do not exhaust Wollstonecraft's book. Her teleological movement toward reason is in direct tension with the epistemology structuring the critique which, paradoxically, pushes her teleological argument forward. Passion and reason imbricate this epistemology not diachronically but, rather, synchronically. That is, at any given moment Wollstonecraft's feminist critique involves a reflexivity that resists any simple progress from passion to reason.

Wollstonecraft dramatizes this reflexivity, and the new complex dialectic between reason and passion it engenders, in the remarkable "Pisgah vision" she has right after the passage on the "regulation of the passions." "Pisgah" refers to the name of the mountain from which Moses was allowed to view the Promised Land; a Pisgah vision, then, was a mode of political prophecy that late-eighteenth-century writers used to articulate their own feelings about the fate of the French Revolution—and, by extension, the political future of Europe and England. One of the most famous visions of that period was that of Dr. Richard Price, an ardent supporter of the Revolution; Burke's *Reflections* is in large part a vehement attack on Price's vision.[55] Wollstonecraft's own *Rights of Men* defends Price against Burke; her use of the vision is thus no mere biblical allusion but, rather, her own contribution to a specific form of political discourse with which she was intimately familiar. At once an elaboration and critique of this form, this contribution structures itself around Wollstonecraft's complex perception of the dialectical interplay between reason and passion.

After Wollstonecraft's statement on how reasonable men should actually thank the "force of their passions, nourished by false views of life," these lines follow:

> But if, in the dawn of life, we could soberly survey the scenes before as in perspective, and see every thing in its true colours, how could the passions gain sufficient strength to unfold the faculties?
>
> Let me now as from an eminence survey the world stripped of all its false delusive charms. The clear atmosphere enables me to see each object in its true point of view, while my heart is still. I am calm as the prospect in a morning when the mists, slowly dispersing, silently unveil the beauties of nature, refreshed by rest.
>
> In what light will the world now appear?—I rub my eyes and think, perchance, that I am just waking from a lively dream. (110; chap. 5)

Wollstonecraft has introduced a vision that apparently simulates the telos of her Christian diachronic narrative, in which she has reached—indeed, climbed to—a vantage point from which her perspective is influenced by neither "false delusive charms" nor "a lively dream." Instead, the charms of that dream will become the subject of her newly found, clear vision. By echoing the "*false* views of life," these "false delusive charms" present themselves as the erroneous but necessary catalysts for passion which will bring people to reason.

Wollstonecraft first views "the sons and daughters of men pursuing shadows, and anxiously wasting their powers to feed passions which have not adequate object—if the very excess of these blind impulses, pampered by that lying, yet constantly trusted guide, the imagination, did not, by preparing them for some other state, render short-sighted mortals wiser without their own concurrence; or what comes to the same thing, when they were pursuing some imaginary present good" (110; chap. 5). At first this passage appears to reproduce Wollstonecraft's teleological narrative, with the "excess of these blind impulses" preparing people for the state of reason. Yet we can also read this passage another way, in which the exact moment of sublation of passion by reason is never clear; that is, the blind impulses and lying imagination "render short-sighted mortals wiser without their own concurrence"—while these mortals are *in* error and negativity. These mortals are not prepared for reason by realizing their error; rather, they reach preparation the more they are in error and the more they cannot see their error. Passion and reason still relate but in a way that problematizes any easy shift from one to the other.

The next part of Wollstonecraft's vision reinforces this more problematic reading. The vision blasts "the ambitious man consuming himself by running after a phantom" and observes how hard it would be for him to change his way even if he could clearly see the fallacy of his situation (111; chap. 5). Wollstonecraft then observes: "But, vain as the ambitious man's pursuits would be, he is often striving for something more substantial than fame—that indeed would be the veriest meteor, the wildest fire that could lure a man to ruin.—What! renounce the most trifling gratification to be applauded when he should be no more! Wherefore this struggle, whether man be mortal or immortal, if that noble passion did not really raise the being above his fellows?" (111; chap. 5).

Again, there is "something more substantial" in, not beyond, the ambitious man's pursuits—something that neither preempts nor coincides with the desire for fame, that which by itself would "lure a man to ruin." Here Wollstonecraft's irony folds in on itself. Mocking both the pettiness of fame and those who would dismiss fame as only petty, she describes fame as the "trifling gratification" that deals with death. "That noble passion," then, neither works toward nor depends on a release from the blindness of fame; instead, it raises the individual even as it works through its earthly double, the desire for fame.

The next part of Wollstonecraft's vision appears to retreat from this new problematic of passion's role. Discussing the follies of love, Wollstonecraft describes the process in which an individual creates a desired object with "imaginary charms." When those charms disappear—when the individual is no longer in error—it is reason that saves the mistaken passion from devolving into mere lust:

> And would not the sight of the object, not seen through the medium of the imagination, soon reduce the passion to an appetite, if reflection, the noble distinction of man, did not give it force, and make it an instrument to raise him above this earthy dross, by teaching him to love the centre of all perfection; whose wisdom appears clearer and clearer in the works of nature, in proportion as reason is illuminated and exalted by contemplation, and acquiring that love of order which the struggles of passion produce? (111; chap. 5)

Here we are raised "above this earthy dross" and taught "to love the centre of all perfection" by reflection, contemplation, and reason, all of which appear at and beyond the level of passion's struggles. Wollstonecraft has apparently reverted to her teleological narrative of God and reason. Yet in the next paragraph she completely scrambles this narrative:

> The habit of reflection, and the knowledge attained by fostering any passion, might be shewn to be equally useful, though the object proved equally fallacious; for they would all appear in the same light, if they were not magnified by the governing passion implanted in us by the Author of all good, to call forth and strengthen

the faculties of each individual, and enable it to attain all the experience that an infant can obtain, who does certain things, it cannot tell why. (111; chap. 5)

Wollstonecraft has, in effect, turned her teleological narrative inside out. First, she has transformed it into a *genetic* narrative, giving originary presence, moreover, not to reason but to "the governing passion implanted in us" by God. The process initiated and managed by this passion marginalizes reason even more so with the figure of the child, whose actions operate outside of the child's cognition, even as their existence calls forth Wollstonecraft's approval. While not simply erasing her teleological narrative, the genetic model does heighten the sense of disequilibrium the entire vision brings to bear on it, even at the moment when the vision appears most ready to fall back into that narrative.

Just as disorienting as the genetic model is the passage's doubling of passion. Not only does Wollstonecraft invoke the primary "governing passion," she also contrasts "any passion" and the knowledge (of passion? or reason?) it attains with the "habit of reflection"—only then to collapse the main difference between them. She associates both of these epistemological modes with error; both can be turned on objects that are "equally fallacious," and both modes can still be productive, as long as they are redeemed, "magnified," by the "governing passion."

It is this leveling of the hierarchy between reason and passion which Wollstonecraft finally recuperates out of the dizzying deployment of both these terms in her vision. Thus, even if we could foresee the error passion will bring, and "had the cold hand of circumspection damped each generous feeling before it had left any permanent character, or fixed some habit, what could be expected, but selfish prudence and reason just rising above instinct? Who that has read Dean Swift's disgusting description of the Yahoos, and insipid one of Houyhnhnm with a philosophical eye, can avoid seeing the futility of degrading the passions, or making man rest in contentment?" (112; chap. 5).

Yet Wollstonecraft's point does not seem to be that we can or should find a middle ground between, or a synthesis of, Swift's Yahoos and Houyhnhnms. Instead, the moral is the dialectical limit reason and passion impose on each other's perceptual powers. Wollstonecraft stresses this limit with startling force when she turns her moral on the truth claims of the Pisgah vision she has just had. Thus, before the passage on Swift she writes,

> I descend from my height, and mixing with my fellow-creatures, feel myself hurried along the common stream; ambition, love, hope, and fear, exert their wonted power, though we be convinced by reason that their present and most attractive promises are only lying dreams. (111–12; chap. 5)

Several paragraphs later she adds:

> The world cannot be seen by an unmoved spectator, we must mix in the throng, and feel as men feel before we can judge of their feelings. If we mean, in short, to live in the world to grow wiser and better, and not merely to enjoy the good things of life, we must attain a knowledge of others at the same time that we become acquainted with ourselves—knowledge acquired any other way only hardens the heart and perplexes the understanding. (112; chap. 5)

Though Wollstonecraft recognizes that a descent from her vision will be into the error and "lying dreams" of passion, she still descends. She does so not only because she must but also because of her recognition of the undependability of her position within that vision. What is her position in that vision but that of the "unmoved spectator" above the throng that she observes but with whom she does not mix? The knowledge and wisdom that Wollstonecraft wants us to acquire echo those parts of her vision which imply that reason and insight are unknowingly found in, not through, passion and error. As such, the position of this knowledge and wisdom is radically antithetical to the epistemological position of the Pisgah vision—a vision that, for all intents and purposes, is the telos, the utopian vantage point of reason and clarity toward which Wollstonecraft's Enlightenment narrative moves.

Wollstonecraft's vision and its aftermath allegorizes a fundamental and irreducible tension in *The Rights of Woman* between a diachronic longing for an unambiguous political progress from passion to reason and a synchronic apprehension of the shifting epistemological boundaries between passion and reason, wherein reason functions not as a final goal but, rather, as a constant imperative toward critique, toward even the unmasking of its own dependency on the shadowed "wisdom" of passion. (We can recall that, much in the same way, the gender indeterminacy of the sentence "Men do not always act like men" is set off by the intervention of *understanding*.) As a reflexive meditation on the exigencies and duplicities of vision, this passage is as powerful an example of "literariness," the insight into blindness and insight, as the one Paul de Man valorizes in the work of Wollstonecraft's own subject, Jean-Jacques Rousseau. More important, as an example of blindness and insight explicitly taking place within the context of a feminist politics, the passage is as powerful a working out of Romantic ideological self-inscription as those that Jerome McGann identifies—a simultaneous acknowledgment and critique of Wollstonecraft's text's own imaginary reifications which is given all the more force by her unreflective use of *man* as the human agent of the Pisgah vision.

Thus, Wollstonecraft's use of passion and reason, her critique of the Rousseauistic Romantic imagination, and her deployment of gender all resist her monumentalization as one who repressed her female Otherness in favor of a male identity of Enlightenment rationality. Indeed, the complex circulation of political, epistemological, and gender signs in *The Rights of Woman* reflect a discursive deftness that exceeds the aporia of writing Mary Jacobus finds only in Wollstonecraft's fragmentary *The Wrongs of Woman,* insofar as *The Rights of Woman* uses the errancy of language to press for an explicitly political, oftentimes didactic rhetoric. Perhaps the most uncanny thing about *The Rights of Woman* is that the text's (still unacknowledged) theoretical density and its given identity as political praxis occupy the same space without scandal. That is a doubling, repressed or unrepressed, from which we might do well to learn.

## IV

Learning from a past intellectual figure is, however, precisely what the history of Wollstonecraft's reception problematizes. That is, the lesson of "Wollstonecraft" as a monumentalized literary persona appears first and foremost to be the basic discontinuity between her theoretical teachings and the critical methods used by the generations of Wollstonecraft interlocutors to come after her. The question then becomes whether it is a simple matter of choice for Wollstonecraft readers to overcome this discontinuity or whether that discontinuity speaks to a larger, more complicated predicament that underwrites but also exists beyond Wollstonecraft studies. While McGann's revisionary strategies evinced a historical condition that was best understood through the aporias of language, here it is useful to characterize this predicament not only through a dialectic between history and language. As necessary is the concept of the hegemonic, a concept that links the pedagogical discontinuity in Wollstonecraft's transmission both to the nondialectical character of feminist readings of Romanticism and to the larger question of feminist theory's own late-twentieth-century conceptual and institutional modernity.[56] To assert this particular set of hegemonic relations is to reorient discussion of the problem of interpretive choice in Wollstonecraft studies away from a nongendered conception of the linguistic and the historical; it is, in fact, to discuss this problem as an effect of gender difference. It is to make the problem of literary historiography the problem of feminist studies.

One could argue that my main point here has been to insist on the play of gender outside this hegemony of feminism's discontinuous transmissions, much in the same way that Wollstonecraft insists on the play of gender beyond the reified opposition between masculine Enlightenment reason and feminine Romantic passion. There is, however, another reaction to this hegemony beside the notion of overcoming its narratives of discontinuous transmissions, of bridging dialectically the gaps between feminism's present theoretical realizations and its objects of study from the past. This other response is that of a simple recognition, a perception of a broad aspect of feminist studies which cannot be solely contained by either the language of a critique or an approbation. I refer to the resistance in feminist studies to the theoretical, institutional, and disciplinary logic of one of the key ideas in this present study: the logic of the representative figure.

This resistance can be glimpsed not only in the way Wollstonecraft is denied a certain theoretical influence in feminist studies but also in how the notion of a primary representative figure in Romanticist feminist studies seems a misguided, counterintuitive approach to the field—a predicament that has a singular force until we consider how the proposition of electing a primary representative figure for feminist theory provokes the same response. That is, neither anyone in the past, such as

Wollstonecraft, nor anyone in the present, occupies the position of the monumentalized voice of feminism. At all these different levels, then, we find a deflection of the critical scene that underwrites how de Man and, to a lesser degree, McGann make a particular set of critical practices intelligible through their own representative presence—and how they further make the intersection of Romanticism and theory in the last twenty-five years readable as the appropriation of such representative figures as Shelley, Rousseau, and Heine. Thus, while the assumption of a dialectical reading strategy operates throughout this chapter, the way in which feminist studies obstructs this strategy as an individuated agon between a single past and present writer provides a metacommentary on the gendered assumptions of that strategy—on the possibility that the univocal function of the representative figure describes a logic that is at once monumental and patriarchal.

To suggest, however, that feminism does resist the representative figure does not mean that that resistance exists uncontested. Indeed, one could argue that it is precisely because there are so many representative voices in feminism that the logic of the representative figure seems so irrelevant or unstable. One could further argue that this long-standing heterogeneity in feminism actually anticipates the growing decentered, localized character of literary and cultural practice throughout the humanities—a contemporary predicament that might then signal the end of one way of discussing, and legitimating, such disciplinary formations as Romanticism and theory. It remains to be seen the degree to which such claims are realized; at the very least, however, their acknowledgment demonstrates how the representative figure introduces questions of gender, with all their attendant implications of entrapment and empowerment, and not only into the dynamics of how literary historiography configures the past. As important is how the representative figures installs such questions within the academic literary institution's own self-design, in how it configures the disciplinary *epistēmē* of the present.

Within the present the representative figure may also shed light on what some have considered to be the problematic relationship between feminism and the "rest" of male-dominated theory. The powerful influence of gender studies notwithstanding, many critics have noted how the representative voices of feminism often as not seem to be the representative voices of poststructuralism, Marxism, or psychoanalysis.[57] The idea of a "pure" feminism untouched by the overlapping boundaries of these other discourses becomes a particular case of the phantasmic modernity that also binds Romanticism and theory together. But, insofar as the phantasm of a pure feminism is tied to the absence of a representative figure, its ghostly state may then be perceived as something more than either a lack or reified occultation; it might actually be the state of an institutional or theoretical advantage rather than an impasse that demands to be overcome. Appropriately enough, Wollstonecraft returns as a participant in this debate, insofar as some critics have tried to "solve" the relation between feminism and theory by attributing to the former the concreteness of a praxis at odds with the abstract existence of the latter.[58]

Along these lines it is not much of an exaggeration to say that Wollstonecraft has been thought of as a feminist activist precisely because of her supposed theoretical unsophistication. But to read her this way is to obfuscate the very point she makes when she appropriates an eighteenth-century discourse of reason which was considered as patriarchal as theory is by some today. It is to forget the point that Wollstonecraft makes in the second epigraph to this chapter: that the emulation of "masculine virtues" need not "lead women astray." Rather, such a strategy both exposes and derealizes various gendered assumptions, such as the putatively intrinsic "masculine" nature of a particular virtue or a theoretical disposition. We thus return to the final lesson of Wollstonecraft, her denial of the opposition between theory and praxis—a repudiation resulting in a critical practice that fittingly defines Wollstonecraft's "enchantment of literary pursuits." Oddly enough, and it is hoped, such a lesson might be available to us unencumbered by the full force of the pedagogical compulsions of the representative figure, precisely because of the history of Wollstonecraft's reception and its hegemonic link to feminism's other discontinuous transmissions. If that is the case, Wollstonecraft will edify us not as the occulted origin of our thought and actions but as simply one who thinks and acts on how theory and praxis originate in each other—an exercise achieved through both reason and passion.

## Chapter 5

# American Askesis

## Harold Bloom, Ralph Waldo Emerson, and the Blinding of America

I surely know that as soon as I return to Massachusetts I shall lapse at once into the feeling, which the geography of America inevitably inspires, that we play the game with immense advantage; that there and not here is the seat and centre of the British race; and that no skill or activity can long compete with the prodigious natural advantages of that country in the hands of the same race; and that England, an old and exhausted island, must one day be contented, like other parents, to be strong only in her children.
>                    Emerson
>                    *English Traits*

And I think Nietzsche particularly understood that Emerson had come to prophesy not a decentering, as Nietzsche had, and as Derrida and

> de Man are brilliantly accomplishing, but a peculiarly American *re-centering,* and with it an American mode of interpretation, one that we have begun—but only begun—to develop . . .
> Bloom
> *A Map of Misreading*

# I

Fittingly, the work of Harold Bloom especially coincides with and complicates the topoi and paradigms in the present study. No work on the relation between theory and Romanticism can afford not to consider Bloom, whose long career converges with so many of the important markers of both topics as institutionalized fields of study in America's universities. From his first book, the archetype-inflected *Shelley's Mythmaking* (1959), to his influential anthology *Romanticism and Consciousness* (1970), Bloom can be seen as part of the 1950s and 1960s revitalization of Romantic studies associated with the post–World War II generation of Romantic scholars. Through the wedding of his ongoing interest in Romanticism to his theories of influence and misprision in the 1970s, however, Bloom can also be seen as part of the '70s and '80s revision of Romantic studies undertaken by the post-Vietnam generation of postmodern Romanticist theorists. Yet again, precisely because of his oftentimes intellectually agonistic relationship with the other members of the so-called Yale School and because of his disassociation with the institutionalized boom in literary theory in the '80s, Bloom might also be said to encompass contrasting phases of theory's development in the American university. He can, in other words, be associated with both the initial impact of theory on our critical landscape and with the reaction against theory which, some might argue, increasingly informs the academy today.

Bloom's career thus spans many of the institutional ruptures and breaks that I have identified as the disciplinary logic of fantastic modernity within both Romantic studies and theory itself. Moreover, Bloom's widely known theoretical polemics about poetic influence, revision, ephebes, and progenitors would seem to dovetail nicely with the themes of Romantic appropriation, reception, and transmission which underwrite the dialectical working out of that logic through the mediation of Romanticism by present and past Romanticists. It is, however, the institutional form of Bloom's theories which poses the first of several crucial reasons why Bloom swerves away (fittingly enough, again) from the interests of this present book.

For, while Bloom's theories of poetic revision and influence do affiliate him with the "new wave" of theoretically informed Romanticists of the '70s and '80s, those same theories do not especially portray Bloom in an institutional agon with the post–World War II generation of Romanticists. Unlike de Man and especially McGann, Bloom's work does not by and large set itself up as a metacritical intervention into the transmission of Romantic knowledge. If anything, Bloom's assertion of an anxiety of influence is a self-conscious polemic for itself as the embodiment of an imaginative, visionary Romanticism that most powerfully continues the argument for Romanticism which Abrams, Frye, and others initiate after World War II. If there is a break between Bloom and the members of this earlier generation, it is more in the sense of his Romanticism surpassing theirs. Thus, unlike de Man, McGann, or many contemporary feminist Romantic scholars, Bloom does not especially worry the distinction between a Romantic and a Romanticist. The disidentification with Romanticism which Jon Klancher argues is a hallmark of contemporary Romantic historiography has never been part of Bloom's theoretical self-description. If anything, Bloom would most likely perceive such a disidentification as he does T. S. Eliot's earlier modernist appraisal of the Romantics: as a willful dismissal of a tradition that cannot be denied, a dismissal that reflects the ignorance of a lesser writer rather than the powerful misprision of a strong poet.

Arguably, Bloom devalues in much the same way the larger theoretical wagers that subtend de Man's, McGann's, and feminist critics' various revisions of Romanticism: how deconstruction, ideological criticism, and feminism construe their own interventionary modernities by asserting theory's ability to effect change in this world. This "revolutionary" sense of theory's modernity as an oppositional formation is obvious enough in the millennial aspirations of feminist and Marxist-inflected criticism. While clearly a more complicated philosophical and political proposition for deconstruction, a similar self-representation of deconstruction as an insurrectionary practice is evinced in Derrida's attack on the Western *epistēmē* and, at a more obviously political level, the various arguments, pro and con, for applying deconstruction to leftist use. In contrast to such political discussions about Derrida and de Man, there has never been a sustained debate about whether Bloom's work is actually a political praxis, precisely because such a controversy seems beside the point when reading Bloom. Indeed, it seems highly counterintuitive to associate Bloom with deconstruction, Marxism, and feminism as part of the disciplinary theory boom of oppositional criticism in the academy in the '80s. Bloom himself, moreover, actively champions such disaffiliation from the institutional mainstream, a position that in turn echoes his dismissal of theory's larger ambitions as a narrative of postmodernism's realized oppositional modernity.[1]

Bloom's dismissal of this revolutionary stance in academic theory also problematizes his relation to one of the key methodological categories of this study, the representative figure. For, if Bloom does not see his thought as institutionalizing the same moment of postmodern modernity as the other theorists and theories, he also does not see his writing as providing a blueprint for an iconoclastic cadre of Bloomian ephebes: "I neither want nor urge any 'method' of criticism. It is no concern of mine whether anybody else ever comes to share, or doesn't, my own vocabularies of revisionary ratios, of crossings, of whatever" (*A,* 38). It is thus difficult to discuss Bloom as if he represents a certain "school" of theory, as Paul de Man represents American deconstruction and Jerome McGann represents a historically oriented, left-inflected materialist criticism in contemporary Romantic studies. Yet there is also something about the sheer scope of Bloom's writings, the way he selects and absorbs sources as eclectic and varied as Gnostic criticism, the Bible, and psychoanalysis, which makes it difficult to divorce Bloom entirely from the semiotic force of a representative figure. Thus, if feminists and feminist Romanticists appear to operate in a discursive hegemony that resists the logic of the representative figure, Bloom appears to be a representative figure who resists representing any one major critical movement or school of thought consistently; his constituency seems to be everyone and no one at the same time. I have thus chosen to describe him as representing a "Bloomian pragmatics" that speaks not so much to a specific theoretical movement as to a particular critical disposition within Bloom himself: a visionary investment in a human self that cannot be reduced to the forces of history, nature, or language.

Aside from identifying this overriding disposition in Bloom, the term *Bloomian pragmatics* also serves two other uses. First, insofar as *pragmatics* intimates a simultaneous accommodation and ultimate denial of linguistic skepticism, this term foregrounds how Bloom's revisionary theories place him within an internecine disciplinary conflict. That is, while Bloom might not really intervene in the transmission of the Romanticism of the post–World War II generation of Romanticists, he does challenge the North American reception of linguistically oriented "Franco-Heideggerian" Continental theory (*A*, 16–51, 330–36). Second, insofar as *pragmatics* also suggests Bloom's loose affiliation with an American tradition of intellectual thought, the term stresses the nationalistic troping that supports and underwrites Bloom's challenge to the American institutionalization of Continental theory, his own literary history of Romanticism, and his own singular version of the fantastic dynamics of literary modernity.[2] For, if Bloom's anxiety of influence creates a Romanticism in which each strong poet tries to assert his (and it usually is "his") original modernity through a strong misreading of literary precursors, that agonistic Romanticism is recuperated in a narrative structure that allows for the transmission of British Romanticism to America in the nineteenth century. Thus, Bloom's narrative of a temporal struggle between precursor and ephebe does not structure itself around a break with a previous generation of Romantic scholarship. Rather, it coheres around a conflict with his European poststructuralist contemporaries, who are impaired by their inheritance of a confused German Romanticism; more important, the narrative also coheres around a continuity between a past British Romanticism, a nineteenth-century American Romantic literature and culture, and a twentieth-century American poetic and critical consciousness.[3] Thus, Bloom's revisionary theories eschew associating the reading of Romanticism with the interventionary identity of the oppositional critic. Rather, Bloom takes from the post-Miltonic identity of a Protestant, revolutionary Romanticism a radical inwardness that, in its voyage across the Atlantic in the nineteenth century, forges a romance of the self which is less revolutionary than migratory in the de facto force of its literary historical pronouncements.[4]

Organizing and grounding all these connections among the various aspects of Bloom's thought is Ralph Waldo Emerson, the Bloomian author of the American self. Emerson is the key transitional figure for

Bloom's history of Romantic poetry, which, as *The Ringers in the Tower* (1971) and other works narrate, moves from the British Romantics to Emerson, Whitman, Dickinson, Crane, Stevens, Ashbery, and Ammons. Emerson is also crucial for the complementary but less visible genealogy of American critical thought which *Agon* tells, one that begins with Emerson and then moves on to James, Peirce, Burke, Rorty, and, implicitly, Bloom himself. For Bloom these two genealogies coincide, in that America's intellectual theorists will resist the Continental heirs of Nietzsche and Heidegger by espousing the same American "truth" that Emerson asserts in his strong poetic transference of British Romanticism onto American soil: the existence of a poetic self vehemently prior to literary precursors, indeterminate language, and historic tradition. As the origin of both of these genealogies, Emerson is for Bloom the central prophet of this American truth.

Somewhat paradoxically, then, Bloom is able through Emerson to fashion a migratory narrative that culminates in an American individual identity that at its most hyperbolic repudiates all past cultural and historical restraints—that transforms, as it were, a British "anxiety of influence" into an "American Sublime." Bloom thus reads Emerson for the various complications that inhere in such a repudiation, for the way in which Emerson oftentimes simultaneously exalts an American self and inadvertently acknowledges the impossibility of that self's radically aboriginal stance. The centrality of such a vatic self remains constant, however, as does the migratory narrative that underwrites this new Romantic self as an American phenomenon. Indeed, these constants have a hegemonic force in Bloom's reading of Emerson, a force that disallows a more sociohistorically oriented transcoding of either Bloom's vatic self or his Romantic migration. Yet this hegemonic force is dialectically challenged by Emerson's own *English Traits* (1856), a work that Bloom has really never addressed. Coming out of Emerson's lecture tour of the British isles in 1847–48, *English Traits* both proleptically literalizes Bloom's poetic migratory narrative and reverses it.

Emerson's book literalizes Bloom's narrative by taking as its subject the English people and their history, a history whose trajectories explicitly and implicitly establish the national destiny of the American people. Yet *English Traits* also reverses the direction of Bloom's poetic migration through Emerson's actual journey across the Atlantic to England, a journey that places Emerson in the position of an outside observer who is able to meditate on the spatial and temporal contradictions that inhere in the misleadingly straightforward narrative of America's inevitable rise and England's inevitable decline. Emerson dramatizes these contradictions through social, economic, and political categories that Bloom usually avoids, and thus Emerson's text dialectically confronts Bloom's migratory narrative of poetic transmission with a historicism that is necessarily inflected in sociopolitical terms. In this confrontation *English Traits* dramatizes how both it and Bloom's romance of the American self participate in a metaphysical legitimation of the historical circumstances that determine the specific modernity of America. Moreover, by imbuing this dramatization with an apparent, partial reflexivity, *English Traits* demonstrates how Emerson and Bloom both practice a particularly American form of cultural analysis, one whose singularity lies in the self-fulfilling prophecy of an American Romanticism defined by a dialectic of visionary critique and ideological blockage.

Because of this dialectic, *English Traits* reveals its historical knowledge not only through the obvious social form of Emerson's meditation but also at a more inchoate level of explanation. In order to comprehend that inchoateness fully, however, we need first to recognize a specific correspondence between Emerson's conception of the self and Bloom's: their mutual investment in what the former describes as the "infinitude of the private man," a conception of the individual self which either incorporates, subsumes, or emblematizes a sense of larger collective historical processes.[5] By recognizing the complicated ways in which this figure operates in Bloom and Emerson, we can connect *English Traits* historically to both the industrial rationalization of nineteenth-century England and the American reception of British Romanticism during the American Civil War. Because of that figure, Bloom's assertion of an original, individual self is set not simply against the strong influence of a literary precursor but against the past, present, and future destinies of a historical subjectivity defined in collective and heterogenous terms.

## II

In a perceptive critical evaluation of Bloom from the late 1980s, Jonathan Arac suggestively distinguishes Bloom from the two prevailing options for literary studies after World War II:

Of the critics who defined their identities in the postwar years, Harold Bloom was one of the most useful. He taught us much about reading romantic and more recent poems, but such individual readings only extended New Criticism, which Bloom in other ways reached beyond. Northrop Frye's archetypal criticism made the totality of literature, rather than the individual poem, the unit of effective wholeness, but Bloom challenged both Frye and New Criticism in opening for exploration a middle range, a human scale: individual poets rather than single poems or all poetry.[6]

For Bloom the "unit of effective wholeness" is indeed the individual poet, a vatic self particularly rhapsodized in the Emersonian canon that Bloom constructs. I want to complicate Arac's placing of this Bloomian individual self in a "middle range" of literary exploration, however, insofar as I believe the difference between this self and Frye's more global sense of literary studies is not as absolute as it first seems.

In noting that Bloom interrogates poetry on "a human scale," Arac inadvertently touches on the most widespread negative evaluation of Bloom's critical work: the claim that Bloom's emphasis on the individual poetic self renders his criticism unable to engage systematically with the larger collective processes of history.[7] Yet Bloom's conception of the vatic self necessarily derives its cultural authority from its intimate connection to the very sociohistoric realm that this self simultaneously denies. Bloom's apolitical stance, then, is but one part of a more complex dynamic: his apparently atomistic conception of the self actually incorporates its own negative critique, through its recognition of the collective and socially heterogeneous energies that the individual poetic self channels and ultimately recontains. This dynamic—and the complications it creates in Bloom's thought and in the reception of his work within literary theory and Romantic studies—is perhaps best exemplified in Bloom's account of the American Sublime, in which his categories for narrating individual poetic agon are confronted and confounded by the cosmic sense of collective destiny which informs the definition of the vatic self within American Romanticism. Making this point means reoccupying two of Bloom's notorious revisionary ratios: *daemonization,* the psychic defense of repression, and *askesis,* the defense of sublimation.

To use Bloom's terms, the dynamic operative within a vatic self that paradoxically expresses both atomistic and collective energies can best be described as a daemonization of the individual self which simultaneously involves an askesis, a "curtailing," of the social world.[8] It should be immediately pointed out that this description reorganizes and reorients the specific meanings of these Bloomian terms. *Daemonization* and *askesis* are two of the notoriously difficult revisionary ratios that allow Bloom in *Anxiety of Influence* (1973), *A Map of Misreading* (1975), and *Poetry and Repression* (1976) to describe how poets psychically, linguistically, and poetically struggle with their literary precursors. While dialectically paired with two other different ratios, daemonization and askesis are also successive phases in the narrative of changing tropological responses that a poem might have in its agon with its literary influences. Within this narrative a poem's askesis reacts to its prior daemonization, the poetic moment of strong repression which disavows previous origins while insisting on the creative and imaginative presence of the new poet's aboriginal self. In its askesis the poem reacts to the disturbing grandeur of such a daemonization by sublimating the poet's struggle with his precursor in a self-purgation that curtails both the present and past writers' poetic powers. Thus, Bloom's ratios are usually understood to define discrete stages in the workings of influence at an individual level. As they relate to Bloom's conception of the vatic self, however, these terms also intimate collective energies at work in ways that defy and confound the distinct stages of daemonization and askesis which Bloom proposes. A reoccupation of these two ratios would therefore recognize the daemonization of the vatic self as repressing not only the individual literary precursor but also an entire social world. Similarly, as a *simultaneous* askesis, this individual repression of the social would curtail rather than assert poetic capability, insofar as that capability is connected to a collective rather than solipsistic sense of existence. For Bloom askesis turns toward solipsism; it does so, however, because the poet's self-disciplining, ascetic purgation leaves him little else with which to engage. In contrast, I would suggest an askesis already at work within the ratio of daemonization, a solipsism that operates through the daemonic disavowal of anything primary beyond the self, through the recontainment of the collective by the private.

The collapse of these two revisionary ratios relates crucially to Bloom's American Sublime, his term for the deeply nativist strain of Emersonian American Romanticism. While Bloom states that his final ratio, the transumption of *apophrades,* "is the mystery of misprision, of deep poetic influence in its final phase," he most closely associates the American Sublime with the hyperbolic condition of daemonization, the ratio most powerfully invested in the obviation of all previous origins.[9] Yet this singular association is problematized by the key image that Bloom uses to define the American daemonic self in Emerson and others writers: the cosmic giant.

By "cosmic giant" I mean the troping of a collective, historical infinitude within the individual form of a single gigantic body. Oftentimes this body will literally circumscribe a nation's landscape as Blake's Albion does or as the gigantic figure in Emerson's "Nature" (1836)—which Bloom names "America"—does in *Agon:* "America was a larger form than nature, filling nature with his emanative excess" (*A,* 165). Bloom explicitly connects the giant only to the hyperbolic existence of daemonization and the American Sublime and not to the process of askesis. As the simultaneous embodiment and circumscription of a nation's geography and population, however, the cosmic giant actually delineates the same relation between the atomistic and the collective that Bloom's vatic self conveys: the collective social world is both repressed and signaled by its privatized recontainment within the individual, personalized body of the giant.[10] The cosmic giant thus actually emblematizes the simultaneous daemonization of the individual self and askesis of social energy which inheres in the Bloomian exaltation of the vatic self.

In *Poetry and Repression* Bloom inadvertently uses a theme that demonstrates this more complicated and contrary relation between the daemonic giant and the ratio of askesis. Bloom explicitly links the figure of the cosmic giant to the hyperbolic American Sublime through an optical thematic that travels across history and national borders: "Giantism as a trope, whether in Milton, or in Emerson and his descendants, is related to sightlessness, or rather a repressive process that substitutes itself for tropes and defenses of *re-seeing,* which I take as a synonym for *limitation,* in my particular sense of the Lurianic *zinzum* or 'contraction'" (*PR,* 252–53). The gist of this typically difficult and esoteric passage is the linking of the giant to a blindness that Bloom then reinterprets into his revisionary system of ratios and tropes. Within that system the giant's "sightlessness" is positively opposed to "re-seeing," a category of images and tropes which "limit meaning more than they restore or represent meaning" (*MM,* 6). An askesis, or curtailment, is, then, a re-seeing, whereas the sightless gigantic daemon is a "re-aiming," a trope that performs the restitution of meaning in a poetic text. In a contemporaneous response to Paul de Man's concepts of blindness and insight, Bloom imagines a cosmic giant whose blindness to the impossibility of his self-rebegetting enables the gloriously daemonic selfhood of the American Sublime.

It is important to stress here the link between the giant and sightlessness, since positive and negative optic images play a number of complex, contradictory roles in Bloom's various discussions of askesis and the specifically daemonic American Sublime. Through this complicated framework Bloom engages with Emerson's own well-known interest in figures of giantism and sight. In *Agon,* for example, Bloom invokes the cosmic giant of "Nature" as the former being that Emerson remembers man to be, a being who once "filled nature with his overflowing currents."[11] For Bloom Emerson's giant reveals the promise of an excessive former American self, a promise that goads our present dwarflike state with glimpses of past and potentially future glories. For Bloom, moreover, Emerson crucially depicts the keeping of this promise in visual terms. That is, Emerson asserts that the self will signify its expansion by *correcting* the optic condition in which the "axis of vision is not coincident with the axis of things, and so they appear not transparent but opaque."[12] Bloom thus argues for the explicit connection in "Nature" between the American daemonic giant and Emerson's transcendentalist language of the transparent eyeball, an existential condition of transparency opposed to the opaqueness of a diminutive, secondary self at the mercy of primary, exterior forces. For Bloom Emersonian transparency is thus a "dialectic of imaginative autonomy," the transparency of a primary self.[13]

Bloom thus links Emerson's giant to a new visual condition that markedly contrasts with the negative optics of "giantism" in *Poetry and Repression.* For, if in that earlier book the giant's sightlessness enables the restitution—the re-aiming—of poetic meaning, in *Agon* Emerson's notion of the "blank . . . in our eye" actively blocks the promise of Emerson's giant, the final anticipation in "Nature" that, as Bloom writes, "we will be restored to the perfect sight of our truly knowing self" (*A,* 169). Thus, Bloom's daemonic American Sublime tropes its hyperbolic figure as both a blindness and a new system of vision. What makes this contradiction more than a mistake, local incoherence, or reductive cliché is the fact that Bloom's ratio of askesis also exhibits this paradoxical use of optic imagery. Thus, in *The Anxiety of Influence* Bloom describes how askesis "posits a new kind of reduction in the poetic self, most generally expressed as a purgatorial blinding or at least a veiling" (*AI,* 121). In *A Map of Misreading,* however, askesis is also associated with perspectivism, the necessarily visual orienting effect that occurs when metaphor asserts the distance between inner and outer forms (*MM,* 100–101). Insofar as perspectivism is a confusion caused by metaphor's ostensibly false resemblances, one could argue that the contradictory visual roles attached to askesis and daemonization actually cohere into a rather stable pattern, in which the perspectivism of askesis is actually a curtailing blindness, while the sightlessness of daemonization is actually the transparent "perfect sight of our truly knowing self." Yet these contradictory optics could just as well evince a more radically unstable condition, in which the veiling of askesis coincides with the sightlessness of daemonization and hyperbolic transparency is as confused a visual position as metaphoric perspectivism. What Bloom's contradictory optical images might actually suggest, in other words, is the enormous epistemological strain involved in preventing the collapse of daemonization and askesis into each other.

Far from preventing our analysis of Bloom and Emerson, however, this underlying confusion in Bloom's ratios allows us to thematize more exactly the figural form of an ideological critique of the cosmic giant in these writers—to thematize, for example, the giant's curtailment of its social energies as the question of whether a body of land attached to a national name (like Bloom's Emersonian giant America or Blake's Albion) occasions a new system of social seeing, a new optical arena that either blocks or enables a sociopolitical, historical apprehension of destiny. Testing these options is Emerson's *English Traits,* a work that on a number of levels thematizes the challenge of making intelligible a national name, a national imaginary, a national body. Furthermore, the specific conclusions that *English Traits* draws about such intelligibility dialectically engage with Bloom's own migratory narrative of British and American Romanticism, with the repressed collective histories that undergird the strange rhetorical appeal of his narrative's representative force.

The obvious social and cultural dimensions to *English Traits* should make clear that this dialectical engagement does not simply mean the arduous recovery of an Emerson who is more "politicized" than Bloom. This critical move is simply the obverse side to the transumption of Emerson as an apolitical Bloom, a nineteenth-century booster for a self absolutely removed from history and politics. Such a debate over Emerson's political consciousness is in fact an integral part of Emersonian scholarship, beginning with Oliver Wendell Holmes's conservative biography of Emerson, traversing the middle part of this century with the difference between Ralph Rusk's action-oriented and Stephen Whicher's transcendentally disengaged Emersons, and continuing with the sociohistoric evaluations of such contemporary critics as Cornel West and Sacvan Bercovitch.[14] Thus, while Bloom's intensely personalized reading of Emerson does not explicitly depend on past and present Emersonian scholarship, the character of that scholarship does contextualize Bloom's work. That is, Bloom is able to recognize a historically and theoretically complex Emerson as the backdrop for his admittedly more singular reading of the New England sage. Bloom can, in other words, acknowledge the many historical and political events that interact with Emerson's writings, as he also acknowledges the moments when Emerson writes in a mood far removed from the American Sublime.[15] Hence, what follows necessarily approaches *English Traits* by matching the book's tropes and images to the aporia of the cosmic giant, with all the curtailments, repressions, and blindnesses that we identified in Bloom. This match demonstrates the mechanism of such curtailments: how the sociohistoric world most significantly relates to its recontainment in an especially intense and inchoate manner, the meanings of which are not solely conveyed by the more obvious social engagements of Emerson's book.

This more volatile flux of signs also necessarily resignals a linguistic presence that has so far been overshadowed by this chapter's focus on the main opposition between a primary individual self and a more social, historicized collectivity. Language especially conditions the eruption of a crucial passage that occurs after Emerson's trip to Stonehenge, one whose outburst is paradoxically a momentary aphasia in Emerson's prose. In that scene—a conversation with English friends followed by a vision of "America"—language registers within a Lacanian symbolic rather than a de Manian allegorical mode, tying the rationalized, industrial modernity of England to a larger set of historical coordinates in and beyond Emerson's text. This narrative of modernity allows *English Traits* to signify what actually follows it, a future registered at the level of Romanticism's transmission and the more thoroughgoing trauma of the American Civil War. The narrative thus extends and complicates the scholarly work done by Len Gougeon and others, of an Emerson deeply involved in the 1850s with the crisis of slavery which precedes a nation's war with itself.[16] It is within this historical space that the cosmic selves in Emerson's book and Bloom's writings most vividly and profitably unravel into language—a language that is accessible, however, only as the text of history.

## III

Emerson's reliance on the paradoxical tropings of an atomistic versus collective entity is by no means confined to *English Traits*. The sense of an individual figure incorporating or typifying a larger cosmic, collective experience certainly underwrites the book Emerson wrote before *English Traits,* his much better-known *Representative Men.* As David M. Robinson has argued, however, one of the main results of *Representative Men* is Emerson's disenchantment with this explicit representative methodology.[17] In *English Traits,* at any rate, the notion of "great" representative men is not the only way in which Emerson narrates his epistemology of the individual's absorption of the collective; it also appears in a number of dispersed, disconnected scenes as well as in other, more stable categories. The category in *English Traits* which most obviously and systematically engages with this epistemology is, of course, race.

To account for the success of the English people, Emerson often relies on a model of intelligibility which embodies traits within a single figure—a type. As Julie Ellison notes, this mode of personifying intelligibility has its humorous consequences, as when the strength and industry of the English economy is mockingly literalized in the corporal beefiness and robustness of the English citizen. At a more disturbing level, as Philip Nicoloff has argued, much of this mode of intelligibility is founded on racial and racist scientific theories of the nineteenth century. In response to Nicoloff, Robinson asserts that *English Traits* retains in places a skeptical stance toward such theories, which in turn signifies Emerson's resistance to such racial discourses as a rationalization for antiabolition forces.

In contrast, Cornel West has recently argued that Emerson's exaltation of the human self, a "unique variant of the North Atlantic bourgeois subject," is "in part, dependent on and derived from his view of the races"; because of this link, a number of Emerson's pieces, including his antislavery writings, are racist.[18] Yet West also goes on to argue another point about Emerson's conception of race and self, one that *English Traits* especially and surprisingly exemplifies:

> The major significance of race in Emerson's reflections on human personality has to do with relation to circumstances, fate, limits—and ultimately history. Emerson's slow acknowledgment that there are immutable constraints on the human powers of individuals resulted primarily from his conclusions regarding the relation of persons to their racial origins and endowments. As a trope in his discourse, race signifies the circumstantial, the conditioned, the fateful—that which limits the will of individuals, even exceptional ones.
> 
> ... Therefore Emerson's first noteworthy attempt to come to terms with history, circumstances, or fate occurs not in *The Conduct of Life* (1860) in which his classic "Fate" appears, but rather in *English Traits* (1856).[19]

West has in effect imaged race in Emerson as an inverse of the askesis associated with the cosmic giant: not the curtailment of the social by the individual but, rather, the curtailment of the individual by the larger social forces of history. West correctly applauds this meaning of race for what it is in *English Traits,* a tentative yet significant trope for historical consciousness which, however, can only imagine history as a negative force impinging on the individual, while the individual as an ideological force constraining history still remains invisible. This premature historical sense in *English Traits* thus acts as an only partly choate articulation of a more capacious self-reflexivity that would acknowledge the possible ideological coincidence between the concept of race and the image of the cosmic giant—a more varied and complex sense of the way in which the curtailment of a collective social world is troped, one in which an entire race is defined by an individual type even as individuals are defined by the larger category of race.

This incomplete, inchoate reflexivity informs my two main examples of social askesis in *English Traits:* Emerson's meditation on the relation of land to national identity in chapters 2, 3, and 4 and his dinner conversation with English friends after his visit with Carlyle to Stonehenge in chapter 16. In both cases the object of this inchoate reflexivity is, appropriately enough, the very question of perception, of *seeing* a sociohistoric world contained, screened, or blocked by the image of land and nation that intimates it.

In the second example of the dinner party and Stonehenge, this visual challenge explicitly coheres around the image of a personified country, much like Bloom's America and Blake's Albion. In the first example, however, the components of the cosmic giant are present in relatively disconnected forms. Land and self are not hyperbolically or metaphorically combined but, instead, metonymically linked as the sequential chapters 3 and 4 on "Land" and "Race." That one is still unavoidably linked to the other is made clear at the end of chapter 3, when Emerson somewhat wryly imagines a personified English nature who asserts: "My Romans are gone. To build my new empire, I will choose a rude race, all masculine, with brutish strength."[20] While Emerson later qualifies this hypertrophied, gendered view of the English people, here he intimates a hyperbolic identification between England's land and its people which underscores English identity throughout the rest of the book.

The chapter on land, moreover, self-consciously describes the contemporary result of this identification in visual terms:

> As soon as you enter England, which, with Wales, is no larger than the State of Georgia, this land stretches by an illusion to the dimensions of an empire. Add South Carolina, and you have more than an equivalent for the area of Scotland. The innumerable details, the crowded succession of towns, cities, cathedrals, castles and great and decorated estates, the number and power of the trades and guilds, the military strength and splendor, the multitudes of rich and of remarkable people, the servants and equipages—all these catching the eye and never allowing it to pause, hide all boundaries by the impression of magnificence and endless wealth. (*ET,* 519–20)

The point is, of course, that the "illusion" that "catches the eye"—the multivaried sight of English society and commerce which hides the actual physical size of England's boundaries—is the truth of Great Britain's empire. The eye, then, looks out on the populated land of England and sees a deceptive screen that in fact signifies a more authentic English reality, much as Bloom's blind giant occasions a truer sense of vision in Emerson's transparent self.

If, however, in this instance the paradoxes of sight work themselves out into an ostensibly successful cultural analysis, they follow an earlier moment in *English Traits* in which a succession of topographic images both signals and repudiates the images' recuperation into a larger narrative. I refer not only to the images of land in chapter 3 but also to the images of Emerson's voyage across the Atlantic in chapter 2. The relation between these images counterbalances what critics agree to be the book's general tone toward its English subject—measured respect and amusement, devoid of any real display of insecurity. If there is in fact any place in which Emerson appears to be uncomfortable, it is when he is literally at sea, traveling to England. A series of images of ship life and of the ocean—some humorous, some serious—conveys Emerson's strong sense of literal and figurative disequilibrium (*ET*, 515–16). This desultory feeling of travel ends with the intuitive sensing of British land, when England's "genius was felt." The comforting distinction between the hostile ocean and England's welcoming borders is problematized, however, by Emerson's own anecdote about how England assumes "strict sovereignty of the sea" (517) and by his description of England as a land marked by the "constant rain," "multitude of rivers," "darkness of its sky," and famous "London fog" (520–21). Emerson further likens England's shape to a ship, a sign of how "these Britons have precisely the best commercial position in the whole planet" (522). Thus, in its ecological, mercantile, and geopolitical existence, England is not so much separated as conjoined to the "dread sea" of chapter 2.

An odd dissonance thus occurs, in which the topographic connection between English land and sea is simultaneously stressed and ignored by Emerson's contrasting attitudes toward England and the ocean proper. One could, easily enough, interpret this dissonance through Bloom as a displaced anxiety over English cultural and national influence, an anxiety given all the more force by its juxtaposition with chapter 1, in which Emerson calmly recounts his first trip to England and his meetings with the slightly doddering Coleridge and somewhat eccentric Wordsworth.[21] It is, however, the very structure of this displacement which is more crucial, in the sense that, along with the later passage of the images of English empire which "catch the eye," this dissonant water imagery thematizes at only a partially coherent, reflexive level the epistemological and ideological challenge of comprehending what is being perceived—the "difficulty," as Emerson puts it, "in making a social or moral estimate of England" (*ET*, 519).

That this "estimate" affects more than a hermetically sealed entity labeled "England" is made clear in a short paragraph that falls between the descriptions of Emerson's Atlantic crossing and those of England's land. Vision is again invoked in what would obviously be a casual secondary reference except for its strange emphatic placement at the end of chapter 2. The land being viewed, moreover, is not simply England proper:

> As we neared the land, its genius was felt. This was inevitably the British side. In every man's thought arises now a new system, English sentiments, English loves and fears, English history and social modes. Yesterday every passenger had measured the speed of the ship by watching the bubbles over the ship's bulwarks. To-day, instead of bubbles, we measure by Kinsale, Cork, Waterford and Ardmore. There lay the green shore of Ireland, like some coast of plenty. We could see towns, towers, churches, harvests; but the curse of eight hundred years we could not discern. (*ET*, 517)

Thus, between the Atlantic ocean and English land lies another transitional boundary, the Irish towns of "Kinsale, Cork, Waterford, and Ardmore," which allow Emerson and his fellow passengers to calculate the growing nearness of England's own harbor ports. Near to but not England, Ireland's countryside paradoxically signals as the "British side" the imaginary of an empire defined by its English traits. Retroactively commenting on the supplementary role of Ireland as England's border, however, are the paragraph's last lines, which dispute the simultaneous vision of Ireland as England and as a "coast of plenty." Instead, hovering behind or beyond the sight of "towns, towers, churches, harvests," is the "curse of eight hundred years," the brute fact of English rule over Ireland since the Norman Conquest.

Thus, if the later vision of English land is a physical illusion that conveys the reality of the English empire and if, conversely, the previous images of a dread sea fail to cohere with those of the land into a consistent signifier of what England means to Emerson; then the "curse of eight hundred years" presents a third asymmetric version of a partially reflexive perception in *English Traits*. That is, the image of the "green shore of Ireland" is immediately apprehended as a negative signifier for what cannot be discerned within it, the oppressive history of Ireland as a de facto and de jure colony of England. The isolated character of Emerson's oddly prominent yet offhand remark complicates, moreover, the force of this negative signification. For, if the asserted opacity of Ireland's coast refers to a complex historical subject beyond Emerson's sight, the failure either to follow up or elaborate on his remark questions the reflexivity behind that assertion of opacity—whether, in other words, the metacritical awareness of those lines really "sees" what it claims the visual sighting of Ireland cannot show.

The complexity of this exposed yet hidden object is already evinced by the ambiguous resonances attached to Emerson's "curse." Obviously enough, the curse can refer to the centuries-old suffering that the Irish have undergone under English rule. But *curse* could just as well apply to the ostensibly onerous burden that the English have endured as caretakers of such an unruly region—an interpretation that would be supported by the unflattering images of the Irish made elsewhere in *English Traits*. Furthermore, a third candidate for *curse* would situate Emerson's remark within a historical narrative instanced by an event occurring during the same decade as Emerson's tour of England: the Great Famine in Ireland of 1845–48. The curse of eight hundred years would, then, culminate in the explosion of Irish immigration to the United States in the 1840s—a situation that Emerson, Boston's first son, experienced firsthand.[22] Ireland's coast acts, then, as a screen for more than that country's ills; what Emerson's lines also turn their reflexivity upon, and, conversely, what they only partially expose, is a larger historical template that includes not only England but, more important, America itself.

What the ambiguity of *curse* emphasizes, moreover, is the possibility that this historical template might be built upon ideological opacities beyond the visual screen of the Irish shore. Placing the Irish immigration to the United States within the context of an "Irish problem" that England has had to endure invokes a historical and political analysis necessarily different from one that situates the migration within the context of Ireland's oppression by England—as would placing the immigration within a combination of both contexts. It is, however, precisely this choice among historical contexts, between what is an ideological mystification and what is not, which the curse leaves unresolved. In doing so, Emerson's words further exacerbate the odd double sense of his "negative" discernment, in which his viewing of Ireland intimates a larger social narrative whose complexity and spiraling historical connections are immediately curtailed.

And, insofar as Ireland does in a displaced form suggest the literally displaced Irish in the United States, the odd double sense of this short paragraph also allegorizes the main narrative action of *English Traits:* that in looking on England—or, in this case, Ireland—Emerson sees America—an America, however, whose social and historical complexity he can only partially comprehend. As the negative optics involved in viewing Ireland imply, moreover, I mean a more complicated and conflicted vision of America than the one usually associated with the recognition of English success in *English Traits,* that is, the well-known prediction of this chapter's first epigraph, in which America's inhabitants, as the migratory heirs to the English people, inherit the latter's national success after England's inevitable decline.

Emerson's reference to the Irish curse already complicates this historical plot in two ways. First, by simply signaling in displaced fashion the Irish immigration to the United States, Emerson's curse implies a more complex and heterogeneous sense of America's growing population than that realized by the grand migratory *récit* of England's people becoming America's. Second, and more important, this very association of America with a heterogeneous migratory population contradicts and thus draws attention to one of the main oppositions that *English Traits* uses to define America against England: the dichotomy between American homogeneity and English heterogeneity.

That is, while one might assume that the migratory arc from England to America would involve the travel of a homogenous population to a heterogenous one, *English Traits* images the very opposite. Far from making England the pure origin of one people, Emerson explicitly commends the mixed character of a population formed by the many different invasions of England's island coast: "Neither do [the English] appear to be of one stem, but collectively a better race than any from which they are derived. Nor is it easy to trace it home to its original seats. Who can call by right what races are in Britain?" (*ET,* 527). This sense of English heterogeneity operates, moreover, at other levels than race. Thus, in one of the most direct comparisons between the two countries, it is the homogeneity of American intellectual life which is contrasted with the variety of the English mind: "In America, we are apt scholars, but have not yet attained the same perfection [as the English]: for the range of nations from which London draws, and the steep contrasts of condition, create the picturesque in society, as broken country makes picturesque landscape; whilst our prevailing equality makes a prairie tameness" (561–62).

Within this quote *prevailing equality* implies not so much a populist sentiment as a cultural condition first and foremost defined by its opposition to the "picturesque" experience of English life. It is no simple coincidence, moreover, that *English Traits* conveys this experience through the images of a "broken country" and "picturesque landscape." The disjointed experience of a broken country—of a landscape that does not cohere visually into a single seamless uniform whole—refers, in fact, to an experience that recuperates at another level the challenge to historical seeing which Emerson's chapters 2, 3, and 4 express. Indeed, the triangulation of "broken country" with "range of nations" and the "steep contrasts of [English] society" echoes the coordinates of the "illusory" vision of England which in chapter 3 conveys the truth of the empire's dynamic commercial existence. As important is how "broken country" also replays the disjointed, separate way in which different sense perceptions assault the cornea, a disconnected sensorium that subtends the formalist logic of Emerson's contrasting responses to the maritime images of chapters 2 and 3. This compartmentalization of Emerson's senses and thoughts, when added to the vision of an England that is heterogeneous in the dynamism of its commerce, architecture, and people, signals the object of study of *English Traits,* what Emerson largely means by "England" and what his accounts reflexively demonstrate he can only partially see: the thoroughgoing reorganization of material life and human society brought on by the advancing stages of capitalism, what Max Weber termed the technological and industrial "rationalization" of human life.[23]

As the most commercially and industrially advanced of the world's nations, England epitomizes for Emerson this technological and capital reification. This contemporary historical experience thus underwrites—indeed, overrides—the other more local historical references attached to Emerson's descriptions of England's rationalized character, from the eighteenth-century resonances of the varied lifestyle inherent in a picturesque worldview to the aboriginal racial heterogeneity of the English people. If anything, these earlier temporal references refer in displaced form to a historical predisposition in the English character, one oriented toward a *technē* intent on effecting a human reality dominant over nature: "[In England] art conquers nature and transforms a rude, ungenial land into a paradise of comfort and plenty. England is a garden. . . . The solidity of the structures that compose the towns speaks the industry of ages. Nothing is left as it was made. Rivers, hills, valleys, the sea itself, feel the hand of a master" (*ET,* 518).

*English Traits* is not short on contemporary allusions to this phenomenon of rationalization. Many critics have noted, for example, how Emerson is both fascinated and unsettled by England's nineteenth-century technological prowess.[24] As important are the equally numerous references to another defining English trait, the obsession with property, the "national life-blood": "The rights of property nothing but felony and treason can override. The house is a castle which the king cannot enter" (*ET,* 588). One of the main subjects of the chapter on "Wealth," the topic of property gives the many references to technology a more ruthlessly monetary resonance, implying an English contemporaneity originating not only in the inventive will of its people but also in larger economic forces. This is not to say, however, that *English Traits* is able explicitly, consistently, or systematically to make these connections so as to articulate a sustained critique of England which would approximate one by Weber, say, or Marx. Property acts less as the overtly theorized cause of England's rationalized modernity and more as an especially prominent emblem of that modernity's accelerating realization. As the aggressively physical, juridical, and economic carving up of land, property most forcefully conveys the compartmentalization and separation of physical and mental reality into the variety of juxtaposed, autonomous experiential states that define English life—exactly what *English Traits* replicates through the thematics of Emerson's optical imagery and the disconnections of its formal structure.

Questions of property—of who own what and of the proper relation between a piece of land and a country—vividly inform the next example of social askesis: Emerson's trip to Stonehenge and subsequent dinner with English friends. The Stonehenge episode also throws into sharp relief the ambivalence of *English Traits* toward England's modern rationalization, the degree to which Emerson's reaction to this modernization oscillates between profound admiration and intense disquiet. This ambivalence comments, furthermore, on the relation of America to England's contemporary rationalized state. For the question remains of what vision of America inheres in this view of England, whether America's "prairie tameness" remains consistently opposed to England's heterogeneous and compartmentalized existence as a literally "broken country."

Oddly enough, *English Traits* appears to transfer the homogeneity of America's prairie tameness to the symbolic resonances of Stonehenge during Emerson and Carlyle's visit. That homogeneity seems to mark the monument as the pure, idealized origin of England's national imaginary, what Emerson claims, essentially, when he irreverently describes Stonehenge as the "old egg out of which all [England's] ecclesiastical structures and history had proceeded" (*ET,* 648). As such an originating landmark—as the legitimating mark of English propriety before English property—Stonehenge operates in Rousseauian fashion as a cultural artifact steeped in the primal, and primary, authority of nature. It is as such a monument that Stonehenge thus appears to merge with its natural surroundings: "Within the enclosure grow buttercups, nettles, and all around, wild thyme, daisy, meadow-sweet, goldenrod, thistle and the carpeting grass. Over us, larks were soaring and singing—as my friend said, 'the larks which were hatched last year, and the wind which was hatched many thousand years ago' " (648–49). As Carlyle's words indicate, this natural aura also seems to fill Stonehenge with a temporal originality existing outside of, indeed before, historical time, an existence that collapses both temporal and spatial differences. Thus, the Stonehenge episode brings together the "oldest religious monument in Britain in company with her latest thinker" (646). Likewise, Emerson later writes: "The old sphinx put our petty differences of nationality out of sight. To these conscious stones we two pilgrims were alike known and near. We could equally well revere their old British meaning" (649–50). Thus, Stonehenge stands as a primary pure presence, a homogeneous origin that marks the beginning of England's ever-accelerating, multivaried historical domination over nature.

Yet, while Emerson participates in this occulted representation of Stonehenge, his book also resists the monument's mystifying force. This resistance occurs most obviously through the skeptical, amused tone that punctuates his otherwise sympathetic portrayal of the English monument. Emerson's book also indicates this resistance in two other, more complicated ways, both of which connect Stonehenge to England's rationalized present. The first has to do with another central issue in *English Traits:* the question of the book's relation to British Romanticism.

Julie Ellison has argued that *English Traits* self-consciously attempts to distance itself from the English Romantics, so much so that in its "attempted judiciousness" Emerson's work feels "both more neoclassical and more Victorian than romantic."[25] Certainly, the English Romantics are rarely mentioned; when they are, as in the reminiscences of chapter 1, Emerson's amused, respectful tone is definitely not that of an adoring ephebe. Given this admiring but cool response to the Romantics, it is oddly striking that the chapter after the one on England's premier cultural monument, Stonehenge, should be mostly about William Wordsworth. Emerson's thoughts on the British poet are, once again, both complimentary and critical; in their sense of summation they very well might, as Ellison insists, "imply a Victorian point of view, from which romanticism appears like a great but long-lost moment."[26] The elegiac tone of Emerson's appraisal could, however, just as well refer to a more immediate set of circumstances, chiefly Wordsworth's death in 1850, right between Emerson's tour and the writing and publication of *English Traits.* In that sense this later section on Wordsworth is an elegy for him, superimposed on the past contemporaneity of Emerson's 1847–48 tour and his last meeting with the poet.

More important, such an elegy would also mark another event inextricably tied to Wordsworth's death: the textual rebirth of his life through the posthumous publication of his autobiographical work *The Prelude,* a poem very much about the imaginative coincidence between self and nation. A crucial meditation on this coincidence is, of course, book 13 of the 1850 edition, in which Wordsworth remembers his 1793 walk across Salisbury Plain, when he sees "Our dim ancestral Past in vision clear" (l. 320).[27] What Wordsworth poetisizes here is his literal and imaginative journey across the national imaginary of England, a temporal and spatial topos of which, as Emerson scientifically relates, Stonehenge is the center. Thus, *The Prelude* lays claim, among other things, to the merging of Wordsworth and a national selfhood, a simultaneity that makes the vision of Stonehenge and Salisbury Plain the vision of William Wordsworth.

Thus, in immediately turning to Wordsworth after Emerson and Carlyle's trip to Stonehenge, *English Traits* retroactively signals an odd doubling of that excursion, in which the two could be walking about the ancient Druidic scene that Emerson relays or about the Stonehenge that Wordsworth, through *The Prelude,* first and foremost *owns.* That Wordsworth's tale of the "Sacrificial Altar" distinctly differs from Emerson's more eclectic account only increases the dissonance of the representational doubling, the semantically intolerable sense that two Stonehenges lay claim to a space defined by its homogeneous existence before property. Thus, far from simply relegating the Romantic poet to a "great but long-lost moment," Emerson's elegiac account of Wordsworth also has the paradoxical effect of suggesting Emerson and Carlyle's trip to be a journey across a piece of land vividly contemporaneous with the symbolic resonances of Wordsworth's English life, *The Prelude.*[28] If a Bloomian anxiety of influence is at work here, it is more properly subsumed under the question of patrilineal inheritance. On whose property, in other words, does Emerson walk? Whose property does he write about? As a topos shot through and defined by such questions, Stonehenge belies its simultaneous depiction in chapter 16 as a pure, idealized transcendence of the rationalized partitioning of England's reality.

This transcendence is also resisted in a second manner, which focuses not so much on the inner representational inconsistency of Stonehenge as the monument's relation to the rest of England. In the space of two pages, after leaving Stonehenge, Emerson and Carlyle travel through three remarkably contrasting sites: a "wretched sheep-walk" that signifies for Carlyle England's latest economic depression, the magnificent Wilton Hall belonging to the Earls of Pembroke, and the Salisbury Cathedral. The juxtaposition of these three contrasting images with Stonehenge demonstrates how the latter, even as a pure origin of homogeneous identity, is merely one site among many compartmentalized realities that constitute modern English life. That the transportation through these scenes is itself so varied—dogcart, coach, and train—merely enforces this disorienting sense of technological, spatial, and epistemological separation.

The grounds of Wilton Hall deliver a miniature reflexive allegory of this mixture of heterogeneous identity and human *technē:* "We crossed a bridge built by Inigo Jones, over a stream of which the gardener did not know the name (*Qu.* Alph?); watched the deer; climbed to the lonely sculptured summer-house, on a hill backed by a wood; came down into the Italian garden and into a French pavilion garnished with French busts; and so again to the house, where we found a table laid for us with bread, meats, peaches, grapes and wine" (*ET,* 653). What Wilton Hall can only allegorize, of course, is a version of modernization which merges seamlessly with the centuries-old imperatives of aristocratic privilege and well-being: an aesthetic artifice that controls nature as well as Kubla Khan's Xanadu; an international variety of settings, architecture, and commodities; and a table of plenty whose commodities signify the success of a commercial island and empire. Sealed off from the success of this artificial *technē* (we might recall Emerson's earlier description of England as a "garden") is the other side to this ever-accelerating era of hegemonic instrumentality: the cognizance attached to the sheep walk of "so many thousands of English men [who] were hungry and wanted labor" (652). That *English Traits* draws no explicit connection between these two scenes merely reaffirms the rationalized condition of separate, disconnected realities which England experientially signifies in more and more complex ways.[29] What the gap between Wilton Hall and the sheep walk further conveys is how this experience is also ideological, in the sense that Wilton Hall's existence benefits from—perhaps depends on—its separation from the sheep walk. In that sense the Weberian rationalization that *English Traits* portrays feeds off itself, operating as both symptom and cause of England's compartmentalized realities.

The extent of this rationalization can also be measured by setting the contemporaneity of Wilton Hall's wealth alongside the more primitive instrumentality of the sheep walk, the "timelessness" of Stonehenge, and the six-hundred-year-old existence of Salisbury Cathedral. Time itself has become localized by the onrushing historical development of England, a land in which different episodes of architecture and cultural and social significance exist synchronically yet independently alongside one another. Indeed, as Emerson's travels with the dogcart, coach, and train show, it is the very phenomenological experience of time which is now being calibrated along contrasting discrete modes of apprehended speed and immediacy. The fairly stable, linear projections of England's historical development and of the attendant narrative of migration to America are thus in tension with the contrasting epistemological and ontological result of England's progress: an increasing spatialization and diversification of time, in which the temporal in *English Traits* can range from the eternal in Stonehenge to the instantaneous rush of Emerson's train passing Clarendon Park. Thus, if England's modernization implies a certain routinization and regulation of its resources, the experience of modernization in Emerson's work also records the opposite: a heterogeneous temporality that constantly reorganizes and recomplicates the futurity it at once projects.

A rather straightforward version of the future is reintroduced, however, through the questions that Emerson is asked by his English friends after his Stonehenge trip: "Whether there were any Americans?—any with an American idea—any theory of the right future of that country?" Emerson's answer is, however, anything but straightforward, beginning with a disclaimer that does not so much enlighten as obfuscate his meaning: "I said, 'Certainly yes—but those who hold it are fanatics of a dream which I should hardly care to relate to your English ears, to which it might be only ridiculous—and yet it is only true' " (*ET,* 654). Emerson's rambling account about the "dogma of no-government and non-resistance" is appropriate, however, for this answer is merely a prelude to his true response, an even more inchoate evocation not directed toward his dinner mates. Instead, Emerson has a private vision that irrupts into his very thoughts as he is being questioned:

> My friends asked many questions respecting American landscapes, forests, houses—my house, for example. It is not easy to answer these queries well. There, I thought, in America, lies nature sleeping, overgrowing, almost conscious, too much by half for man in the picture, and so giving a certain *tristesse,* like the rank vegetation of swamps and forests seen at night, steeped in dews and rains, which it loves; and on it man seems not able to make much impression. There, in that great sloven continent, in high Alleghany pastures, in the sea-wide sky-skirted prairie, still sleeps and murmurs and hides the great mother, long since driven away from the trim hedge-rows and over-cultivated garden of England. And, in England, I am quite too sensible of this. Every one is on his good

behavior and must be dressed for dinner at six. So I put off my friends with very inadequate details, as best as I could. (654–55)

Several points can immediately be made about Emerson's vision. First, as the land of America coheres into the sleeping body of the "great mother," the vision explicitly structures itself around a figure that closely approximates the cosmic giant, the individual embodiment of an entire nation's topos and soul. Second, unlike other versions of the cosmic giant associated with Emerson—such as Sacvan Bercovitch's notion of the Emersonian man as America, the *"natura-prophetica,"* or Emerson's own image of Daniel Webster as the giant America—this figure for the American continent is distinctly gendered in feminine terms.[30] Third, accompanying this feminine gendering, and in spite of, or because of, the maternal resonances, is an unmistakable eros that displays itself in nature's fecund *"tristesse"* and the "great sloven continent," an unsettling erotic frisson that Emerson's words do not adequately explain. And, finally, that ineffable quality dominates the entire passage's import, making Emerson's words mean, if anything, a set of circumstances and emotions "too strange for conversation."[31] Thus, despite the vividness of its images, the passage has a strange aphasic quality to it, one that acts as a literal irruption within the narrative intelligibility of *English Traits,* a radical blockage against the knowledge that Emerson's book works toward—a knowledge that, simultaneously, the opacity of the vision seems both to contain and to strive to convey. Emerson's imaginary "sighting" of the American great mother thus seems to outrun the semantic meaning of the vision, leaving only a deep, inarticulate affect that Emerson can only deflect, with "very inadequate details," away from his English friends.

There is, however, a historical and linguistic logic that links the twin identities of Emerson's American continent as a land before language and a land before man. Within such a logic America's great mother acts as an emblem for a presymbolic Lacanian reality, a land before the intelligibility of language as it is authorized by the name of the father. Within the rationalized parameters of *English Traits,* however, the name of the father necessarily coincides with the language of patrilineal inheritance, what imprints on the body of Albion as the readability and intelligibility of property's discourse. In Emerson's vision, then, the great mother's presymbolic ineffability also stands in for a nonindustrialized, nondeveloped reality opposed to the modernized rationalization of Great Britain—a condition that within this vision is reduced to the determinedly nonsublime images of "trim hedge-rows," "over-cultivated garden," and "dinner at six."

However, the fact that "man" cannot "make much impression" on the body of the American continent does not seem solely to assert an absolute, eternal difference between England and America. Rather, man's puny presence in America also helps to incite the strong erotic character of the great mother. Thus, the eros of Emerson's vision can be recuperated at another level as a partially choate historical anticipation, an only semi-sensate awareness of America's own future of rationalization and modernization, where the sleeping body of America will in fact awake and conjoin with the partitioning force of patrilineal discourse, the historical language, the historical reality, of property. That this erotic anticipation is only partially choate—that it remains incompletely verbalized to Emerson's English friends, his readers, and himself—speaks to the immensely conflicting responses such a massively contradictory historical event invokes. Emerson's writings dramatize such complexity through the mediating forms of his lifelong themes and concerns, from his changing attitudes toward the marketplace, science, and technology, to his horror at American jingoism, to his constant faith in the redemptive power of the American west. The aphasic quality of Emerson's vision in *English Traits* thus signals more than the great mother's presymbolic state. It also refers to the vision's self-reflexive message: its recognition of the vast span of historical thinking it can never fully represent.

What the erotic anticipation of Emerson's vision does manage to signal indirectly is the intimate ontological relation between England's and America's developed and undeveloped states of existence—how a vision of America's pristine, "natural" condition necessarily calls forth, no matter how inchoately, the proleptic sense of that country's own future modernization. Thus, within Emerson's vision the sublimity of the great mother covertly merges with its opposite, the historical sublimity of a future rationalization which Emerson's fascination with English industry elsewhere signals but which the "trim hedge-rows" here censor. We might also recall how the logic of Emerson's earlier decree about the future ascendancy of America over England would also necessitate confronting the possibility of America's rationalized future—what, paradoxically, the inchoateness of Emerson's vision also promptly evades.

At another more mystified level, however, the connection between American nature and English industry is similar to that between Stonehenge and the rest of England, in which both America and Stonehenge act as the pure, homogeneous origin that is necessary for a history of modernization and heterogeneous development. Recently, Gayatri Spivak has discussed the implications of that role of primal origin for the United States in grimly materialist terms:

> Is it banal to remind ourselves that this new [American] start or origin could be secured because the colonists encountered a sparsely populated, thoroughly precapitalist social formation that could be managed by prepolitical maneuvers?
>
> ... Let me therefore ask you to imagine that, because India was not a sparsely populated, thoroughly precapitalist social formation easily handled through prepolitical maneuvers and the manipulation of chattel slavery, in other words because it was not possible to establish a settlement colony there, no apparent origin could be secured and no Founding Fathers could establish the United States of India, no "Indian Revolution" against Britain could be organized by foreign settlers.[32]

Spivak's remonstrance thus enables us to reread the natural state of Emerson's great mother not as an idealized entity whose pure aboriginal condition authorizes a historical modernization similar to England's but, rather, as a set of material and historical circumstances that enable the particular course of American modernization through the absence of physical, political, and social impediments similar to those thrown up by Great Britain's other great colony, India.

That many have retroactively transformed these material and historical circumstances into a metaphysical legitimation of America's specific modernity arguably subtends a large portion of the history of American literature. Through its images of land, people, and land cohering into people, *English Traits* at once participates in, complicates, and critiques that history. Distilled into an even more pure form, in which an aboriginal nature is replaced by an even more primary self, this history of metaphysical legitimation is also the history of Harold Bloom's

American Sublime. Bloom replaces, as it were, Emerson's erotic anticipation of the great mother with a more explicit existential frisson for the American self; looking out upon the embodiment of a nation's land, Bloom concentrates on the individual form at the expense of the slovenly landscape that the form collects and attempts to bring into view. What *English Traits* pointedly reminds us, however, is how much a conception of that land is necessarily linked to larger historical forces and, thus, how much Bloom's Emersonian American self is metonymically linked to what it attempts—heroically, fatally—to transcend.

There is, finally, one other historical coordinate that impinges on Bloom's American Sublime as a more immediate underpinning to Emerson's vision of the great mother. For, between Emerson's 1847–48 English tour and the publication of *English Traits,* another event occurs in the United States, one that brutally foregrounds the implication of impressing upon a body the name of a father, the law of property: the Fugitive Slave Act of 1850. As David M. Robinson relates, Emerson's vision of the great mother dates from the journal he kept during his English visit; Robinson thus sees its publication in 1856 as actually offering an earlier optimistic vision of America's future which is set against the much darker prophecies that are presented in Emerson's bitter attacks against the Fugitive Slave Act in 1851 and 1854. But, given the proleptic narrative of rationalization which structures the vision of the great mother and the explicit reference that Emerson makes to the "manacles" of the North's economic interests in 1851, another reading of the great mother emerges.[33] In such a reading, contrary to Robinson, Emerson's alternate images of America's future would actually exist intolerably and inseparably together in the published vision of 1856. The aphasic quality of the passage's lines would then also speak to the cognitive dissonance that cannot overcome the possibility that the erotic anticipation of the conjoining of nature and property might in fact be realized in the despised Fugitive Slave Act, by the manacles of economic interest which work themselves out in the form of the North's moral compromise. The opacity of Emerson's vision thus finally becomes the aporia of Emerson's own political and philosophical categories, those with which he faced his nation and confronted its future. To call this aporia Emerson's failure is, however, to miss the point of its eruption in *English Traits;* it is to miss the fact that it is Emerson looking at the opacity of his vision, repeating the relentless optical structure that operates throughout this book and also in the images of daemonization and askesis which Bloom reorganizes into his formulation of America's vatic self. Thus, in contrast to Bloom, Emerson realizes a vatic self that is defined by its radical, negative self-critique.

Yet, if this definition of the vatic self in *English Traits* distinguishes Emerson from Bloom, the self-incapacity of that definition links the text to Emerson's more famous works, especially his essays. As Sharon Cameron has argued, many of those essays are structured around what she calls "disassociation," experience as an oblique, contingent phenomenon that denies the immediacy of both human affect and apprehension.[34] This sense of disassociation, of obliquity, underwrites the inchoate reflexivity of the vision of the great mother and underscores the opacities of the vision's historical and social critique. The energetic awareness of this limited reflexivity allies *English Traits* to the particular force that Cameron identifies in Emerson's great essay "Experience" (1844): in both of these works disassociation does not simply keep "ideas that challenge central premises, however imperfectly, at a remove"; rather, this very marginalization—what I have described as recontainment—is foregrounded so as to "preserve what is dismissed."[35] Coupled with the social energies of *English Traits,* this consciousness of liminality gives us a new way to read the trajectory in "Experience," from the essay's beginning statement, "Our life is not so much threatened as our perception," to these later, surprisingly bracing words: "We have learned that we do not see directly, but mediately, and that we have no means of correcting these colored and distorting lenses which we are, or of computing the amount of their errors. Perhaps these subject-lenses have a creative power; perhaps there are no objects. Once we lived in what we saw; now, the rapaciousness of this new power, which threatens to absorb all things, engages us."[36]

In both passages the "threat" remains the same. What changes is the latter passage's newly empowered but equally vertiginous acceptance of this threat: the "rapaciousness of this new power," which, in *English Traits,* at least, is registered as a historical real that is preserved and signaled precisely by the inchoateness of its irruption, its relegation to, in Cameron's words, "some liminal place."[37] For Cameron these dynamics of (non)representation and disassociation cohere around an intensely privatized narrative, the paradoxical liminality and preservation of Emerson's grief over his son Waldo's death. What the juxtaposition of *English Traits* and "Experience" suggests—and what Emerson's dialectical refunctioning of Bloom's nexus of giants, sight, and sightlessness necessarily invokes—is the relocation of this Emersonian narrative in the sociohistoric realm of political analysis.

The larger historical scope of this analysis in *English Traits* becomes more clear when the book is linked to Emerson's abolitionist activities in the 1850s, to the American Civil War that follows the text by five years, and, oddly enough, to the American Romantic concerns of Bloom. That is, in light of the Bloomian questions of migration and transmission, it is simply difficult to read *English Traits* and not connect its vision of England with the question of English support for the Confederacy during the American Civil War; it is difficult not to associate the Carlyle of Stonehenge with his racist "Occasional Discourse on the Nigger Question" (1849) and with the 1864 letter that Emerson sends him attacking his past antiabolition views.[38] Through its historical proximity to Emerson's abolitionist activities and the future American Civil War, *English Traits* thus claims as its subject not only the future of the United States but also the bifurcation of that future into a struggle between the North and South.

And, contrary to Bloom, the migration of British Romanticism to the United States does not simply arc over to New England during this struggle. As the sinking ship *Sir Walter Scott* in Mark Twain's *Huckleberry Finn* (1884) attests, the Confederate's neofeudal imaginary had its own investments in the reception and appropriation of British Romanticism aside from the American Sublime that Bloom projects onto Emerson, Whitman, and Thoreau. In contrast to the neofeudal parameters of the Confederacy's reception, the investments that *English Traits* has in England are oriented reflexively and inchoately toward a terrible, sublime future; as the context of the Fugitive Slave Act demonstrates, however, the immediate effect of that rationalized future is a cataclysm that fatally involves the Confederacy's Romantic reimagining of its own economic and social life.[39] Emerson's vision of the great mother uncannily predicts this grim historical nexus of events, through its canny, knowing representation of its own inchoate reflexivity. In this intense oscillation between historical knowledge and historical aphasia, Emerson's text performs a social askesis that simultaneously gestures toward the history contained within and beyond the work's repressions and curtailments. In doing so, *English Traits* both enacts and qualifies the structure of social blindness which informs Bloom's own migratory history of Romanticism and America. Emerson's book explicitly imparts to that history some of the sociohistoric coordinates that are heard only implicitly in the vatic self's visionary pronouncements, the collective traumas of history that Bloom transmutes into the poetic authority of the individual life.

## IV

> A great town hanging pendent in a shade,
> An enormous nation happy in a style,
> Everything as unreal as real can be,
>
> In the inexquisite eye.
> > Wallace Stevens
> > "An Ordinary Evening
> > in New Haven"

> Who has chosen me
> to reconstruct this eye of God,
> to understand the signs
> of this dispossession?
> > Jay Wright
> > "The Eye of God, the Soul's
> > First Vision"

The subject of Bloom's most recent meditation on the American Sublime and the Evening Land, *The American Religion* (1992), is the particularly American mixture of self-assertion and religious faith—the fact that Americans believe that "God loves her and him on an absolutely personal and indeed intimate basis"—which Bloom sees concretized in the "peculiarly American varieties of spiritual experience," ranging from the Mormons to Christian Scientists to Southern Baptists to Jehovah's Witnesses.[40] At the beginning of his book Bloom attaches his study to the arc of a specific historical moment: "Our war against Iraq, just completed, was a true religious war, but not one in which Islam was involved spiritually, on either side. Rather it was the war of the American Religion (and of the American Religion abroad, even among our Arab allies) against whatever denies the self's status and function as the true standard of being and value" (*AR,* 16). These are remarkable sentences. Behind this scenario is Bloom's description of what he sees as the key political formation in the United States of his time: the Republican Party's alliance with the religious Right, a relation that is a "parody" of the American religion (270).

In making this argument, moreover, Bloom accomplishes two other feats. First, by tracking one possible set of consequences of the American apotheosis of the self, Bloom carries out, no matter in how displaced a form, what amounts to a self-critique. For, in these sentences and in Bloom's later thoughts on "Bushian Gnosticism," the critic admits that, while "American Orphism has led on to what is most distinctive in our cultural and aesthetic achievement . . . it may have had a miserable fallout upon our political morality." Amazingly, then, for readers of the Bloom of the '70s and '80s the book's author faces one consequence of his own Orphic desires: how the cultural and poetic migration of Romanticism to America has in his own account effected an "American Gnosticism [that] continues to rejoice in its social inutility" (*AR,* 58). With those words Bloom could just as well be harshly evaluating the early '80s Bloom of *Agon.* Similarly, in perhaps an even less displaced form of self-knowledge, Bloom defines the legacy of African-American religion as a "central dilemma" that is the "inevitable paradigm now for all similar American quests." He thus asks: "Is the self to be made free of itself, or free of other selves? The goal is to be made free for God, however you interpret *that* freedom, but do you deny the self for a community, past or present, or do you affirm the self by evading community?" (254). Bloom could just as well be asking these questions of his own vatic self. Here our response to Bloom has been that the community will inhere even in the self's evasion or curtailment of the community.

The second feat that Bloom accomplishes is that he explicitly joins the American Sublime to his own moment of national and international history. Far from merely contextualizing the spiritual character of the "American Religion," moreover, Bloom's invocation of the Persian Gulf War intimates the opposite: that an understanding of the American Religion actually contributes to the grave, grim span of historical knowledge signaled by America's war with Iraq. It is thus no coincidence that, after citing the Persian Gulf War, Bloom immediately refers to Emerson's famous angry reaction in 1847 to American's war with Mexico, the latter "being the Iraq of that American moment" (*AR,* 16). This analogy between Mexico and Iraq allows for the implicit parallel between Emerson and Bloom, one that places the vatic self within the historical moment of a national crisis—indeed, a national failure. The gravity of this crisis allows Emerson and Bloom to speak of a vatic self whose authority does not go against but, instead, coincides with a collective history. One could say that it is precisely this coincidence that Bloom's Romantic readings of Emerson from the '60s to the '80s have tried on the whole to contain, absorb, or transcend. Here, however, Bloom reverses this movement, making the American romance of self part of the collective experience that leads a nation to war.

This reversal may also partially speak to Bloom's own changing role as an intellectual in the United States. As his changing publishers indicate, Bloom has increasingly moved away from a specialized academic audience to occupy the position of a "public intellectual."[41] His citation of Emerson might then also signal an acknowledgment of some of the social responsibilities that Emerson accepts, as Cornel West argues, in occupying the nineteenth-century American role of a Gramscian "organic intellectual."[42] For Bloom, however, this transition has in many ways been problematic. Indeed, if anything, this more public role for Bloom arguably demonstrates what has been a constant in Bloom's career: the odd way in which the cultural authority of the Bloomian self is haunted by what it curtails or contains, a larger sense of collective history. It is this paradoxical situation that explains why Bloom, in his supremely self-willed iconoclasm, has still retained for so long the stature of a representative figure. It also explains why Bloom's investment in a poetic self often coincides with his immersion in texts that assert the collective destinies of a people, from the Kabbalah of *Kabbalah and Criticism* (1975) to the Old Testament of *The Book of J* (1990). This situation could thus underwrite a present scenario in which Bloom departs from an ostensibly elitist academy, whose categories are paradoxically politicized and historicized, for a more wide-ranging intellectual situation in a public sphere paradoxically more diffuse and depoliticized in its cultural conversations, a sphere that could quite conceivably be circumscribed by the main preoccupation of Bloom during the years of his explicitly academic writing: the possibility of a primordial vatic self existing before the demands of language, nature, history, and the human community. The explicitly topical issues in *The American Religion,* however, suggestively complicate this very scenario.

Bloom's citation of Emerson in *The American Religion* also signals another aspect of the former's conjoining of history and the American Sublime: his willingness to engage with contemporary issues and thus to confront the future. Thus, like Emerson's vision of the great mother, Bloom's estimation of his present object of study leads to a sighting of the future. Unlike this particular image of Emerson's, however, Bloom's visions are more particularized and more choate in the grimness of his tone. In terms of the nation, he writes that his "fear is that we will never again see a Democrat in the Presidency during my lifetime." In terms of the world he writes: "We export our culture abroad, low and high, and increasingly we export the American Religion as well. If Woodrow Wilson proves correct, and we were intended to be a spirit among the nations of the world, then the twenty-first century will mark a full-scale return to the wars of religion" (*AR,* 57–58, 265). The migratory narrative of Romanticism completes itself, as it were, transforming itself into the more global, more apocalyptic trajectories of the American empire.

Bloom's prophecies recall Emerson's in two more ways, however. First, as in Emerson's vision, Bloom's predictions willingly step into history and thus immediately demonstrate the limitations, the opacities, of their own sightings. Bloom has, after all, lived to see a Democratic presidency. We might also wonder whether Bloom's retranslation of the social world into a religious dilemma is as circumscribed as his own specific predictions. Second, however, as with the inchoateness of Emerson's vision, the opacities of Bloom's prophecies signal a larger historical template that deepens the resonances of his futurity. It is not too difficult, in other words, to match Bloom's concerns with those of a more materialist, leftist analysis, in which the world's religious wars and the rise of fundamentalism in the United States would be symptomatic of the ongoing convulsions of late capitalism's global market—what Bloom inadvertently allegorizes as the "export of the American religion." It is certainly not difficult to connect the general tone of Bloom's analysis to more "properly" Marxist metanarratives, which must engage unsentimentally and thoroughly with the possibility of confirming more "mystified" intimations of the future's bleak trajectories.

If anything, then, Emerson's and Bloom's engagements with the future differ only in the degree of their reflexivity. Emerson's vision of the great mother readily signals a double sense of opacity and vision in its inchoate tropings and analysis. In contrast, Bloom's predictions carry in their assertive clarity more of the daemonization, the conviction of a self that can truly see. Both Emerson and Bloom stand, then, as two sides to a self-consciously American form of cultural analysis, one whose singularity is based on an American exaltation of a "Romantic" self and of what that self sees, an exaltation that simultaneously signals its knowing as a form of blockage and its limitations as a sign of what lies beyond its ken. This analysis's self-representation as American, as singular, is then the self-fulfilling sign of this doubleness, of limited vision and visionary opacity.

*The American Religion* would, then, be another version of this cultural analysis in Bloom, one whose topical soundings contrast starkly with the more normatively submerged sense of collective authority which Bloom's romance of the poetic self contains, hides, and redirects. It is, of course, quite easy to make too much out of these soundings and of the new course in Bloom that they seem to imply. Bloom himself might simply respond that *The American Religion* is religious and social criticism, a book's whose coordinates necessarily differ from those of his intensely poetic and literary meditations of the '70s and '80s.[43] Connecting *The American Religion* to these other works, however, is a migratory narrative of Romanticism which defines the American Sublime in terms of an unwavering, hyperbolic selfhood. And, surprisingly enough, this migratory narrative leads Bloom in *The American Religion* not only into the historical world but also toward the category of a historical future. For the moment, at least, the vatic self's prophecies do not cohere around the burdens of a poetic past but gaze, instead, no how matter how grimly or bleakly, forward.

# Epilogue

# Fantastic Futures, Postmodern Jacobins

> Without this *non-contemporaneity with itself of the living present,* without that which secretly unhinges it, without this reponsibility and this respect for justice concerning those who *are not there,* of those who are no longer or who are not yet *present and living,* what sense would there be to ask the question "where?" "where tomorrow?" "whither?"
> Jacques Derrida
> *Specters of Marx*

The last chapter on Bloom and Emerson concludes by foregrounding one reoccurring topic of this book: the relation of modernity to the category of the "future" in postmodernism. This topic necessarily confronts the attendant problem of Romanticism's and theory's intellectual prospects *in* the future: whether these two formations of literary and critical practice will retain any particular force within or beyond North America's academic institutions or whether new discursive practices will relegate Romanticism and theory to an "antiquity" of reified knowledge, separate and distinct from the "immediacy" of the '90s fin-de-siècle *epistēmē*. Admittedly hyperbolic, perhaps impossible to answer, these issues do have the merit of demonstrating how their intelligibility depends on the very categories they try to interrogate: "modernity," "futurity," "immediacy," and "antiquity." Returning to a formulation that we earlier revised, we might then say that the thinking through of a postmodern future is necessarily a Romantic project.

For, if through the concept of modernity we have troped both Romanticism and theory as simultaneously asserting and obstructing historical difference, we also acknowledged earlier how Romanticism has been identified with teleological historical thinking—with the very categories that allow us to wonder about the "future" of Romanticism and theory in a spatialized, atemporal postmodernism. Given a political dimension, this "Romantic" insertion of linear historical thinking into a spatialized postmodernism can be described as both the effect and cause of a postmodern Jacobinism.

Within the specific texts of *Fantastic Modernity* this Jacobinism has been associated with a futurity that has been treated in a variety of locally contrasting, asymmetric ways. In chapter 2 "The Triumph of Life" shows how both Shelley's and de Man's challenges to historical thinking belong to a two-hundred-year-old tradition of Jacobin-inflected thought, one that critiques the epistemological and ontological assumptions of its own political designs. In chapter 3 the focus is on the political and methodological confusions that occur when current Romanticist historicism allows an uninterrogated continuity to exist between Romantic Jacobinism and Marxist thought. This confusion radically separates McGann's Enlightenment progressive futurity from Heine's more grim prophecy of the past's influence on the future. Far from simply obstructing further historical action, however, this bifurcation challenges Marxism to face how its critical powers might image a future more negative than positive in its emancipatory potential. Simultaneously, this bifurcation also intimates a form of Enlightenment Romanticism which might actually critique Marxist thought from the position of a postmodern Left. In chapter 4 Mary Wollstonecraft's *Rights of Woman* partakes of an Enlightenment utopian politics that is complicated not only by a derealizing, circulating economy of gender but also by a self-reflexive, synchronic critique of the diachronic teleology associated with the millennial aspirations of such politics. In chapter 5 Bloom ignores an explicit

Romantic Jacobinism in order to exalt an American vatic self, whose migratory relationship to British culture is transmuted by Emerson's *English Traits* into the history of modernization in nineteenth-century America and England. Oddly enough, however, Bloom's romance with the American Sublime orients itself toward the future in *The American Religion,* in a bleak vision that is nevertheless beholden not to the past but to a future world.

The future thus circulates among these various texts in a variety of ways—as a mystified lacuna within critical thought as well as a breach into the hypostatizations of the critical mind; as the romance of a utopian millennialism as well as the trauma of a dystopian critique. The one constant to this circulation of the future is, then, how critical praxis is oriented, no matter how problematically, toward a modernity not solely contained by the coordinates of the past and present. More so than the specific, contradictory engagements between Jacobinism and various postmodern theories, this orientation defines the significance of postmodern Jacobinism, as the insistent pressure of a different, contingent future on a historically denuded postmodern present.

I want to conclude by suggesting how such a pressure might affect the world beyond the academy by citing several passages that describe two different events separated by almost exactly two hundred years, two irruptions into historical time, one in 1789 and the other in 1989. The first passage comes from William Hazlitt:

> The change in the belles-lettres was as complete, and to many persons as startling, as the change in politics, with which it went hand in hand. There was a mighty ferment in the heads of statesman and poets, kings and people. According to the prevailing notions, all was to be natural and new. Nothing that was established was to be tolerated. . . . Authority and fashion, elegance or arrangement, were hooted out of countenance, as pedantry and prejudice. Every one did that which was good in his own eyes. The object was to reduce all things to an absolute level; and a singularly affected and outrageous simplicity prevailed in dress and manners, in style and sentiment. A striking effect produced where it was least expected, something new and original, no matter whether good, bad, or indifferent, whether mean or lofty, extravagant, or childish, was all that was

aimed at.... The licentiousness grew extreme.... The world was to be turned topsy-turvy.[1]

Hazlitt's subject is, of course, the cultural convulsions that followed the French Revolution. Two points can be made about his account. First, regardless of Hazlitt's oftentimes wry tone, his passage conveys a historical imaginary whose antiauthoritarian tenets are based on the heady sense of a suddenly unpredictable future, a future whose contingencies allow for any number of opportunistic, hyperbolic changes. The reflexive harnessing of that headiness for a revolutionary imperative—"nothing that was established *was to be* tolerated"—is the political result of the future's presence within this modernity, a modernity that has been retroactively designated many times over as Romanticism.

This retroactive condition also speaks to my second point. Hazlitt's quote appears in this epilogue as a *double* citation: it is also Thomas McFarland's proof for his anecdotal linkage of the 1950s and 1960s revitalization of Romantic studies to the social and cultural turbulence, the "Romanticism," of the 1960s countercultural movement. Thus, Hazlitt's quote is not simply exemplary as a description of the power of the future's contingency in the present. As a citation for the 1960s by McFarland, Hazlitt's passage also exemplifies one crucial way that historical knowledge about Romanticism is constructed—through a Romantic *quotation* that anchors an unknown future in a present suddenly known by its putative Romanticism. Thus, this strategy of citing Romanticism's "unknown future" as a means of understanding the 1960s not only associates a historical study with a Romantic form of knowledge; equally important, such a citational strategy also involves a Romantic *methodology* grounded in the very practices of historical mediation and representation which have been the focus of this book.

McFarland's citation of Hazlitt—the Romantic textualization, as it were, of the historical conjunction between 1789 and the 1960s—occasions the next passage that I want to examine. The mediation of Romantic futurity sets up semiotic resonances between Hazlitt's passage and this journalistic account from 1989:

In the intoxication of the moment it was not difficult to believe that a state of revolutionary immortality had been attained and that some important but indefinable success was just around the corner. The atmosphere, however illusory it might ultimately prove to be, recalled Woodstock in its nonviolence and sense of giddy liberation, and the Paris Commune in the conviction among the demonstrators that the "people" had finally risen up to secure the country's heartland from forces of reaction.[2]

This passage by Orville Schell describes "China's Spring" in Tiananmen Square, shortly before the events of 3 and 4 June 1989. Like the headiness of Hazlitt's "topsy-turvy" world, the "intoxication" of Tiananmen can also be interpreted as the heady sense of an unknown future that suddenly conditions the present's symbolic realm, its social, political, and cultural soundings. Like Hazlitt's passage, Schell's account creates a historical trajectory that asserts the contemporaneity of the revolutionary imperatives of 1789 in the late twentieth century. Yet, just as McFarland uses Hazlitt's words to refer to the French Revolution and the American 1960s, the references to Woodstock and the Paris Commune in the Tiananmen passage also indicate how this contemporaneity is not a historical phenomenon arrived at transparently or naturally. Instead, this contemporaneity evinces a constitutively *textual* historical knowledge in a historical will that searches for a deeper, more profound signifying logic that might order the links between Tiananmen and past Romantic mediations and confirm the uncanny formal parallels between 1789 and 1989. The importance of this logic lies, however, not only in the moral and political urgency of its realization but also in its dependency on such mediations and formal parallels. The correspondence beween Hazlitt's and Schell's passages is Romantic, then, because of the futurity impinging on both passages and because of the mediated nature of that correspondence.

This mediated nature allows a Romantic futurity to exist in the postmodern world by placing that futurity within the context of a postcolonial, post-Anglo-European history. Yet it also necessarily asserts the allegorical nature of that placement. By *allegory,* I mean here both de Man's and Jameson's use of this term—as a reflexive dramatization of language's signifying inauthenticity *and* as a necessary transcoding for a purported nontextual, historical real, the necessary language of historical intelligibility.[3] The Romanticism constructed by theory exhibits this dual allegorical nature as an especially vivid postmodern cultural *arti-*

*fact.* If Romanticism is able to continue to influence the multiplying histories of this planet, it will do so as such an artifact. Romanticism will, in other words, condition the difference between a postmodern apprehension of the future as a simulacrum and a postmodern Jacobinist appropriation of the future as a strategy—a strategy defined by the open possibilities of a world no longer understood by the hegemonic claims of the West.

This formulation requires one large qualification. Artifact or no, a discourse so heavily encoded as Western accommodates itself neither simply nor innocently to the hybridity and alterity of postcolonial history. One could argue that later historical events already amply demonstrate the limited influence of a revolutionary "future" at work in Tiananmen in 1989—a point emphasized by Schell's own rhetoric of intoxication. Yet the danger then becomes whether this ephemeral sense of China's future's potential *is* the larger hegemonic effect of Romanticism as a Western discourse of modernity, in the sense that "China's Spring" becomes intelligible *only as* the reification of a Romantic action accomplished in vain. Certainly, then, Romanticism's relevance to the world will depend on its ability to stress the complicated series of discursive mediations, appropriations, and revisions that already define its presence in the North American university. Only such an emphasis— one that increasingly includes not only Romanticism's transhistorical but also its cross-cultural transmissions—will expose the naturalizing, totalizing tendencies within Romanticism's significations as well as occasion the possibility of its historical knowledge being cathected by someone besides the Western critical subject.[4]

Such a subject and its discourses, however, will not remain untouched by this larger sense of mediation and reception. We can glimpse one consequence for the discourses of modernity in a final example, another correspondent's account of a moment during the Tiananmen Square protests, a conversation between the journalist and a Chinese student.

> "You see, over there?" [the student] said. "That's the Great Hall of the People. And here?" He pointed straight down, into the ground. "This is the People's Republic of China, where we have the People's National Congress and the People's Liberation Army.
> "And . . ." He wasn't pausing for effect, only trying to find the

right words in English, though it was impossible for an American not to be stunned by what he said next. *"We are the people."*[5]

I would venture that the "stunned" figure of the American also encompasses the shock of the Western subject faced with the dialectical image of modernity.[6] What is stunning, moreover, is not the indeterminacy of historical events—the aporetic relations among the past, present, and future—but, rather, the momentary shocking *readability* of the student's explicit ordering of his surroundings, the stunningly clear architecture of his spatial and temporal signs. Here, then, is the fantastic logic of modernity—fantastic, however, not as an illusion but as a recognition, a realization of emancipatory referents which all too often the Western subject can only express as cant, as the intelligibility of moribund, reified thought.

For the last twenty-five years the particularly cathected relation between Romanticism and theory, as a cryptonormative formation of modernity, has attempted its own academic, university-bound versions of such emancipatory discourse. This relationship might very well be over for a variety of reasons that range from the changing fortunes of each field of study to the increasingly embattled position of intellectual labor in the United States. Giving up on this relationship means, however, forgoing one intellectual source for a postmodern Jacobinism that defiantly insists on a contingent category of change and possibility in a futureless world. Such possibilities appear in the semiotic shock, the fantastic clarity, of the student's words—not least in their chastening, dialectical remonstrance of modernity's phantasmic nature within Western discourse, not least in their assertion of how so much of what the West signifies by emancipatory change remains unrealized.

# Notes

### Introduction: Fantastic Modernity

1. See Jonathan Arac, *Critical Genealogies: Historical Situations for Postmodern Literary Studies* (New York: Columbia UP, 1987); Clifford Siskin, *The Historicity of Romantic Discourse* (Oxford: Oxford UP, 1988); and Herbert Lindenberger, *The History in Literature: On Value, Genre, Institutions* (New York: Columbia UP, 1990). My argument differs from these critics' in stressing the trope of fantastic modernity and the methodology of dialectical reading. See, however, Lindenberger's discussion of modernity, theory, and Romanticism (61–84). As his discussion of Schiller demonstrates (62–67), Lindenberger emphasizes a Romantic model of modernity similar to M. H. Abrams's *Natural Supernaturalism: Tradition and Revolution in Romantic Literature* (New York: Norton, 1971), one structured by loss and recovery, whereas *Fantastic Modernity* configures modernity as a potential revolutionary rupture that does not necessarily represent itself as a loss. See also Thomas A. Vogler, "Romanticism and Literary Periods: The Future of the Past," *New German Critique* 38 (1986): 131–60.

2. Marilyn Butler, *Romantics, Rebels, and Reactionaries: English Literature and Its Background, 1760–1830* (Oxford: Oxford UP, 1981), 1.

3. The ongoing revision of acknowledging who is and is not a Romantic further signals the mediated nature of Romanticism; for a discussion of the latest change in the Romantic canon, the archival rediscovery of a number of late eighteenth- and early-nineteenth-century female writers, see chapter 4.

4. Jürgen Habermas uses *cryptonormativism* to describe how Foucault's "theory can give no account of the normative foundations of its own rhetoric"

(Habermas, *The Philosophical Discourse of Modernity* [Cambridge: MIT P, 1990], 294). Habermas uses this term in defense of a modernity that is synonymous with the promise of a recuperated Enlightenment rationalism under assault from postmodern antifoundational thinking. While my study necessarily engages at points with this long-standing definition of modernity, I decline the fixity of Habermas's framework and goals. What I take from *cryptonormativism* is the sense that many postmodern theories implicitly refer to a project of change that is oftentimes explicitly denied by their theoretical assertions.

5. For two histories of the concept of modernity, see Matei Calinescu, *Five Faces of Modernity: Modernism,* Avant-Garde, *Decadence, Kitsch, Postmodernism* (Durham: Duke UP, 1987); and Robert P. Pippin, *Modernism as a Philosophical Problem: On the Dissatisfactions of European High Culture* (Oxford: Basil Blackwell, 1991). For the argument that modernity is the *Neuzeit* of a new eighteenth-century historical consciousness, see Reinhart Koselleck, *Futures Past: On the Semantics of Historical Time,* trans. Keith Tribe (Cambridge: MIT Press, 1985). For two more linguistically oriented works that especially stress modernity as an aporia, see the essays "Literary History and Literary Modernity" and "Lyric and Modernity" in Paul de Man, *Blindness and Insight: Essays in the Rhetoric of Contemporary Criticism,* 2d ed. (Minneapolis: U of Minnesota P, 1983). All further references to *Blindness,* abbreviated *BI,* will appear in the text.

6. For a gloss on Nietzsche's use of this term, see Gianni Vattimo, *The End of Modernity: Nihilism and Hermeneutics in Postmodern Culture,* trans. Jon R. Snyder (Baltimore: Johns Hopkins UP, 1988), 24–25; Vattimo quotes the title of a chapter from Friedrich Nietzsche's *Twilight of the Idols,* trans. R. J. Hollingdale (London: Penguin, 1968).

7. For three other accounts of Romanticism's twentieth-century institutional history, see Lindenberger, 23–43; Jon Klancher, "Romantic Criticism and the Meanings of the French Revolution," *Studies in Romanticism* 28 (1989): 463–91; and Jon Klancher, "English Romanticism and Cultural Production," in *The New Historicism,* ed. H. Aram Veeser (London: Routledge, 1989), 77–88.

8. Lindenberger, 42–43; see David Wagenknecht, ed., "How It Was," *Studies in Romanticism* 21 (1982): 553–71, for ten scholars' memories of teaching Romanticism in the 1950s. See also Klancher's point in "Cultural Production" that the installation of Romanticism occurs along national disciplinary lines, in that it is more specifically *English* Romanticism that rises in academic stature during this time (82–84).

9. New Criticism's hegemonic rise in the fifties and sixties also, of course, associates Romanticism and modernism. While an intriguing narrative in its own right, the New Critical appropriation of Romanticism and modernism is peripheral to this account in the sense that New Criticism did not really affect the revitalized Romanticist *scholarship* of this period. That is, while during this time academics were certainly teaching Romantic poems as examples of New Critical organicism, the professional 1950s Romanticist—with the exception of Wellek—was neither reading, studying, nor writing about Romanticism as a

New Critic. Both Abrams's literary history and Frye's neostructuralist approach are, for example, critical projects readily distinguishable from, if not outright hostile to, their New Critical colleagues' programs.

10. Fredric Jameson, "Periodizing the 60s," in *The 60s without Apology*, ed. Sohnya Sayres, Anders Stephanson, Stanley Aronowitz, and Fredric Jameson (Minneapolis: U of Minnesota P, 1984), 204–9; see also Fredric Jameson, *Postmodernism, or The Cultural Logic of Late Capitalism* (Durham: Duke UP, 1991), 32–38.

11. My use of the term *postmodern theory* thus refers to this general boom in theory and not solely to more specific usages of postmodernism and postmodernity. Thus, while certainly part of this general theoretical movement, Paul de Man actually resisted *postmodernism* as an enabling term for his deconstructive project. See Paul de Man, *The Resistance to Theory* (Minneapolis: U of Minnesota P, 1986), 119–20.

12. For a discussion of the sociohistoric use of this idea during the late eighteenth and early nineteenth centuries and of its latter-day reification in Romantic studies, see James K. Chandler, "Representative Men, Spirits of the Age, and Other Romantic Types," in *Romantic Revolutions: Criticism and Theory*, ed. Kenneth R. Johnston, Gilbert Chaitin, Karen Hanson, and Herbert Marks (Bloomington: Indiana UP, 1990), 104–32. See also Mark Patterson, "Emerson, Napoleon, and the Concept of the Representative," *ESQ* 31 (1985): 230–42.

13. For two discussions that touch upon much of what I mean by this mutual transformation, see Marjorie Levinson's elegant "transhistorical" use of Althusser's concept of "structural causality," in the introduction to *Rethinking Historicism: Critical Readings in Romantic History*, ed. Marjorie Levinson (Oxford: Basil Blackwell, 1989), 1–17; and Dominick La Capra's historical application of "transference," in *Soundings in Critical Theory* (Ithaca: Cornell UP, 1989), 6, 35–41.

14.
We never really confront a text immediately, in all its freshness as a thing-in-itself. Rather, texts come before us as the always-already-read; we apprehend them through sedimented layers of previous interpretations, or—if the text is brand-new—through the sedimented reading habits and categories developed by those inherited interpretive traditions. This presupposition then dictates the use of a method (... "metacommentary") according to which our object of study is less the text itself than the interpretations through which we attempt to confront and appropriate it. (Fredric Jameson, *The Political Unconscious: Narrative as a Socially Symbolic Act* [Ithaca: Cornell UP, 1981], 9–10)

## Chapter 1: Fantastic Reflexivities, Dialectical Transmissions

1. Jürgen Habermas, "Modernity versus Postmodernity," *New German Critique* 22 (1980–81): 3.

2. Herbert Lindenberger, *The History in Literature: On Value, Genre, Institutions* (New York: Columbia UP, 1990), 67.

3. Ernesto Laclau and Chantal Mouffe, *Hegemony and Socialist Strategy: Toward a Radical Democratic Politics* (London: Verso, 1985), 2.

4. Jürgen Habermas, *The Philosophical Discourse of Modernity* (Cambridge: MIT P, 1987), 294.

5. See, for example, Jacques Derrida, "The Law of Genre," *Critical Inquiry* 7 (1980), 61–62; and Vogler, 131–33.

6. Earl Wasserman, "The Grounds of Knowledge," *Studies in Romanticism* 4 (1964): 17–34. For the argument, however, of a more conflicted side to Wasserman's take on the question of indeterminacy, see Arac, 103–4.

7. Fredric Jameson, *Postmodernism, or The Cultural Logic of Late Capitalism* (Durham: Duke UP, 1991), 95–96.

8. Ibid., 48; Jameson's essay originally appears in *New Left Review* 146 (1984): 59–92. See also Jameson's comment about the dissolution of the subject-object dialectic in Anders Stephanson, "Regarding Postmodernism—A Conversation with Fredric Jameson," in *Universal Abandon? The Politics of Postmodernism*, ed. Andrew Ross (Minneapolis: U of Minnesota P, 1988), 7.

9. Jameson, *Postmodernism*, 3. For his discussion of cognitive mapping, see 51–54.

10. Ibid., 54. For his reformulation of the Lacanian and Althusserian gap between the symbolic and the real, see Jameson, *The Political Unconscious: Narrative as a Socially Symbolic Act* (Ithaca: Cornell UP, 1981), 34–35.

11. For two critical works that tie Keats's poem to the question of a historical consciousness, see Philip Fisher, "A Museum with One Work Inside: Keats and the Finality of Art," *Keats-Shelley Journal* 33 (1984): 85–102; and, more recently, A. W. Phinney, "Keats in the Museum: Between Aesthetics and History," *Journal of English and Germanic Philology* (1991): 208–29. For a discussion of how "Ode on a Grecian Urn" reflects Keats's larger reception of Hellenic culture, see Martin Aske, *Keats and Hellenism* (Cambridge: Cambridge UP, 1985), 110–27.

12. Kenneth Hudson, *Museums of Influence* (Cambridge: Cambridge UP, 1987), 23; Joseph Rosenblum, "Hellenism," in *Encyclopedia of Romanticism: Culture in Britain, 1780s–1830s*, ed. Laura Dabundo (New York: Garland, 1992), 256. For two other histories of the British Museum during this time, see Edward Miller, *That Noble Cabinet: A History of the British Museum* (Athens: Ohio UP, 1974), 64–91; and Alma S. Wittlin, *Museums: In Search of a Usable Future* (Cambridge: MIT Press, 1970), 101–5. For a recent overview of both the Hellenic revival in England and scholarship of this phenomenon, see Marilyn Gaull, *English Romanticism: The Human Context* (New York: Norton, 1988), 182–207.

13. The history of the museum in France is at once more simple and complex, in that the French Revolution initiates both a more stark contrast between aristocratic privilege and public display *and* the groundwork for Napoléon's conflation of state and self in the Musée Napoléon in the Louvre (Wittlin, 15,

83–85). It was, in fact, the Musée Napoléon that first exposed many English to the possible scope of museum collections, when individuals such as J. M. W. Turner, Henry Fuseli, and Fanny Burney had the opportunity to visit the museum during the Treaty of Amiens in 1802 (Hudson, 4).

14. For the latest and most sophisticated discussion of class anxiety in Keats's work, see Marjorie Levinson, *Keats's Life of Allegory: The Origins of a Style* (Oxford: Basil Blackwell, 1988); for an account of how Keats obtained his various inspirations for the urn, see Ian Jack, *Keats and the Mirror of Art* (Oxford: Clarendon Press, 1967), 214–24.

15. Aske, 3; Fisher, 85.

16. John Keats, *Complete Poems,* ed. Jack Stillinger (Cambridge: Harvard UP, 1982), 283.

17. See Raymond Williams, *Culture and Society: 1780–1950* (New York: Columbia UP, 1983), xiii–xx; and Raymond Williams, *Marxism and Literature* (Oxford: Oxford UP, 1977), 14–17.

18. Aske, 1.

19. Vogler, 159–60.

20. See, for example, the offhand labeling of Romanticism's fascist resonances as well-worn doxa in Northrop Frye, "The Drunken Boat: The Revolutionary Element in Romanticism," in *Romanticism Reconsidered; Selected Papers from the English Institute,* ed. Northrop Frye (New York: Columbia UP, 1963), 13.

21. A. O. Lovejoy, "The Meaning of Romanticism for the Historian of Ideas," *Journal of the History of Ideas* 2 (1941): 257–78 (hereafter "MR").

22. Leo Spitzer, " *'Geistesgeschichte'* vs. History of Ideas as Applied to Hitlerism," *Journal of the History of Ideas* 5 (1944): 191–203 (hereafter *"G"*).

23. In linking these two debates, I mean not only the specific argument between Lovejoy and Spitzer but also the general debate over the cultural identity of fascism that was part of the American intellectual scene at that time. The specific debate between Lovejoy and Spitzer has been made more readily available to us through the publication of Alban K. Forcione, Herbert Lindenberger, and Madeline Sutherland, eds., *Leo Spitzer: Representative Essays* (Stanford: Stanford UP, 1988). See also Geoffrey Green, *Literary Criticism and the Structures of History: Erich Auerbach and Leo Spitzer* (Lincoln: U of Nebraska P, 1982), 111–14.

For a number of different views—and accounts—of de Man's wartime past, see Werner Hamacher, Neil Hertz, and Thomas Keenan, eds. *Responses: On Paul de Man's Wartime Journalism* (Lincoln: U of Nebraska P, 1989).

24. See, for example, the role of Romanticism in Cynthia Chase's "Trappings of an Education toward What We Do Not Yet Have," in Hamacher, Hertz, and Keenan, 44–79.

25. See Jonathan Culler, " 'Paul de Man's War' and the Aesthetic Ideology," *Critical Inquiry* 15 (1989): 777–83. See also chapter 2, n. 9.

26. A. O. Lovejoy, "Reply to Professor Spitzer," *Journal of the History of Ideas* 5 (1944): 204 (hereafter "RS").

27. Thus, in much the same way that, for Spitzer, the Romantic method of *Geistesgeschichte* is on trial, so too, in the de Man debate, is deconstruction both the object of critical debate and, in some cases, also the method employed in that debate.

28. Similarly, Jerome McGann's accusation of Paul de Man's idealism rests on an assumption of the "clear line of demarcation" between sociohistoric conditions and the (il)logic of textuality. See Jerome McGann, *Social Values and Poetic Acts: A Historical Judgement of Literary Work* (Cambridge: Harvard UP, 1988), 108–9.

29. This nascent possibility does not erase, however, the probably more immediate reason why Lovejoy employed such language—the desire among early-twentieth-century literary critics to introduce scientism into their disciplines in order to revitalize the humanities and make them equal to the natural sciences. See Paul Bové, *Intellectuals in Power: A Genealogy of Critical Humanism* (New York: Columbia UP, 1986), 41. For an argument that this scientific impulse still operates in contemporary theory, see Roger Seamon, "Poetics against Itself: On the Self-Destruction of Modern Scientific Criticism," *PMLA* 104 (1989): 294–305.

30. See, for example, Martha R. Herbert, in collaboration with Richard Levins, "Marxism and Biology," in *The Left Academy: Marxist Scholarship on American Campuses,* ed. Bertell Ollman and Edward Vernoff, 3 vols. (New York: Praeger, 1984), 123–53; and Paul Feyerabend, *Farewell to Reason* (London: Verso, 1987).

31. Such a reception history would have to be broad and complicated enough to include studies of how Ludwig Uhland and other Romantic poets were received by the jingoistic German *Gymnasein* during Heinrich Heine's time, the deployment of Romanticism during the Weimar intellectual period, and of such figures as Carl Schmitt, the anti-Romantic political and legal theorist who held a variety of party posts within the Third Reich. I know of no study that examines the deployment of Romanticism during the Weimar period, though a book that sets the context for such a study would be Dagmar Barnouw, *Weimar Intellectuals and the Threat of Modernity* (Bloomington: Indiana UP, 1988). See also Carl Schmitt, *Political Romanticism,* trans. Guy Oakes (Cambridge: MIT Press, 1986); and Klancher's discussion of Schmitt in "English Romanticism," 83–84.

32. See Daniel J. Wilson, *Arthur O. Lovejoy and the Quest for Intelligibility* (Chapel Hill: U of North Carolina P, 1980), 195–96. Lovejoy had also vigorously lobbied for American support of Great Britain and France during World War I; his academic writing after the United State's entrance into the war was explicitly partisan and political, to the point of being "little more than a propaganda tract" (Wilson, 122–28). I mention this fact neither to impugn the essays of Lovejoy I am dealing with here nor to critique (or praise) his politics; rather, my point is to show how the relation between ideas and political effects was more diverse and complex in Lovejoy's writings than Lovejoy's response to Spitzer implies.

33. Wilson, 198.

34. Between "The Meaning of Romanticism" and "*Geistesgeschichte,*" for example, another debate occurred in the *Journal of the History of Ideas* between Jacques Barzun and Peter Viereck over each other's methodological use of Romanticism and national socialism. See Jacques Barzun, "Peter Viereck's *Metapolitics: From the Romantics to Hitler," Journal of the History of Ideas* 3 (1942):107–10; and Peter Viereck, "Reply," *Journal of the History of Ideas* 3 (1942): 110–12. Also, in the same issue that featured Lovejoy's essay "The Meaning of Romanticism," four of the other five articles were about either political, social, or economic aspects of Romanticism; of those four, two considered the link between Romanticism and fascism (Goetz A. Briefs, "The Economic Philosophy of Romanticism," *Journal of the History of Ideas* 2 [1941]: 279–300; and Eugene N. Anderson, "German Romanticism as an Ideology of Cultural Crisis," *Journal of the History of Ideas* 2 [1941]: 301–17.) Thus, Lovejoy's article was no lone voice but, rather, part of a larger institutional recognition—in the form of the *Journal*—of a field of inquiry constituted by the intersection of Romanticism, politics, and fascism. For a discussion of Viereck and how the connection between fascism and Romanticism was reappropriated itself through the French Revolution, see Klancher, "Romantic Criticism," 479–86.

35. The cumulative index of the *Journal of the History of Ideas* shows, for example, eleven references to fascism, national socialism, and related subjects for the first five volumes of the journal, from 1939–44: Esther F. Kandel and Elizabeth Rapaport, *Journal of the History of Ideas: Cumulative Index* (New York: Journal of the History of Ideas, 1966). The number of articles about fascism drops dramatically during the next twenty years, indicating that the institutional recognition of this subject was historically specific and that the institution has since forgotten the recognition.

36. The link between politics and scholarship was so much an issue in the study of Romanticism and fascism that Peter Viereck (n. 34) was forced in his reply to say, "But I cannot permit to pass unchallenged his grave charge that I 'unfastidiously' distort the 'rules of evidence,' apparently in order to bolster my support of anti-Nazi interventionism" (111). Thus, what writers are doing when they critique Romanticism and fascism becomes the critical object of contention which composes a large part of their critiques.

37. For one interpretation of Spitzer's investment, see Green, 85–86.

38. Of course, the emigré does not solely express either literally or symbolically the fact of the transmission of the West's culture. The more ugly alter ego of the emigré is the third world colonialist, whose transmission of culture to lands beyond Europe is not a preservation of but, rather, an invasion by the West. See Roberto Fernandez Retamar, "Caliban: Notes towards a Discussion of Culture in Our America," trans. Lynn Garafola, David Arthur McMurry, and Robert Marquez, *Massachusetts Review* 15 (1974): 7–72.

## Chapter 2: Disfiguring Monuments

1. Jerome Christensen, " 'Like a Guilty Thing Surprised': Deconstruction, Coleridge, and the Apostasy of Criticism," *Critical Inquiry* 12 (Summer 1986): 771.

2. Ibid., 769–71.

3. Indeed, Christensen's essay is in fact a critique of Frank Lentricchia's belief in the simple equivalence of linguistic and political apostasy (ibid.). See Frank Lentricchia, *Criticism and Social Change* (Chicago: U of Chicago P, 1983), 38–40.

4. For an assertion of the importance of "Shelley Disfigured" for understanding de Man's relation to history, see Jacques Derrida, "Like the Sound of the Sea Deep within a Shell: Paul de Man's War," in *Responses: On Paul de Man's Wartime Journalism,* ed. Werner Hamacher, Neil Hertz, and Thomas Keenan (Lincoln: U of Nebraska P, 1989), 152.

5. Lindsay Waters, "Introduction," in Paul de Man, *Critical Writings: 1953–1978,* ed. Lindsay Waters (Minneapolis: U of Minnesota P, 1989), lii.

6. Tilottama Rajan, "Displacing Post-Structuralism: Romantic Studies after Paul de Man," *Studies in Romanticism* 24 (1985): 468–69. For Rajan's own Bakhtinian-inflected version of such a reading-oriented deconstructive practice, see Tilottama Rajan, *The Supplement of Reading: Figures of Understanding in Romantic Theory and Practice* (Ithaca: Cornell UP, 1990), 1–35.

7. For another argument that explicitly links deconstruction's early institutional practice to a late 1960s and early 1970s skepticism in political and social authority, see Jonathan Arac, *Critical Genealogies: Historical Situations for Postmodern Literary Studies* (New York: Columbia UP, 1987), 98–99.

8. Jerome McGann, *The Romantic Ideology: A Critical Investigation* (Chicago: U of Chicago P, 1983), 21–31. All further references to *Romantic,* abbreviated *RI,* will appear in the text.

9. See Christopher Norris, *Paul de Man: Deconstruction and the Critique of Aesthetic Ideology* (London: Routledge, 1988), 33–38; Geoffrey Hartman, "Blindness and Insight," *New Republic,* 7 March 1988, 26–31; and Culler.

10. "Wordsworth and Hölderlin," in *The Rhetoric of Romanticism,* ed. Paul de Man (New York: Columbia UP, 1984), 65. Norris also cites "Wordsworth and Hölderlin" in order to prove in de Man's early works a resistance to a history based on "secular change," an attitude toward history that is then opposed in his later works and the earlier "Rhetoric of Temporality" by his deconstruction of the aesthetic ideology (Norris, 1–17). Norris uses "Wordsworth and Hölderlin" to demonstrate de Man's perception of the belatedness of thought, or "reflection," in relation to deeds, which Norris describes earlier as a diachronic situation in which "these principles [of action and thought] exist in a kind of reciprocal dependence where neither could begin to articulate its claims by virtue of this constant oscillating rhythm" (15–16). I will argue that de Man's writings also demand that we read this belatedness, and even more strongly this oscillation, as a synchronic predicament, one that then separates "secular

change" from an unmediated "Titanism" (16) and restores the former to the status of a problem to be investigated—exactly the problematic status, I would suggest, of Norris's own depiction of "The Rhetoric of Temporality" as a form of political action.

11. All quotations from "The Triumph of Life" are from the critical edition by Donald H. Reiman, *Shelley's "The Triumph of Life": A Critical Study* (Urbana: U of Illinois P, 1965) (hereafter "TL"). For a discussion of the poem's complex textual history, see 241.

12. See Harold Bloom, *Shelley's Mythmaking* (New Haven: Yale UP, 1959), 220–75; and Kenneth Neill Cameron, *Shelley: The Golden Years* (Boston: Harvard UP, 1974), 472–73.

13. The archetypical example of this approach is Harold Bloom's analysis of the poem in *Shelley's Mythmaking,* 220–75. With a vigor that anticipates his later critical method, he wrestles with past readers of Shelley over many of the specific lines of the poem, recovering and reconstructing the lines' meaning through a close reading that is critical, interpretive, and emendatory. Bloom constructs what he believes to be the complete poem of which "The Triumph of Life" is a fragment: a poem that is a vision, in which history is inscribed in "mythpoeia" and in which the completed poem also completes another reconstructed structure, a whole that includes most of Shelley's major works, in which one can read a progression of Shelley's mythpoeia toward the only conclusion possible, the "antimyth" of "The Triumph of Life."

Bloom is one of two critics de Man mentions ("SD," 70 n. 3) to exemplify critical methods that assume the fragmentary nature of Shelley's work must be answered. Opposed to Bloom, whom de Man typifies as believing the poem would have ended pessimistically as antimyth, is M. H. Abrams's optimistic evaluation of the poem in Abrams, 441.

14. Paul de Man, "Shelley Disfigured," in *Deconstruction and Criticism,* ed. Harold Bloom et al. (New York: Continuum, 1979), 39–40. All further references to "Shelley," abbreviated "SD," will appear in the text.

15. De Man treats this trope most fully in his piece on Wordsworth's *Essay upon Epitaphs,* "Autobiography as De-Facement." See de Man, *Rhetoric of Romanticism,* 67–81. See also Cynthia Chase's essay "Giving Face to a Name: Paul de Man's Figures," in Cynthia Chase, *Decomposing Figures: Rhetorical Readings in the Romantic Tradition* (Baltimore: John Hopkins UP, 1986), 82–112.

16. I take these and the following phrases of "The Triumph of Life" from the pasages of the poem (352–57; 394–411) that de Man quotes in his argument about Rousseau ("SD," 45, 54).

17. The difference between "The Rhetoric of Temporality" and "Shelley Disfigured" can, then, be gauged by the latter's stress upon the impossibility of the figure's suspension as opposed to the former's emphasis upon the suspension of its methodology of historical revison of the symbol alongside its ahistorical analysis of irony. That is, the point of "Shelley Disfigured" is the simultaneous decomposition and sinking of the shape, whereas the point of "The Rhetoric

of Temporality" is the ongoing suspension of a historical method as a possible option for critical thought. That it is this historical method that has been memorialized by the readers of "The Rhetoric of Temporality" as *the* lesson of the essay speaks to a logic of monumentalzation which paradoxically proves and resists—that is, escapes—what "Shelley Disfigured" asserts.

18. It is precisely this performative power of language which Cynthia Chase argues de Man is diagnosing as the condition "of the possibility of Nazism," in his essay "Aesthetic Formalization: Kleist's 'Uber das Marionettheater.' " See Chase, "Trappings of an Education toward What We Do Not Yet Have," in *Responses: On Paul de Man's Wartime Journalism,* ed. Werner Hamacher, Neil Hertz, and Thomas Keenan (Lincoln: U of Nebraska P, 1989), 43–79. For a more reserved commentary on the politics of that same essay by de Man, see Dominick La Capra *Soundings in Critical Theory* (Ithaca: Cornell UP, 1989), 131.

19. While it is not at all clear that the shape does sink, see Cameron (n. 11), 470, for a reading that supports de Man's contention that the "arch of victory" is the rainbow.

20. "The history of Rousseau interpretation is particularly rich in this respect, both in the diversity of the tactics employed to make him say something diferent from what he said, and in the convergence of these misreadings toward a definite configuration of meanings. It is as if the conspiracy that Rousseau's paranoia imagined during his lifetime came into being after his death, uniting friend and foe alike in a concerted effort to misrepresent his thought" (de Man, *BI,* 112).

21. Peter France, *Rousseau: Confessions* (Cambridge: Cambridge UP, 1987), 17.

22. Jean Jacques Rousseau, *The Reveries of the Solitary Walker,* trans. Charles E. Butterworth (New York: New York UP, 1979), 4–5, 7.

23. Irving Babbitt, *Rousseau and Romanticism* (Boston: Houghton Mifflin, 1919).

24. Edward Duffy, *Rousseau in England: The Context for Shelley's Critique of the Enlightenment* (Berkeley: U of California P, 1979), 33.

25. James K. Chandler, *Wordsworth's Second Nature: A Study of the Poetry and Politics* (Chicago: U of Chicago P, 1984), 98–104. See also Duffy, 34–35.

26. Duffy, 37–53.

27. This reading is largely indebted to Edward Duffy's *Rousseau in England,* which connects the light of Enlightenment reason with the light imagery of "The Triumph of Life" (106–51). Duffy, however, sees the "shape all light" as a positive force, a symbol of poetic imagination and Keatsian negative capability (128), an "obscure tenour" ("TL," 432) which opposes Rousseau's wrongheaded desire for Enlightenment reason and clarity, "something more definite and precise" (Duffy, 131).

28. Duffy, 130.

29. Ibid., 125.

30. Edmund Burke, "Letter to a Member of the National Assembly," *The Works of the Right Honorable Edmund Burke* (Boston: Little, Brown, 1889), 4:26.

31. Ibid., 4:24.

32. W. J. T. Mitchell, "Visible Language: Blake's Wond'rous Art of Writing," in *Romanticism and Contemporary Criticism,* ed. Morris Eaves and Michael Fischer (Ithaca: Cornell UP, 1986), 50; and Edmund Burke, *Reflections on the Revolution in France* (Garden City: Anchor Books, 1973), 90, 265. All further references to *Reflections,* abbreviated *RRF,* will appear in the text.

33. Burke, "Letter to a Member of the National Assembly," 4:25.

34. For Rousseau, see Duffy, 86. The most famous example of the Burke revival, which only became known years later, was Wordworth's inclusion and homage to Burke in the 1820 version of *The Prelude.*

35.
> Both Rousseau and Burke, approached and interpreted in the light of 1789 and what followed, have become in some degree symbols, and have entered what might be called the "mythology" of European history.... And as a rule the admirers and critics of Burke and Rousseau, though they agree in little else, are of one mind when it comes to locating the position of each in respect of the Revolution. Alfred Cobban writes of Rousseau that "his name was inevitably associated with the revolution, both with the popular disorders in which it began, and the excess of governmental authority in which it ended. For both these developments in turn he has been made chiefly responsible." Edmund Burke is viewed by friends and foes alike as the most eloquent spokesman of the counter-revolution, and he predicted and opposed both the phases Cobban describes above. (David Cameron, *The Social Thought of Rousseau and Burke: A Comparative Study* [Toronto: U of Toronto P, 1973], 165)

Cameron quotes Alfred Cobban from his *Rousseau and the Modern State,* rev. ed. (New York: George Allen and Unwin, 1964), 20.

36. "[The French Assembley acts] amidst the tumultuous cries of a mixed mob of ferocious men, and of women lost to shame . . ." (*RRF,* 81).

37. As Rousseau writes, "Là se firent les prémiéres fêtes, les pieds bondissoient de joye, le geste empressé ne suffisoit plus, la voix l'accompagnoit d'accens passionnés, le plaisir et le desir confondus ensemble se faisoient sentir à la fois" (Jean-Jacques Rousseau, *Essai sur l'origine des langues* [Bordeaux: Ducros, 1970], 123).

38. Burke's outcry could just have well been directed against the later installation of Rousseau in the pantheon of the Revolution's heroes; the procession toward the pantheon was a literal triumph that bore Rousseau's ashes. See the cover illustration of Chandler's book *Wordsworth's Second Nature, The Apotheosis of J. J. Rousseau and His Conveyance to the Pantheon (October 11, 1794),* from the *L'ancien moniteur,* 1794.

39. W. J. T. Mitchell, *Iconology: Image, Text, Ideology* (Chicago: U of Chicago P, 1986), 144.

40. Burke also exposes the mobility—and thus perhaps the instability—of his own iconoclastic vocabulary, by calling Reverend Peters a Catholic idolater, for example, the "Pontiff" (*RRF,* 79).

41. See Fredric Jameson, *The Political Unconscious: Narrative as a Socially Symbolic Act* (Ithaca: Cornell UP, 1981), 281–300, for one treatment of libidinal Utopian vision and collective history.

42. Arac, 110. For a discussion of deconstruction's investment in the concept of "rigor," see 97–110.

43. The Arc de Triomphe was begun in 1806 but was not completed until 1835. But another arch was built during Napoléon's reign, celebrating Austerlitz, at the Tuileries. (Napoléon originally wanted to build four triumphal arches in Paris, celebrating Marengo, Austerlitz, peace, and religion.) The arches were also part of a larger imperial discourse that flourished during Napoléon's reign, the Empire style of architecture which changed Paris. See Vincent Cronin, *Napoleon Bonaparte: An Intimate Biography* (New York: William Morrow, 1972), 302–18. For a discussion of the continuation of the rhetoric of the French Revolution in French and Western notions of politics and education, see Jean-François Lyotard, *The Postmodern Condition: A Report on Knowledge,* trans. Geoff Bennington and Brian Massumi (Minnesota: U of Minnesota P, 1984), 31–36.

44. De Man refers to the lines

> . . . much I grieved to think how power and will
> In opposition rule our mortal day—
>
> And why God made irreconcilable
> Good and the means of good.
> (ll. 228–31; "SD," 47)

Calling this passage on Bonaparte "banal," de Man sees these lines as relevant only insofar as they introduce how the difference between words and deeds operates through the figure of Rousseau and other historical figures ("SD," 47–50); this elision of Bonaparte in relation to historical action and language is precisely what I want to reintroduce in Shelley's poem.

45. This constant substitution of statuary parallels Jerrold E. Hogle's notion of "transference" in his *Shelley's Process: Radical Transference and the Development of His Major Works* (Oxford: Oxford UP, 1988). For Hogle, however, Shelley's "transference"—his "ceaseless transition between elements of thought"—is a liberating, politically progressive force, whereas what I am stressing here is how the substitution of statuary in "The Triumph of Life" functions as a critique of the liberation narrative with which Shelley's poem is trying to coincide. Hogle's specific reading of "The Triumph of Life," moreover, is concerned with the poem's classical and literary allusions, rather than the political ones I identify. See Hogle, 3–27, 319–42.

46. Paul de Man, *The Resistance to Theory* (Minneapolis: U of Minnesota P, 1986), 20.

47. Karl Marx, "The Eighteenth Brumaire of Louis Bonaparte," in *The Marx-Engels Reader,* ed. Robert C. Tucker (New York: Norton, 1978), 595.

48. Chantal Mouffe, "Radical Democracy: Modern or Postmodern?" in *Universal Abandon? The Politics of Postmodernism,* ed. Andrew Ross (Minneapolis: U of Minnesota P, 1988), 31.

49. See, for example, Lentricchia; and Terry Eagleton, *The Function of Criticism: From* The Spectator *to Post-Structuralism* (London: New Left Books, 1984), 100–104.

50. See, for example, Catherine Gallagher's description of the relation between New Left politics and literary studies as based on the political and cultural experience of "simply the collapse of representation itself" and how the role of deconstruction was then "to confirm New Left tenets and, at the very same time when the movement was losing momentum, to provide an explanation for that loss" (Gallagher, "Marxism and the New Historicism," in *The New Historicism,* ed. H. Aram Veeser [London: Routledge, 1989], 39–40).

51. See, for example, Ernesto Laclau's argument that one type of critique of de Man and *Le Soir* assumes an a priori definition of fascism in its analysis of de Man's early life and writings (Laclau, "Totalitarianism and Moral Indignation, *Diacritics* 20 [1990]: 88–95; Laclau directs his comments toward John Brenkman, "Fascist Commitments," in Hamacher, Hertz, and Keenan, 21–35; and John Brenkman and Jules David Law, "Resetting the Agenda," *Critical Inquiry* 15 [1989]: 804–11).

52. Marx, 595.

## Chapter 3: Allegories of Praxis

1. Herbert Lindenberger, *The History in Literature: On Value, Genre, Institutions* (New York: Columbia UP, 1990), 42–43.

2. Ibid., 43. For Lindenberger's historical objections to this term, see 83, 237.

3. I take the term *oppositional criticism* with all its attendant questions of inflation, validation, and inspiration from Gerald Graff, "Co-optation," in *The New Historicism,* ed. H. Aram Veeser (London: Routledge, 1989), 168–81; my own point of intervention begins, as it were, with Graff's citation of the book jacket of Walter Benn Michaels's *The Gold Standard and the Logic of Naturalism: American Literature at the Turn of the Century* (Berkeley: U of California P, 1987), in which Philip Fisher declares Michaels's book a break with an "exhausted oppositional criticism" (180).

4. I thus limit this discussion to critiques that are carried out within and by the academic community; the accusation of formalism is, in other words, rarely part of the heightened rhetoric of humanist and conservative critics attacking political and historical criticism during the so-called culture wars.

5. I would argue that one example of the former critique of "formalist poli-

tics" is Sam Weber's essay on Fredric Jameson in Weber's book *Institution and Interpretation* (Minneapolis: U of Minnesota P, 1987), 40–58. Two versions of the latter critique of formalism in New Historicism are Carolyn Porter, "Are We Being Historical Yet?" *South Atlantic Quarterly* 87 (1988): 743–86; and Alan Liu, "The Power of Formalism: The New Historicism," *ELH* 56 (1989): 721–71.

6. See, for example, Michael Ryan, *Marxism and Deconstruction: A Critical Articulation* (Baltimore: Johns Hopkins UP, 1982); and Gregory S. Jay, "Values and Deconstructions: Derrida, Saussure, and Marx," *Cultural Critique* 8 (1987): 153–96.

7. Jon Klancher, "English Romanticism and Cultural Production," in Veeser, 77. "Romantic opposition" refers, of course, to both an apolitical tendency among Romantic writers and the *reification* of that tendency among Romanticists in both the nineteenth and twentieth centuries.

8. Ibid, 80. See also Liu, 730–33.

9. Klancher, "English Romanticism," 77.

10. Ibid. See also Liu, 752.

11. Louis Montrose, "Professing the Renaissance: The Poetics and Politics of Culture," in Veeser, 26–27.

12. See Clifford Siskin, *The Historicity of Romantic Discourse* (Oxford: Oxford UP, 1988), 30–36, 56–62; Liu, "The Power of Formalism"; Alan Liu, *Wordsworth: The Sense of History* (Stanford: Stanford UP, 1989), 500–502; and Marjorie Levinson, "Back to the Future: Wordsworth's New Historicism," in *Rethinking Historicism: Critical Readings in Romantic History,* ed. Marjorie Levinson (Oxford: Basil Blackwell), 18–63. It has become more and more apparent that Levinson's work does not readily fit into the New Historicist mode; see Klancher's use of her project in "English Romanticism," 80–81.

The reflexive presence of an autocritique has also become increasingly visible in McGann's recent works, in the guise of his pseudonyms, "J. J. Rome" and "Anne Mack." See Jerome McGann, "Rethinking Romanticism," *ELH* 59 (1992): 748–53.

13. While decisively non-Foucaultian, the work of Walter Benn Michaels can thus be associated with that of Mark Seltzer and Philip Fisher and contrasted—no matter how reductively—to the adamantly revisionist Americanist work exemplified in *Boundary 2* 17 (1990). See Donald Pease's introductory essay, "New Americanists: Revisionist Interventions into the Canon," for an explicit argument for such revisionism (1–37).

14. Christopher Norris, *Paul de Man: Deconstruction and the Critique of Aesthetic Ideology* (London: Routledge, 1988), 5–17, 26.

15. See Siskin; and Frances Ferguson, "On the Numbers of Romanticisms," *ELH* 58 (1991): 471–98. See also the discussion of de Man, McGann, and Siskin in Paul Hamilton, " 'A Shadow of Magnitude': The Dialectic of Romantic Aesthetics," in *Beyond Romanticism: New Approaches to Texts and Contexts, 1780–1832,* ed. Stephen Copley and John Whale (London: Routledge, 1992), 11–31.

16. I thus associate Romanticism with the Enlightenment in the most general manner, with the latter simply defined as the *overarching* hegemonic discourse surrounding the eighteenth century's two bourgeois revolutions and Anglo-European calls for social reform. This association is obviously more complicated at a number of different levels, from the theoretical debate over Romanticism's simultaneous antagonism toward and debt to the Enlightenment to the more historically specific debate over, say, the relation of Blake's English radicalism to the politics of the French Revolution. For an introduction to the former issue, see Marshall Brown, "Romanticism and Enlightenment," in *The Cambridge Companion to British Romanticism,* ed. Stuart Curran (Cambridge: Cambridge UP, 1993), 25–47; for an example of the latter, see W. J. T. Mitchell, "Visible Language: Blake's Wond'rous Art of Writing," in *Romanticism and Contemporary Criticism,* ed. Morris Eaves and Michael Fischer (Ithaca: Cornell UP, 1986), 58–59.

17. Crane Brinton, *The Political Ideas of the English Romanticists* (London: Oxford UP, 1926), 4.

18. I refer to the way in which McGann's vocational identity as a Romanticist is initially based on him being a Byron specialist, an identification with Byron which—much like Erdman's with Blake and Cameron's with Shelley—allows McGann to reduplicate, as well as critique, the force of Byron's politics in a contemporary critical setting. Thus, while in *The Romantic Ideology* McGann does demonstrate the ideological blinds of Byron's own ironic imagination, the poet's more important role is to effect a familiar iconoclasm that disputes Abrams's totalizing definition of Romanticism in *Natural Supernaturalism (RI,* 26–27).

19. Graff, 168–81.

20. Such an explanation would then coincide with the material fact of the culmination of a number of Wordsworth-related editorial and biographical projects by the mid-1980s; for an account of such projects, see James K. Chandler, *Wordsworth's Second Nature: A Study of the Poetry and Politics* (Chicago: U of Chicago P, 1984), xx.

21. We should thus note that current uses of historical revisionism in the academy have differing political objectives. Thus, the Americanist attempt to include the diaspora of Native Americans and African Americans in American history has in part the tropological structure of a national confession similar to the German acknowledgment of the Holocaust. This confessional structure is not part of the emancipatory agenda found in Jacobin Romanticist historiography. At the other end of the political spectrum there is the recent attempt at revising—repudiating, that is—the Holocaust, a degraded empiricism whose fetishization of history actually preempts its participation in the problematic of revisionism practiced in 1980s American academic historicism. See Jean-François Lyotard, *The Differend: Phrases in Dispute,* trans. Georges Van Den Abbeele (Minneapolis: U of Minnesota P, 1988).

In *The Romantic Ideology* McGann does explicitly target a version of Enlightenment progressiveness in the form of Shelley's "implacable futurism" *(RI,*

118–23). My argument is that what McGann is able to critique ideologically at one level reappears and informs his politics, methodology, and rhetoric at other levels. That *The Romantic Ideology* is not really remembered for its analysis of Shelley supports, moreover, my explanation for the central role that Wordsworth has occupied in 1980s Romantic revisionism.

22. In *The Romantic Ideology* and his other works McGann often resorts to an antiformalist rhetoric. In *Social Values and Poetics Acts: A Historical Judgement of Literary Work* (Cambridge: Harvard UP, 1988), however, McGann does offer a four-part discursive field for contemporary criticism which explicitly accommodates "formalism (structuralism)" to historicism, deconstruction, and Marxism. The relation among these four discursive modes is dialogic, in that they exist "in relation to each other in a variety of uneasy half-connections, accommodations, and antitheses." Marxism, moreover, subtends the other three's hermeneutic value, holding them up "to the danger of inconsequence" (112–13). My chapter can thus be seen as pushing this dialogic model to the point where we can ask whether the relative stability of Marxist value in McGann is actually problematized by formal and deconstructive aspects of his critical identity and whether that problem is both expressed and generated by the ambivalent relation between his Marxist and historicist modes of inquiry.

23. See Jerome McGann, *A Critique of Modern Textual Criticism* (Chicago: U of Chicago P, 1983); *The Beauty of Inflections: Literary Investigations in Historical Method and Theory* (Oxford: Clarendon, 1985); *Social Values*, 152–94; *The Textual Condition* (Princeton: Princeton UP, 1991); "Rethinking Romanticism," *ELH* 59 (1992): 738–39; and "The Case of *The Ambassadors* and the Textual Condition," in *Palimpsest: Editorial Theory in the Humanities*, ed. George Bornstein and Ralph G. Williams (Ann Arbor: U of Michigan P, 1993), 151–66. See also the role materialism plays, in Klancher, "English Romanticism," 77–82; and Marjorie Levinson, *Wordsworth's Great Period Poems* (Cambridge: Cambridge UP, 1986), 14–57.

24. McGann, *Social Values*, 3, 121; Terry Eagleton, *The Ideology of the Aesthetic* (Oxford: Basil Blackwell, 1990), 9–10. For an exemplary discussion of the contradictory significations of materialism, see Ernesto Laclau and Chantal Mouffe, "Post-Marxism without Apologies," in Ernesto Laclau, *New Reflections on the Revolution of Our Time* (London: Verso, 1990), 103–12; see also Ferguson, 490–96.

25. McGann's example of such a reading is "Poem and Ideology: A Study of Keats's 'To Autumn'," in Geoffrey Hartman, *The Fate of Reading* (Chicago, U of Chicago P, 1975), 124–46.

26. Raymond Williams, *Culture and Society: 1780–1950* (New York: Columbia UP, 1983), 30.

27. This not to say that Williams's book receives an institutional reception that is stable and simple in its consequences. For a discussion of the history of the work's reception, see ibid., x–xi.

28. Ibid., 31–32.

29. Raymond Williams, *Marxism and Literature* (Oxford: Oxford UP, 1977), 75–82.

30. McGann, *Beauty of Inflections,* 62.

31. Roland Barthes, *Mythologies,* trans. Annette Lavers (New York: Hill and Wang, 1977), 123.

32. Hegel is discussed extensively but only as the main progenitor of the totalizing Romanticism that Abrams's reading of the British Romantics exemplifies (*RI,* 36–38, 40–48).

For McGann's own list of the primary critical responses to *The Romantic Ideology,* see McGann, "Rethinking Romanticism," nn. 7 and 8.

33. Heinrich Heine, *Heinrich Heine: Selected Works,* ed. and trans. Helen Mustard (New York: Random House, 1973), 259; all further references to this work, abbreviated *HH,* will appear in the text.

34. McGann sees this correspondence in Heine's earlier measure of Schlegel but is unable to associate this criticism with Uhland. If Schlegel occupies the role of M. H. Abrams, Uhland is equated with the British Romantics and the "actual" populace of the Middle Ages, all whose critical visions project themselves into a future ideological critique of Romanticism occupied by both Heine and McGann (*RI,* 34–35). For a discussion of the "general" leftist appropriation of *The Romantic School,* see Jeffrey L. Sammons, *Heinrich Heine: A Modern Biography* (Princeton: Princeton UP, 1979), 195.

35. Heinrich Heine, *Oeuvres complètes,* 16 vols.(Paris: Levy, 1895), 7:371. This collection is based on the original French editions of *De l'Allemagne* from 1835 and 1855.

Charles Godfrey Leland also cites these lines in Heinrich Heine, *The Works of Heinrich Heine,* 12 vols., trans. Charles Godfrey Leland (London: William Heinemann, 1906), 6:79.

36. Leland, 79 n. 1.

37. This is not to imply that Heine is simply accusing Uhland of being a direct agent of German imperialism; indeed, as an activist on behalf of his homeland of Swabia, Uhland remained throughout his life opposed to the hegemony of Prussia, which was the main agent of German adventurism throughout the century. I would still argue, however, that Heine is describing an effect of Uhland's poetry which connects a certain reading of Germany's past not only to German populist patriotism against Napoleon but *also* to the growth of an imperial German imaginary in that century.

38. Fredric Ewen, "Heinrich Heine: Humanity's Soldier," in *The Poetry and Prose of Heinrich Heine,* ed. Fredric Ewen (New York: Citadel, 1944), 6–7.

39. This irony is exacerbated by the likening by Heine of Uhland's horse to the "steed Bayard," whom Mustard describes as in "romances of chivalry a wonderful bay horse, remarkable for his spirit and for his unique ability to fit his size to his rider" (*HH,* 263). If Bayard is indeed known for magically fitting his rider, what does it mean for Uhland and his new "civic" existence that his horse is dead?

40. A more literal translation of the first part of the first sentence ("Schärferen Blicken als den meinigen will es nicht entgangen seyn") would be "It will not have escaped keener eyes than mine." The difference is slight but crucial, in that Mustard's translation focuses almost all of Heine's satire on those perceiving Uhland; I view his irony as much more uncontrolled, so that, in their hyperbolic condemnation of Uhland, Heine's lines might at first leave Uhland and target his critics but then, precisely because of the amount of condemnation, return to confirm the anachronistic absurdity of the poet's predicament.

41. Leland, 86 n. 1.

42. One could argue that, contrary to Leland, these lines forecast a Germany of Protestant liberalism which will in fact follow the example of France. At the very least, then, these concluding lines operate in an apocalyptic indeterminacy that foregrounds the historical moment of Heine's later readers as much as his prophetic powers; these lines thus operate at the same hermeneutically controversial pitch as the better-known debate that surrounds the conclusion of Heine's *Concerning the History of Religion and Philosophy in Germany,* written at the same time as *The Romantic School,* in which various critics have and have not seen a forecast of twentieth-century German fascism. See Mustard, "Introduction," *HH,* xiv.

We should also further note that, as Heine's ambivalence toward Uhland's Protestant activism implies, a progressive desire for a unified Germany is not simply discontinuous with the will to power of later German political and military adventurism. See n. 37.

43. Heine, *Oeuvres complètes,* 373. Also see Leland, 85.

44. By "text-centered" I mean that, while McGann's readings of the British Romantics do refer to historical events, none of the readings structure themselves around as vivid, specific, and insistent a model of transmission, reception, and intervention as Heine's reading of Uhland. *Like* McGann's reading of Uhland, however, the British poems also interiorize their own self-critiques, which further strengthens the text-centered sense of McGann's hermeneutic. Consider, for example, how Coleridge's "Kubla Khan" "haunts its own precincts with a fear that its genius may be a demon or a tyrant, and its paradise an illusion (or worse)" (*RI,* 103).

45. See Heinrich Heine, *Heinrich Heine: Sämtliche Schriften, Band 5,* ed. Karl Pörnbacher (Berlin: Ullstein Werkausgaben), 493; and Pörnbacher, *Band 6: Kommentar zu Band 5,* 906–7 n. 492. I am grateful to Elke Frederiksen for her invaluable help in these matters.

46. McGann, *Textual Condition,* 10.

47. McGann, "Rethinking Romanticism," 740.

48. For a lucid and powerful account of this aspect of Bloch's thought, see David Kaufmann, "Thanks for the Memory: Bloch, Benjamin, and the Philosophy of History," *Yale Journal of Criticism* 6 (Spring 1993): 143–62.

## Chapter 4: The Other Reasons

1. Mary Jacobus, *Romanticism, Writing, and Sexual Difference: Essays on The Prelude* (Oxford: Clarendon, 1989), 237–39.

2. The occasion for Jacobus's meditation is Kenneth Johnston's acknowledgment of Bloom and Hartman in his study *Wordsworth and the Recluse* (New Haven: Yale UP, 1984), xxv.

3. See, for example, Rey Chow's suggestive distinction between this split's presence in feminist studies and its absence in Marxism, in Rey Chow, "Response," *Polygraph* 6–7 (1993): 209–11.

4. William Wordsworth, *Selected Poems and Prefaces*, ed. Jack Stillinger (Boston: Houghton Mifflin, 1965), 146. For discussions of the relation of the narrator to the later poets and of the general themes of duplication and inheritance, see James K. Chandler, *Wordsworth's Second Nature: A Study of the Poetry and Politics* (Chicago: U of Chicago P, 1984), 162–68; Sydney Lea, "Wordsworth and His 'Michael': The Pastor Passes," *ELH* 45 (1978): 58; and Peter J. Manning, " 'Michael,' Luke, and Wordsworth," *Criticism* 19 (1977): 195–211.

5. Thus, "Michael" recognizes a thwarted entailment and the dislocations impinging upon turn-of-the-century English agrarian life, yet the poem does so only to transcend such discontinuities as a pastoral that traces its own genealogy not back to Pope but, rather, to the "actual misfortunes of a family at Grasmere" (*The Norton Anthology of Literature,* ed. M. H. Abrams, vol. 2, 4th ed. [New York: Norton, 1979], 195 n. 1.) Conversely, the poem's self-interpellation as a pastoral can be seen not only as an interventionary refunctioning and denial of Pope's pastoral bequest but also as a highly conflicted *confession* about the continuity between "Michael" and that bequest, insofar as the narrator's peripatetic wanderings much more resemble the activities of the pastoral shepherd than the labor-intensive life of either Michael, the "actual" Grasmere family, or the georgic farmer. Thus, in its (attempted) seizing of the generic patronymic name, the poem's title—and entitlement—displays its anxiety over the impossibility of its origins.

6. As his essays on Wordsworth in *The Rhetoric of Romanticism* (New York: Columbia UP, 1984) show, de Man does not deny this inheritance, only that it is one of salvational transcendence rather than the linguistic violence of Shelley and Rousseau. One could argue that McGann's and 1980s Romantic historiography is the assertion of Wordsworth's inheritance as the naturalization of political apostasy, a lesson that we must work hard to *avoid.*

Beyond Wordsworth and Romantic studies the flip side to the predicament of a female critic "cross-dressing" as Wordsworth would be the issue of male scholars practicing feminist criticism. This issue approaches from another angle the same derealizing questions of biology and culture which the relation of feminism and Romantic studies addresses. See Alice Jardine and Paul Smith, eds., *Men in Feminism* (New York: Methuen, 1987); and Joseph A. Boone and

Michael Cadden, eds. *Engendering Men: The Question of Male Feminist Criticism* (New York: Routledge, 1990).

7. For the linking of Dorothy's predicament to that of Mary Shelley's, see Marlon Ross, *The Contours of Masculine Desire: Romanticism and the Rise of Women's Poetry* (Oxford: Oxford UP, 1989), 3–5.

8. Thus, Dorothy's predicament also reveals how patrimony elides the metonymic dimension within its legitimating metaphoric dynamics—how patrimony naturalizes, in other words, the authority of its historical contingencies.

9. See, for example, Kurt Heinzelman, "The Cult of Domesticity: Dorothy and William Wordsworth at Grasmere," in *Romanticism and Feminism,* ed. Anne K. Mellor (Bloomington: Indiana UP, 1988), 52–78.

10. The question remains about why feminist Romantic studies appear much later than contemporary feminist studies, which begins to explode in the mid-1970s. I would suggest that a large part of this belatedness is simply the fact of the monopoly that deconstructive and ideological criticism has on Romanticism as exemplary modes of critical practices until the mid-1980s. I would also add that feminist Romantic studies arguably begins much earlier in a displaced form, through feminist works in Victorian studies which touch upon both male and female Romantic writers; the classic example of this criticism would, of course, be Sandra M. Gilbert and Susan Gubar, *The Madwoman in the Attic: The Woman Writer and the Nineteenth-Century Literary Imagination* (New Haven: Yale UP, 1979).

11. Mellor, 3. Issued in 1988, Mellor's anthology is itself part of this disciplinary inception.

12. One large reason for the initial focus upon this "outer" orbit of writers would simply be material; the archival recovery of a wider variety of female writers and their texts begins on a large scale only in the last part of the 1980s. It is thus only in the recent past that such texts have been anthologized and made available to a larger audience. See, for example, Charlotte Smith, *The Poems of Charlotte Smith,* ed. Stuart Curran (Oxford: Oxford UP, 1993).

13. The different ways that Poovey and Homans use Romanticism especially indicate how the intersection of gender and Romantic studies is at this earlier point a particularly instrumental event. For Homans, Romanticism is most explicitly tied to the psycholinguistic quest-romance of the male poet, one that constantly transforms the desired feminine maternal figure into silent nature (Margaret Homans, *Bearing the Word: Language and Female Experience in Nineteenth-Century Women's Writing* [Chicago: U of Chicago P, 1986], 10); for Poovey the concept of Romanticism is mostly a generic and cultural one, tied to the bourgeois expectations of romance novels and a sentimental literature (Mary Poovey, *The Proper Lady and the Woman Writer: Ideology as Style in the Works of Mary Wollstonecraft, Mary Shelley and Jane Austen* [Chicago: U of Chicago P, 1984], 38, 108–9). The point is not that there should be a monolithic use of Romanticism by these critics or that any of them even use Romanticism in one way—only that their diverse uses of *romance* suggests a more dispersed and indeterminate relation between these works than a term such as

*feminist Romanticist studies* suggests. See also, however, Mary Jacobus, "The Buried Letter: *Villette,"* in *Reading Women: Essays in Feminist Criticism* (New York: Columbia UP, 1986), 41–61, which does anticipate the self-reflexive questions about feminism's and Romanticism's relation which I want to pursue.

The other point that needs to be stressed is that these works do not relate to the larger disciplinary history of feminist studies per se in a simply arbitrary manner. Within this larger disciplinary context all these works argue in a variety of ways for a noncontingent relation between the category of gender and literary studies.

14. The key phrase in my description of this archival recovery is "present institutionalized links"; that is, while many of these female writers might have been active members of the same literary culture as our presently canonized Romantics, it is precisely the memory of their links to such a culture which has to be recovered. Thus, their contemporary institutional relation to the mainstream canon necessarily differs from that of the "outer" orbit of female writers already circling the Romantic canon such as Wollstonecraft, Austen, Shelley, and the Brontës.

15. As Marlon Ross argues, "As we recover [the female writers of the late eighteenth and early nineteenth centuries] we must be sure not to examine them in isolation. Too wary of wedding them erroneously to the romantic movement, we may stray too far in the other direction and forget their complex interrelations with romantic discourse" (6).

16. Stuart Curran, "Romantic Poetry: The I Altered," in Mellor, 203. See also Curran, 187–89, for a fuller account of how complex the chronology of these female writers is.

17. See, for example, how Stanley Cavell uses the "ordinary" in Wordsworth and Coleridge to connect Romanticism to a wider tradition of Western philosophy in Stanley Cavell, *In Quest of the Ordinary: Lines of Skepticism and Romanticism* (Chicago: U of Chicago P, 1988), 50–75.

18. For the argument that gender studies should retain the term *Romanticism* on both pragmatic curricular and theoretical grounds—that the rediscovered female writers will most readily be taught in established Romantic courses and that such women can revitalize Romanticism's "revolutionary and utopian" connotations—see Anne Mellor, *Romanticism and Gender* (New York: Routledge, 1993), 210–12.

19. I refer specifically to the first part of Mellor's book, on "masculine Romanticism" (ibid., 13–29); the rest of her text dwells on a wide-ranging feminine Romantic culture constructed by both female writers of the "outer" Romantic orbit and female authors who have been recently rediscovered in the last decade. Likewise, I refer to the first half of Ross's book; the second part of his project engages with how a number of female writers from Mary Tighe to Felicia Hemans responded to the dominant masculine Romantic culture. *Romanticism and Gender* and *The Contours of Masculine Desire* are thus two of the first works to engage explicitly and comprehensively with both of the critical impulses that inform the intersection of feminism and Romanticism today.

20. One recent attempt to manage this dialectical oscillation is to associate the essentialism of biology with "sex," the nonessentialism of culture with "gender," and the political consequences of this distinction with "feminism." By locating the split between biology and culture within gender, I want to explore how gender might actually be subtended by this oscillation—by the fact that a "pure" state of nonessentialism might be itself an essentialist mystification.

21. See, for example, Laura Claridge's critique of how Ross assigns a feminine gender and a particular set of values to Dickens's sentimentalism, in her review of *The Contours of Masculine Desire* (*Keats-Shelley Journal* 40 [1991]: 174); and Mellor's own methodological self-qualification that the opposition between a "feminine" and "masculine" Romanticism is itself deeply grounded in a binary of Sameness and Otherness which historically defines the philosophy of "masculine" Romanticism (Mellor, *Romanticism and Gender*, 3–4).

22. Jacobus, "Buried Letter," 59.

23. Mellor, *Romanticism and Gender*, 4.

24. See Irving Babbitt, *Rousseau and Romanticism* (Boston: Houghton Mifflin, 1919), 133; and Alan Richardson, "Romanticism and the Colonization of the Feminine," in Mellor, *Romanticism and Feminism*, 13–25. Ross responds to Richardson's argument by suggesting how "two interrelated phenomena occur simultaneously: the male writers' colonization of the feminine and their attempt to separate their own self-possessing poetic endeavors from the very feminine which they appropriate" (Ross, 318–19). It is precisely a more *radical* sense of this "simultaneous" movement which I want to insist upon as the ground for a more disruptive sense of how gender circulates throughout these various writers' texts.

25. In recognizing such a surplus, we must, however, keep in mind Jacobus's admonishment about how linguistic indeterminacy means different things for different people: "Let us not forget that while Wordsworth himself is allowed to wander freely in pursuit of signs, for Lucy Gray one slip means the end" (Jacobus, *Sexual Difference*, 266). The point is thus not to create a homogeneous formalism out of gender's semiotic circulation but, rather, to use that circulation to pinpoint more precisely the unequal relations of power which are the brute facts of gender difference. See also Homans's concept of "differential valuation" in *Bearing the Word*, 5.

26. It is thus no accident that one of the most comprehensive and ambitious attempts at such a historiography—Ross's study *The Contours of Masculine Desire*—is also one of the most complex; see his explanation of the "dialectic" created by his "quadruple focus" upon the male High Romanticists, the female writers, the female writers' influence upon the male Romanticists, and masculine Romanticism's influence upon the female writers (Ross, 6). My own interests can be described as intensifying the dialectical exchange between such discrete identities to see whether or not the gendered assignations to such historical and cultural monads become unmoored—and, then, whether the monads' very discreteness comes into question.

27. See, for example, Ross, 37, 207–8; and Richardson, 13. Sentimentality

and sensibility also play a role in Poovey, 18, 38; and Jacobus, "Buried Letter," 59. Thus, if there is a candidate for the *point de capiton* that holds together the contingency of the initial relation between gender and Romantic studies, it would be the topic of "feeling"; this concept does not, however, play a major role in either of Homans's first two works or Jacobus's study *Sexual Difference*. See also Julie Ellison, *Delicate Subjects: Romanticism, Gender, and the Ethics of Understanding* (Ithaca: Cornell UP, 1990). For a recent work on the feelings which does not focus on gender alone, see John Morillo, "Bordering on Enthusiasm: Wordsworth and Crimes of Passion" (MS).

28. Michel Foucault, *Language, Counter-Memory, Practice: Selected Essays and Interviews,* ed. Donald F. Bouchard, trans. Donald F. Bouchard and Sherry Simon (Ithaca: Cornell UP, 1977), 131.

29. Wollstonecraft is, moreover, relevant to the issue of intellectual legacy as an agent of intervention as well as an object of transmission. See, for example, how Wollstonecraft intervenes into the pedagogical structure of transmission and reception which Rousseau's *Emile* devises in Jacobus, *Sexual Difference,* 242–47.

30. Paula McDowell and Susan Lanser have pointed out to me that it would be highly unlikely for any female writer of that time to dedicate her work to her mother; thus, the uncanniness of the absence of Wollstonecraft in Shelley's dedication is not only the emblematic discontinuity between Wollstonecraft and later feminist writers but also the link of that emblem to the overdetermination of cultural and social forces in Shelley's own time. For a meditation on the problematic, and exemplary, relation between Wollstonecraft and a contemporary feminist "daughter," Luce Irigaray, see Jacobus, *Reading Woman,* 276–92.

31. As Katharine M. Rogers writes: "Widely admired during her lifetime, Wollstonecraft shortly after her death was vilified by her enemies and her work was ignored by her friends. Her reputation was so bad by the nineteenth century that several leading feminists repudiated her. . . . Even Wollstonecraft's friend [Mary] Hays omitted her from her five-volume *Female Biography* in 1803" (*Feminism in Eighteenth-Century England* [Urbana: U of Illinois P, 1982], 3, 5).

In the twentieth century this harsh evaluation of Wollstonecraft reaches its nadir with Ferdinand Lundberg and Marynia Farnham's reductive psychoanalytic work, *Modern Woman: The Lost Sex* (New York: Harper and Row, 1947) 144–45, 159–63. Lundberg and Farnham's text if full of such choice pronouncements as "That Mary Wollstonecraft was an extreme neurotic of a compulsive type there can be no doubt. . . . Only deeply disturbed women—disturbed by the nature of their childhood upbringing in the shattered home and the constricted circumstances they encountered in adult life—could have drawn what they supposed was pure wisdom from *A Vindication"* (159, 161–62).

32. Rogers, 3. See also Barbara Taylor, *Eve and the New Jerusalem: Socialism and Feminism in the Nineteenth Century* (New York: Pantheon, 1983), 9–12; and Alice Browne, *The Eighteenth Century Feminist Mind* (Detroit: Wayne State UP, 1987), 170. Wollstonecraft, needless to say, saw a necessary

continuum between her two positions. For a discussion of England's reception of Rousseau, see Duffy, 37–53.

33. Just as Rousseau's *Confessions* affected the interpretation of his political and social theory, so too did Godwin's biography of Wollstonecraft provide anti-Jacobinists and antifeminists with the tools to attack *The Rights of Woman*. For a discussion of the effects of the publication of Rousseau's autobiography in England, see Duffy, 32–53; for a discussion of how Godwin's biography of Wollstonecraft affected her intellectual and political reputation, see Browne, 170–73.

34. Jacobus, "Buried Letter," 59.

35. Thus, Mary Poovey portrays Wollstonecraft's duality in the ideological terms of the two literary discourses open to her as a woman, sentimental fiction and the "how-to" texts of "the proper lady." Relying heavily on Wollstonecraft's biography, Poovey turns Wollstonecraft's life and texts into a seamless narrative of a figure, "Wollstonecraft," who is, on the whole, blind to the limits of the discourses structuring her life and writing (Poovey, 48–113). Likewise, Cora Kaplan sees in Wollstonecraft's supposed privileging of male reason over female sentiment a fear of the female body—a fear that duplicates current debates over the role of female sexuality and pleasure in contemporary feminist agendas (Cora Kaplan, "Wild Nights: Pleasure/Sexuality/Feminism," *Sea Changes: Essays on Culture and Feminism* [London: Verso, 1986], 31–57). Both Kaplan and Poovey primarily associate imagination in Wollstonecraft with a sexuality that the Romantic writer tries to occlude; in contrast, Mary Jacobus associates Wollstonecraft's imagination not only with passion but also with the irreducible errancy, the "madness," of language itself (*Reading Woman,* 33–34). Thus, unlike Poovey, Jacobus looks for the repressed effects of imagination not in Wollstonecraft's biography but, instead, in the rhetorical effects of her writing. Still, Jacobus has not really altered the Wollstonecraft paradigm that she, like Poovey and Kaplan, has inherited. She merely transfers Wollstonecraft's subversive Otherness from Wollstonecraft's biography to her literary works.

An influential recent precursor of this critical plot which emphasizes the duality in Wollstonecraft as one between femininity and masculinity is Margaret Walters's essay "The Rights and Wrongs of Women: Mary Wollstonecraft, Harriet Martineau, and Simone de Beauvoir," in *The Rights and Wrongs of Women,* ed. Ann Oakley and Juliet Mitchell (London: Penguin, 1976), 304–29.

36. For a reading of Wollstonecraft's acknowledgment of female writing, see Jacobus, "Difference of View," 32–33; for a reading of female desire, see Kaplan, 35, 159. For Poovey the movement from *The Rights of Woman* to *The Wrongs of Woman* is both a progress and a decline. On the one hand, Poovey sees *The Rights of Woman* as exhibiting a frustration over the split between Wollstonecraft's professional and sexual identities, a split that the later works confront more directly; yet Poovey also sees this later confrontation hampered by a reification of the bourgeois self which *The Rights of Woman* seeks to deny (80–81, 94–113). For the argument that *The Wrongs of Woman* actually has more in common with *The Rights of Woman* than Wollstonecraft's first novel,

*Mary, A Fiction* (1788), see Laurie Langbauer, "An Early Romance: Motherhood and Women's Writing in Mary Wollstonecraft's Novels," in Mellor, *Romanticism and Feminism,* 209–11.

37. As Denise Riley points out, one can refute the essential nature of "woman" while still believing in some other hypostatized agent, such as "women." (See her study *"Am I That Name?": Feminism and the Category of "Women" in History* [Minneapolis: U of Minnesota P, 1988], 2–3.) In my critique, however, I do not distinguish between the terms *woman, women,* and the *feminine* precisely because I see Wollstonecraft's rejection of the gendered duality between reason and imagination as a rejection of the ontological assumptions that would allow for the reification of all three terms.

38. Mary Wollstonecraft, *A Vindication of the Rights of Woman,* ed. Carol H. Poston (New York: Norton, 1975), 6; intro. All further references to this work will appear in the text. For further reference to other editions I have cited chapters as well as page numbers.

39. See Timothy J. Reiss, "Revolution in Bounds: Wollstonecraft, Women, and Reason," in *Gender and Theory: Dialogues on Feminist Criticism,* ed. Linda Kauffman (Oxford: Basil Blackwell, 1989), 12–21, 39–44. From the same book see also Frances Ferguson's rebuttal to Reiss, "Wollstonecraft Our Contemporary" (51–62).

40. Ernesto Laclau and Chantal Mouffe, *Hegemony and Socialist Strategy: Toward a Radical Democratic Politics* (London: Verso, 1985), 154.

41. "Hegemonic practices are suturing insofar as their field of operation is determined by the openness of the social, by the ultimately unfixed character of every signifier. This original lack is precisely what the hegemonic practices try to fill in. A *totally* sutured society would be one where this filling-in would have reached its ultimate consequences and would have, therefore, managed to identify itself with the transparency of a closed symbolic order. Such a closure of the social is, as we will see, impossible" (ibid., 88). See also 127–34.

42. The quote by Rousseau which Wollstonecraft responds to is: "Educate [women] like men. The more women are like men, the less power they will have over men, and then men will be masters indeed" (Jean-Jacques Rousseau, *Emile,* trans. Barbara Foxely [London: J. M. Dent, 1911], 327).

43. I do not exaggerate when I claim that Wollstonecraft's analysis operates at the level of "forces"; the sentence I cite is in her chapter entitled "Animadversions on Some of the Writers Who Have Rendered Women Objects of Pity, Bordering on Contempt," which, as its title suggests, surveys and evaluates the cultural effect of a century's worth of literature aimed at conferring onto "woman" a single identity.

44. I am indebted to Richard A. Strier for pointing out to me that Wollstonecraft's reference to masturbation ("vices which render the body weak") is specifically aimed not at girls but at boys. Earlier Wollstonecraft does refer to girls who might learn "nasty or immodest habits" from one another in nurseries and boarding schools (127; chap.7).

45. While she does not refer to the same passage on masturbation which I

analyze, the most vivid example of this model of repression, articulated at the level of both style and sexuality, is offered by Kaplan, 34–50.

46. After this passage Wollstonecraft once again refers to the "bad habits which females acquire when they are shut up together," thus stressing that masturbation is a literal fact for girls as well as boys (165; chap. 12).

47. Richard A. Strier has pointed out to me that, for someone like Wollstonecraft, who came out of the Protestant tradition of dissent, this solipsistic imagination would also have been associated with a Catholic sensibility. For a recent reading of Wollstonecraft with a view on sexuality and experience similar to mine, see Langbauer, 210. Also, Wollstonecraft's critique of sentimental fiction is inscribed within the same polemic against female confinement and repression: "There are the women who are amused by the reveries of the stupid novelists, who, knowing little of human nature, work up stale tales, and describe meretricious scenes, all retailed in a sentimental jargon, which equally tend to corrupt the taste, and draw the heart aside from its daily duties. I do not mention the understanding, because never having been exercised, its slumbering energies rest inactive, like the lurking particles of fire which are supposed universally to pervade matter" (183; chap. 13).

Thus, sentimental fiction actually keeps the mind from experience, confining understanding and rendering it passive, much like the way schools restrict the exercise and activities of young girls. (And, while the negative view of fiction does privilege reason over emotion, the analogy between reason and the schoolgirls disrupts any facile reification of the male reason–female emotion split.) In the same vein Wollstonecraft also argues that the reading of sentimental fiction is better than no reading at all, since such fiction at least gives women some experience, even if it is the wrong kind (184; chap. 13).

48. There is evidence that suggests that Wollstonecraft paints this picture of Rousseau with knowledge of his own literary references to masturbation. Consider, for example, this passage from a review of *The Confessions* in the *Analytical Review* which critics have attributed to Wollstonecraft: "his most enthusiastic admirers must allow that his imagination was sometimes rampant, and breaking loose from his judgement, sketched some alluring pictures, whose colouring was more natural, than chaste, yet over which, with the felicity of genius, he has thrown those voluptuous shades, that, by setting the fancy to work, prove a dangerous snare, when the hot blood dances in the veins" (*Analytic Review* 11 [December 1791]; quoted in Duffy, 48). As Duffy writes, "the *Analytical*'s critique of Rousseauean sensibility coincides exactly with the anti-Rousseauean message of [Wollstonecraft's] *Vindication of the Rights of Woman*" (48–49). We can also note the similarity between the *Analytical*'s passage, the Wollstonecraft quote, and this piece from *The Confessions,* in which Rousseau explicitly connects the imagination to masturbation:

> I had preserved my physical but not my moral virginity. . . . The progress of the years had told upon me, and my restless temperament had at last made itself felt. . . . [I] learned that dangerous means of cheating Nature,

which leads in young men of my temperament to various kinds of excesses, that eventually imperil their health, their strength, and sometimes their lives. This vice, which shame and timidity find so convenient, has a particular attraction for lively imaginations. It allows them to dispose, so to speak, of the whole female sex at their will, and to make any beauty who tempts them serve their pleasure without the need of first containing consent. (Jean-Jacques Rousseau, *The Confessions,* trans. J. M. Cohen [London: Penguin, 1953], 108–9)

The most thorough treatment of Rousseau and masturbation is, of course, Jacques Derrida's essay ". . . That Dangerous Supplement . . . ," in *Of Grammatology,* trans. Gayatri Chakravorty Spivak (Baltimore: Johns Hopkins UP, 1974), 141–64.

49. "There is indeed much in [Rousseau's] make-up that reminds one less of a man than a high-strung woman. . . . By subordinating judgment to sensibility Rousseau may be said to have made woman the measure of all things" (Babbitt, 130–32).

50.
> Throughout your letter [i.e., Burke's *Reflections*] you frequently advert to a sentimental jargon, which has long been current in conversation, and even in books of morals, though it never received the *regal* stamp of reason. A kind of mysterious instinct is *supposed* to reside in the soul, that instantaneously discerns truth, without the tedious labor of ratiocination. This instinct . . . has been termed *common sense,* and more frequently *sensibility;* and by a kind of *indefeasible* right, it has been *supposed,* for rights of this kind are not easily proved, to reign paramount over the other faculties of the mind, and to be an authority from which there is not appeal. . . . [This sensibility] dips, we know not why, granting it to be an infallible instinct, and, though supposed always to point to truth, its pole star, the point is always shifting, and seldom stands due north. (Mary Wollstonecraft, *A Vindication of the Rights of Men* [Delmar: Scholar's Facsimiles, 1975], 68–69)

For an extended analysis of Wollstonecraft's critique of Burke's emotional sensibility, see James T. Boulton, *The Language of Politics in the Age of Wilkes and Burke* (London: Routledge and Kegan Paul, 1963), 168–76.

51. Thus Wollstonecraft attacks the assumptions of gender that underwrite Burke's duality between a masculine sublime and feminine beautiful in his study *Philosophical Enquiry into the Origin of Our Ideas of the Sublime and the Beautiful* (1757) and then she asserts how Burke is himself actually inscribed not in the sublime but, rather, in the beautiful (*Rights of Men,* 111–21, 138–42).

Wollstonecraft also associates Burke's sensibility with a "personal pique" and a "hurt vanity"—those very traits of egomania which Burke attacks in Rousseau (110).

52. Elsewhere, in praising the writing of Catherine Macaulay, Wollstonecraft takes pains *not* to associate Macaulay's thought with the masculine: "I will not call [Macaulay's] a masculine understanding, because I admit not of such an arrogant assumption of reason; but I contend that it was a sound one, and that her judgment, the matured fruit of profound thinking, was a proof that a woman can acquire judgment, in the full extent of the word" (105, chap. 5).

53. See Poovey, 58–59; and Chandler, *Wordsworth's Second Nature,* 63. See also n. 45.

54. This is exactly Boulton's final point about *The Rights of Men* (Boulton, 172–76).

55. For a discussion of Price's vision and Burke's repudiation of it, see W. J. T. Mitchell, *Iconology: Image, Text, Ideology* (Chicago: U of Chicago P, 1986), 144–46.

56. For an elaboration of the strong poststructuralist sense of Gramsci's "hegemony," see Laclau and Mouffe, *Hegemony,* 93–148.

57. Annette Kolodny, "Dancing between Left and Right: Feminism and the Academic Minefield in the 1980s," in *Literature, Language and Politics,* ed. Betty Jean Craige (Athens: U of Georgia P, 1988), 27–38.

58. See ibid.; and Janet Todd, *Feminist Literary History* (New York: Routledge, 1988), 1–16.

## Chapter 5: American Askesis

1. Harold Bloom, *Agon: Towards a Theory of Revisionism* (Oxford: Oxford UP, 1982), 19, 39. All further references to *Agon,* abbreviated *A,* will appear in the text. The exception to this apolitical iconoclasm in Bloom is how he has been recuperated, oddly enough, by feminist readings of Romanticism. See Marlon Ross, *The Contours of Masculine Desire: Romanticism and the Rise of Women's Poetry* (Oxford: Oxford UP, 1989), 22–23.

2. While Bloom does explicitly cite his relationship to the pragmatism of Richard Rorty and William James in *Agon* (16–53), his other intellectual touchstones make it difficult to label him as simply the representative figure of American pragmatism in the academy today—a position that Rorty would much more easily occupy. For a discussion of contemporary American pragmatism as a recognizable "school" in the humanities today, see Giles Gunn, *Thinking across the American Grain: Ideology, Intellect, and the New Pragmatism* (Chicago: U of Chicago P, 1992). While Emerson appears often in Gunn's book, Bloom's presence is noticeably, and tellingly, much less strong. See also Cornel West, *The American Evasion of Philosophy: A Genealogy of Pragmatism* (Madison: U of Wisconsin P, 1989). Finally, for a discussion of what is involved in relating pragmatism to Emerson, see David M. Robinson, *Emerson and the Conduct of Life: Pragmatism and Ethical Purpose in the Later Work* (Cambridge: Cambridge UP, 1993), 3–4.

3. For an explanation of Bloom's rivalry with his Continental contemporaries as a Bloomian family romance, see Frank Lentricchia, *After the New Criticism* (Chicago: U of Chicago P, 1980), 326.

4. For two accounts of this migratory narrative of the Romantic self, see David Fite, *Harold Bloom: The Rhetoric of Romantic Vision* (Amherst: U of Massachusetts P, 1985), 91–122; and David Wyatt, "Bloom, Freud, and 'America' " *Kenyon Review* 6 (1984): 59–66.

5. Ralph Waldo Emerson, *Emerson in His Journals,* ed. Joel Porte (Cambridge: Harvard UP, 1982), 236.

6. Jonathan Arac, *Critical Genealogies: Historical Situations for Postmodern Literary Studies* (New York: Columbia UP, 1987), 11–12.

7. See ibid., 21–23; Lentricchia, *After the New Criticism,* 344; Edward Said, "Interview," *Diacritics* 6 (1976): 34; and Fite, 190–91. For an argument that Bloom's theories actually allow for a communal sense of our past, see Donald Pease, *Visionary Compacts: American Renaissance Writings in Cultural Context* (Madison: U of Wisconsin P), 209–13.

8. Harold Bloom, *The Anxiety of Influence: A Theory of Poetry* (Oxford: Oxford UP, 1973), 15. All further references to *Anxiety,* abbreviated *AI,* will appear in the text.

9. Harold Bloom, *A Map of Misreading* (New York: Oxford UP, 1975), 23; and *Poetry and Repression: Revisionism from Blake to Stevens* (New Haven: Yale UP, 1976), 244. All further references to *Map* and *Poetry,* abbreviated *MM* and *PR,* respectively, will appear in the text.

10. This recontainment of the collective world by the giant body of the individual figure is precisely what Fredric Jameson identifies in the Blakean giant that exemplifies the fourth and ultimate level of Northrop Frye's "Theory of Symbols"; see Fredric Jameson, *The Political Unconscious: Narrative as a Socially Symbolic Act* (Ithaca: Cornell UP, 1981), 70–74.

11. Ralph Waldo Emerson, "Nature," in *Selected Writings of Emerson,* ed. Donald McQuade (New York: Modern Library, 1981), 39. Cited in *A,* 165.

12. Ibid., 41.

13. Harold Bloom, *Figures of Capable Imagination* (New York: Seabury P, 1976), 63. I am thus not so much interested in discerning the "truth" of Bloom's interpretation of Emerson's vocabulary of "transparency" as pointing out how that interpretation is linked to a larger visual logic at work in Bloom. One could, of course, argue a position the opposite of Bloom's: that Emerson's "transparent eyeball" evinces a transcendentalism that does not assert but, rather, dissolves the subject's discrete position in the world.

14. See Oliver Wendell Holmes, *Ralph Waldo Emerson* (Boston: Houghton Mifflin, 1885); Ralph Rusk, *The Life of Ralph Waldo Emerson* (New York: Charles Scribner's Sons, 1949); Stephen Whicher, *Freedom and Fate: An Inner Life of Ralph Waldo Emerson* (Philadelphia: U of Pennsylvania P, 1953); David Marr, *American Worlds since Emerson* (Amherst: U of Massachusetts P, 1988), 3–72; West, 17–25; and Sacvan Bercovitch, "Emerson, Individualism, and the Ambiguities of Dissent," *South Atlantic Quarterly* 89 (1990): 623–62. The last three are contemporary readings that all consider the limits of Emerson's political thinking; of the three Marr comes closest to seeing the Emersonian self as a form of absolute apolitical idealism; Bercovitch comes

closest to seeing Emerson's "individualism" as a form of cultural, if not "simply" political, praxis.

For a discussion of how Holmes's work especially erased Emerson's career as an antiabolitionist, see Len Gougeon, *Virtue's Hero: Emerson, Antislavery, and Reform* (Athens: U of Georgia P, 1990), 3, 7–12.

15. See, for example, Bloom's discussion of Emerson's anger at the Fugitive Slave Act in Bloom, "Introduction," *Ralph Waldo Emerson,* ed. Harold Bloom (New York: Chelsea House, 1985), 1–4. For the argument that Bloom mostly conveys the melancholy defeat of the American Sublime's defiance of the past, see Lawrence Buell, "The Emerson Industry in the 1980s: A Survey of Trends and Achievements," *ESQ* 30 (1984): 126.

16. See Gougeon, 86–250; and Robinson, 124–33.

17. Robinson, 89–111.

18. Julie Ellison, "The Edge of Urbanity: Emerson's *English Traits,*" *ESQ* 32 (1986): 96–97; Philip L. Nicoloff, *Emerson on Race and History: An Examination of "English Traits"* (New York: Columbia UP, 1961), 97–135; Robinson, 116; and West, 28–31. See also the connection that Dale T. Knobel makes between Emerson's racial theories and the American sterotype of the immigrant Irish "Paddy," in *Paddy and the Republic: Ethnicity, Nationality in Antebellum America* (Middletown: Wesleyan UP, 1986), 83, 110, 120.

19. West, 31–32.

20. Ralph Waldo Emerson, *English Traits,* in McQuade, 522. All further references to *English Traits,* abbreviated *ET,* will appear in the text.

21. For a reading of chapter 1 as an implicit Bloomian drama of influence, see Julie Ellison, *Emerson's Romantic Style* (Princeton: Princeton UP, 1984), 66–67, 70.

22. As Emerson writes in his 1849 essay "Power," the "necessity of balancing and keeping at bay the snarling majorities of German, Irish, and of native millions, will bestow promptness, address, and reason, at last, on our buffalo-hunter, and authority and majesty of manners" (cited in Jenny Franchot, *Roads to Rome: The Antebellum Protestant Encounter with Catholicism* [Berkeley: U of California P, 1994], 5). See also Knobel's implicit placement of Emerson within the larger reaction of New England "elite culture" against Irish immigration, in Knobel, 70.

23. Jameson describes the term thus:

> For the dynamic of *rationalization*—Weber's term, which Lukács will strategically retranslate as *reification* in *History and Class Consciousness*—is a complex one in which the traditional or "natural" *(naturwüchsige)* unities, social forms, human relations, cultural events, even religious systems, are systematically broken up in order to be reconstructed more efficiently, in the form of new post-natural processes or mechanisms; but in which, at the same time, these now isolated broken bits and pieces of the older unities acquire a certain autonomy of their own, a semi-autonomous coherence which, not merely a reflex of capitalist reification and rationalization, also

in some measure serves to compensate for the dehumanization of experience reification brings with it, and to rectify the otherwise intolerable effects of the new process. (Jameson, *Political Unconscious,* 62–63).

What I especially want to stress in Emerson's book is the sense of isolation and semi-autonomy that comes from the rationalization of the "older unities."

In his own discussion of *English Traits* David M. Robinson anticipates much of my general argument about England's rationalization, including Emerson's sense that this modernization involves American's own future as well (see Robinson, 113–20). Robinson, however, sees *English Traits* as fundamentally a critique of English commercialism, while my argument is that Emerson's reaction is much more inchoate and conflicted. For the assertion that Emerson's book is in fact a "sustained apologia for modern liberal culture," see Bercovitch, "Emerson," 653. See also Ellison, "Edge of Urbanity," 106–7.

24. See Robinson, 113–14; Ellison, "Edge of Urbanity," 106–7; and Phyllis Coe, "Emerson, England, and Fate," in Levin, 98.

25. Ellison, "Edge of Urbanity," 97–98.

26. Ibid., 98.

27. William Wordsworth, *The Prelude: 1799, 1805, 1850,* ed. Jonathan Wordsworth, M. H. Abrams, and Stephen Gill (New York: Norton, 1979), 455.

28. *The Prelude* would certainly have been accessible to Emerson before the publication of *English Traits.* Henry Wadsworth Longfellow mentions the work in his journal in 1850; Emerson mentions it, rather coolly, in his journal in 1858 (Wordsworth, Abrams, and Gill, 561). My argument does not really depend, however, on whether Emerson knew of and read *The Prelude* before the publication of *English Traits,* in the sense that the dissonances of literary property in Emerson belong to a process of modernization which circumscribes the "intentionality" of Emerson's authorial production.

Moreover, these dissonances need not simply reify Wordsworth's claim to Salisbury Plain in *The Prelude;* consider, for example, Sacvan Bercovitch's remark that "several critics have argued that the Scholar [in Emerson's essay 'The American Scholar' (1837)] is the protagonist of an unwritten *Prelude.*" (Sacvan Bercovitch, "Emerson the Prophet: Romanticism, Puritanism, and Auto-American Biography," in Bloom, *Ralph Waldo Emerson,* 36).

29. Emerson in fact qualifies Carlyle's anger over the sheep walk, suggesting in effect that his friend has interpreted the scene incorrectly: "But I heard afterwards that it is not an economy to cultivate this land, which only yields one crop on being broken up, and is then spoiled" (*ET,* 652).

30. Bercovitch, "Emerson the Prophet," 33–34; and Robinson, 131.

31. Ellison, "Edge of Urbanity," 102.

32. Gayatri Chakravorty Spivak, "The Making of Americans, the Teaching of English, and the Future of Culture Studies," *New Literary History* 21 (1990): 783–84.

33. Robinson, 129–31. The image of a "manacled" North is from Emer-

son's 1851 address on the Fugitive Slave Act. See also Gougeon, 152–56, 160–65.

34. Sharon Cameron, "Representing Grief: Emerson's 'Experience,' " in *The New American Studies: Essays from "Representation,"* ed. Philip Fisher (Berkeley: U of California P, 1991), 201–27.

35. Ibid., 227.

36. Ralph Waldo Emerson, "Experience," in McQuade, 326, 343.

37. Cameron, 227.

38. For a discussion of Carlyle's racist views before and during the American Civil War and Emerson's response to them, see Kenneth Marc Harris, *Carlyle and Emerson: Their Long Debate* (Cambridge: Harvard UP, 1978), 155–57; and Gougeon, 180–81, 302–22. For a discussion of Emerson's criticism of the British during the Civil War, see Gougeon, 303–19. Bloom actually does discuss Carlyle's essay in *Agon;* his argument is, however, to interpret the horrific psychosexual and racist images in the essay as signs of "devouring time, Kronos" (*A,* 156).

39. The locus classicus for this view of a Romantic confederacy is, of course, Mark Twain's highly critical set of comments about the pernicious influence of Sir Walter Scott on the readers of the Confederate South (Samuel Clemens, *The Writings of Mark Twain,* 37 vols. [New York: G. Wells, 1923], 12:376–77). While Twain's comments have oftentimes been dismissed as hyperbole, see, for counterarguments, Rollin G. Osterweis, *Romanticism and Nationalism in the Old South* (New Haven: Yale UP, 1949); Grace Warren Landrum, "Sir Walter Scott and His Literary Rivals in the Old South," *American Literature* 2 (1930): 256–76; and James K. Chandler, "The Historical Novel Goes to Hollywood: Scott, Griffith, and Film Epic Today," in *The Romantics and Us: Essays on Literature and Culture,* ed. Gene W. Ruoff (New Brunswick: Rutgers UP, 1990), 264–66. In recuperating Twain's argument, Chandler argues for a conjunction between Scott's Highland novels and the group identity of the earliest forms of the Ku Klux Klan, including the antebellum Knights of the Golden Circle.

40. Harold Bloom, *The American Religion: The Emergence of the Post-Christian Nation* (New York: Simon and Schuster, 1992), 16–17. All further references to *The American Religion,* abbreviated *AR,* will appear in the text.

41. The publisher for Bloom's main works on poetic influence in the 1970s and early 1980s is either Oxford or Yale. The publisher for *Poetics of Influence* (1988), a collection of old and new essays, is Henry R. Schwab; the publisher for *Book of J* is Grove Weidenfeld; the publisher for *The American Religion* is Simon and Schuster.

42. West, 35–41.

43. One constant shared by those earlier works and *The American Religion* is Bloom's disdain for the politicized academy: "Anti-intellectualism pervades American political, social, and moral life, and its answering chorus is the political correctness of the academic pseudo-Left" (*AR,* 43–44).

## Epilogue: Fantastic Futures, Postmodern Jacobins

1. William Hazlitt, cited in Thomas McFarland, "Thoughts on a Twenty-First Anniversary," in "How It Was," ed. David Wagenknecht, *Studies in Romanticism* 21 (1982): 563.

2. Orville Schell, "China's Spring," *New York Review of Books*, 29 June 1989, 6.

3. Paul de Man, *Blindness and Insight: Essays in the Rhetoric of Contemporary Criticism*, 2d ed. (Minneapolis: U of Minnesota P, 1983), 187–208; and Fredric Jameson, *The Political Unconscious: Narrative as a Socially Symbolic Act* (Ithaca: Cornell UP, 1981), 28–35.

4. For two different views on the problems of mediating Western discourse in relation to contemporary China, see Rey Chow, "Violence in the Other Country: Preliminary Remarks on the 'China Crisis,' June 1989," *Radical America* 22 (1988): 23–32; Zhang Longxi, "Western Theory and Chinese Reality," *Critical Inquiry* 19 (1992): 105–30.

5. T. D. Allman, "The Crushing Wheel of China," *Vanity Fair*, October 1989, 236.

6. *Modernity* is, of course, a particularly charged word to apply to a non-European situation, one that resonates with imperialist projects of Western modernization and colonization. A large part of the "shock" of the Western subject comes, then, from the way the force of the student's words exceed these very resonances.

# Index

Abrams, M. H., 41, 42, 70, 75, 90, 96, 108, 146, 191n. 9, 197n. 13, 205nn. 32 and 34; *Mirror and the Lamp,* 5, 13; *Natural Supernaturalism,* 90, 189n. 1, 203n. 18
Adorno, Theodor, 79
aestheticism, 79. *See also* ideology
allegories of praxis, 69, 105, 106
allegory, 41–42, 43–45, 48, 168–69, 186–87. *See also* de Man, Paul
Allman, T. D., "The Crushing Wheel of China," 187–88
Althusser, Louis, 191n. 13, 192n. 10
American Sublime, 8, 149, 151, 152–55, 156, 174, 176, 177, 178, 180, 181, 184, 218n. 15. *See also* Bloom, Harold
anxiety of influence, 146, 148, 149, 152, 168. *See also* Bloom, Harold
apostasy, trope of, 39, 40, 51, 196n. 3. *See also* Christensen, Jerome; de Man, Paul
Arac, Jonathan, *Critical Geneaologies,* 63, 105–51, 189n. 1, 192n. 6, 196n. 7, 217n. 7
Arc de Triomphe, 63, 200n. 43

Aske, Martin, *Keats and Hellenism,* 21, 22–23, 192n. 11
askesis, 144, 152–54, 155, 158, 165–66, 175, 176. *See also* Bloom, Harold
Austen, Jane, 114, 209n. 14

Babbitt, Irving, *Rousseau and Romanticism,* 55, 119, 210n. 24, 215n. 49
Baillie, Joanna, 116
Bakhtin, Mikhail, 79, 87
Barthes, Roland, *Mythologies,* 88
Barzun, Jacques, "Peter Viereck's *Metapolotics,*" 195n. 34
Bercovitch, Sacvan: "Emerson, Individualism, and the Ambiguities of Dissent," 156, 217n. 14, 219n. 23; "Emerson the Prophet," 171, 219n. 28
Betham, Mary, 116
biology and culture, nature and culture, language and culture, language and biology, 110–20
Blake, William, 2, 79, 80, 84, 203n. 16; and Albion, as cosmic giant, 153, 155, 159, 171, 217n. 10

Bloch, Ernest, 106
Bloom, Harold, 5, 6, 8, 9, 47, 108, 145–57, 160, 168, 173–81, 182, 183–84, 216n. 3, 217n. 7, 218n. 21; *Agon,* 147–48, 153, 154–55, 178, 216nn. 1 and 2, 220n. 38; *The American Religion,* 177–81, 184, 220n. 43; *The Anxiety of Influence,* 152, 155; Bloomian pragmatics, 8, 147–48, 216n. 2; *Book of J,* 179; *Figures of Capable Imagination,* 217n. 13; *Kabbalah and Criticism,* 179; *A Map of Misreading,* 144–45, 152, 153, 155; *Poetry and Repression,* 152, 153, 154; *Ralph Waldo Emerson,* 218n. 15; *The Ringers in the Tower,* 149; *Romanticism and Consciousness,* 38, 145; *Shelley's Mythmaking,* 145, 197nn. 12 and 13. See also American Sublime; anxiety of influence; askesis; cosmic giant; daemonization; Romanticism
bluestocking circle, 116
Bolshevism, 5
Bonaparte, Napolèon, 46, 63, 64, 67, 92, 97, 101, 192n. 13, 200nn. 43 and 44, 205n. 37
Bonaventure Hotel, 17, 18, 25
Bornstein, George, *Transformation of Romanticism in Yeats, Eliot and Stevens,* 5
Boulton, James T., *The Language of Politics in the Age of Wilkes and Burke,* 215n. 50, 216n. 54
bourgeois, 65, 81; as class aspiration, 20–22
Brenkman, John, "Fascist Commitments," 201n. 51
Brinton, Crane, 153; *The Politics of the English Romanticists,* 78
British Museum, 20–21, 192n. 12
Brontë, Charlotte, 209n. 14; *Villette,* 118–19
Brooks, Cleanth, 19
Brown, Marshall, "Romanticism and Enlightenment," 203n. 16
Burke, Edmund, 46, 53–63, 121, 199nn. 34, 35, and 38, 200n. 40, 216n. 55; *Letters to a Member of the National Assembly,* 58; *Philosophical Enquiry into the Origin of Our Ideas of the Sublime and the Beautiful,* 215n. 51; *Reflections on the Revolution in France,* 59–61, 132–33, 135, 215n. 50
Burke, Kenneth, 149
Butler, Judith, *Gender Trouble,* 107
Butler, Marilyn, *Romantics, Rebels, and Reactionaries,* 2, 189n. 2
Byron, Lord, 2, 15, 79, 90

Calinescu, Matei, *Five Faces of Modernity,* 190n. 5
Cameron, David, *The Social Thought of Rousseau and Burke,* 199n. 35
Cameron, Kenneth Neill, 79, 80; *Shelley: The Golden Years,* 47, 78, 197n. 12
Cameron, Sharon, "Representing Grief," 175–76
capitalism, 17, 18, 87, 105, 164, 180
Carlyle, Thomas, 159, 166, 168, 176, 219n. 29, 220n. 38; *On Heroes, Hero Worship, and the Heroic in History,* 7; "Occasional Discourse on the Nigger Question," 176
Cavell, Stanley, *In Quest of the Ordinary,* 1, 209n. 17
Chandler, James K.: "The Historical Novel Goes to Hollywood," 220n. 39; "Representative Men, Spirits of the Age, and Other Romantic Types," 191n. 12, *Wordsworth's Second Nature,* 199n. 38, 203n. 20, 207n. 4, 216n. 53
Charles I, 60, 62
Chase, Cynthia: "Giving Face to a Name," 197n. 15; "Trappings of an Education toward What We Do Not Yet Have," 193n. 24, 198n. 18
Chesterfield, Lord, 127
Chow, Rey: "Response," 207n. 3; "Violence in the Other Country," 221n. 4
Christensen, Jerome, 42–43, 51 " 'Like a Guilty Thing Surprised': Deconstruction, Coleridge, and the

Apostasy of Criticism," 38–40, 196n. 3. *See also* apostasy

Claridge, Laura, review of *The Contours of Masculine Desire,* 210n. 21

Coleridge, Samuel Taylor, 2, 83, 90, 161; *Biographia Literaria,* 10, 13; "Kubla Khan," 169, 206n. 44; letter to Mary Evans, 26; *The Statesman's Manual,* 41

collective versus individual, 21–22. *See also* history; self

Continental theory, 148

cosmic giant, optics of, 153–56, 157, 158–60, 163, 171, 176, 217n. 10. *See also* Bloom, Harold

cryptonormativism, 189–90n. 4. *See also* Habermas, Jürgen

Curran, Stuart, "Romantic Poetry: The I Altered," 116

daemonization, 151–55, 175, 181. *See also* Bloom, Harold

de Beauvoir, Simone, 218

deconstruction, 7, 10, 27, 38–40, 42–43, 45–46, 53, 63, 64, 65, 66, 67–68, 70, 72, 83–84, 114, 117, 122, 146–47, 191n. 11, 194n. 27, 196nn. 6 and 7, 200n. 42, 201n. 50, 204n. 22, 208n. 10; American deconstruction, 8, 83, 147. *See also* de Man, Paul; Yale School

de Man, Paul, 6, 7, 8, 9, 13, 15, 27, 35, 39–40, 66–68, 102, 104–5, 108, 117, 122, 140, 142, 145, 146–47, 154, 156, 183, 186, 194nn. 27 and 28, 197n. 13, 198n. 19; "Aesthetic Formulation," 198n. 18; "Autobiography as Defacement," 197n. 15; *Blindness and Insight,* 40–42, 43–44, 54, 64, 190n. 5; "The Resistance to Theory," 64, 191n. 11; "The Rhetoric of Blindness," 54; *The Rhetoric of Romanticism,* 38–39, 207n. 6; "The Rhetoric of Temporality," 38, 40–45, 47, 67–68, 196n. 10, 197n. 17; "Shelley Disfigured," 8, 40, 46–57, 63, 65, 67–68, 70, 72, 76, 196n. 4, 197n. 17;

"Wordsworth and Hölderlin," 44, 45, 196n. 10. *See also* allegory; apostasy; deconstruction; disfigurement; symbol; words (thought) and deeds

Derrida, Jacques, 13, 73, 144, 146; "That Dangerous Supplement . . . ," 215n. 48; "The Law of Genre," 192n. 5; "Like the Sound of the Sea Deep within a Shell," 196n. 4; *Specters of Marx,* 1, 182

dialectical: dialectical historicism, 12; dialectical reading, 2, 4, 9–10, 12, 16–17, 25, 27, 32, 33, 36, 44, 46, 49, 53, 58, 65–68, 70, 81, 89, 90–91, 94, 102, 104, 109, 113, 117, 119, 121, 122, 134, 135, 142, 146, 149–50, 155–56, 176, 188. *See also* past-present dialectic

Dilettanti Society, 20

disfigurement, 46, 49–58, 63, 64, 65, 67, 122. *See also* de Man, Paul; history

Duffy, Edward, *Rousseau in England,* 55–56, 57, 198n. 27, 199n. 34, 212n. 33, 214n. 48

Eagleton, Terry, 80, 84

Elgin Marbles, 20

Eliot, T. S., 146

Ellison, Julie: *Delicate Subjects,* 211n. 27; "Edge of Urbanity," 157, 167, 171, 219nn. 23 and 24; *Emerson's Romantic Style,* 218n. 21

Emerson, Ralph Waldo, 9, 148–51, 152–53, 178–79, 180–81, 216n. 2, 217nn. 13 and 14, 220n. 38; "The American Scholar," 219n. 28; and American self, 148–49; *The Conduct of His Life,* 158; *Emerson in His Journals,* 150; *English Traits,* 144, 149–50, 155–77, 184, 219nn. 23, 28, and 29; "Experience," 175–76; "Fate," 158; "Nature," 155–53; "Power," 218n. 22; *Representative Men,* 7, 157; "Wealth," 165

emigré(s), 27, 35–36, 195n. 38

Enlightenment, 14, 56–57, 64, 67, 78, 81, 87, 91, 106, 120–21, 125, 134,

Enlightenment (*continued*)
140, 183, 203n. 16; reason during the, 57, 123, 124, 129, 141, 198n. 27; revolutionary politics of, 56–65. *See also* Romanticism, revolutionary, of the Enlightenment
Erdman, David, 79, 80; *Blake: Prophet against Empire,* 78
Ewen, Frederick, "Heinrich Heine: Humanity's Soldier," 97

fascism, 5, 12, 26–28, 30–32, 43, 66, 67, 193n. 23, 195nn. 35 and 36
feminism, 6, 8, 107–10, 112–16, 117, 119–23, 126, 135, 140, 141–43, 146–47, 210n. 20, 212n. 35, 216n. 1; feminist studies, 113, 120, 141, 207nn. 3 and 6, 208nn. 10 and 13, 209n. 18; intellectual genealogies of, 8
Ferguson, Frances: "On the Numbers of Romanticism," 78, 202n. 15; "Wollstonecraft Our Contemporary," 213n. 39
Fisher, Philip, 201n. 3, 202n. 13; "A Museum with One Work Inside," 21, 192n. 11
formalism, 67, 72–74, 76–77, 83–84, 87, 89, 104, 201nn. 4 and 5, 204n. 22, 210n. 25
Foucault, Michel, 72, 74, 77, 104, 189n. 4, 202n. 13; *Language, Counter-Memory, Practice,* 122
France, 20, 55–58, 59, 63, 97, 100–101, 102, 103, 122–23, 125, 128; Boulevard Monmartre, 92
France, Peter, *Rousseau: Confessions,* 54
Franco-Prussian War, 101
Frederick William III, 97
French Revolution: of 1789, 10, 12, 14, 39, 55–57, 59, 62, 63, 65, 81, 87, 97, 122–23, 133, 135, 184–86, 192n. 13, 195n. 34, 199n. 38, 200n. 43, 203n. 15; July Revolution of 1830, 101
Freud, Sigmund, 122
Frye, Northrop, 75, 146, 151, 191n. 9; "The Drunken Boat," 193n. 20;

*Fearful Symmetry,* 5; "Theory of Symbols," 217n. 10
Fugitive Slave Act (1850), 174, 176, 218n. 15, 220n. 33
Fukuyama, Francis, 15
futurity, 87, 89, 91, 94, 96–100, 101, 106, 180, 183, 185, 186; progressive, 91, 103, 104, 183

Gallagher, Catherine, "Marxism and the New Historicism," 201n. 50
Germany, 31, 32, 34, 35, 89, 95–103, 206n. 42; imperialism, 89, 97, 205n. 37; nationalism, 98, 195nn. 34 and 35, 206n. 42
Gilbert, Sandra, and Susan Gubar, *Madwoman in the Attic,* 122, 208n. 10
Glorious Revolution of 1688, 60
Gnosticism, American, 178
Godwin, William, 122, 123, 212n. 33
Gougeon, Len, *Virtue's Hero,* 157, 218nn. 14 and 16, 220nn. 33 and 38
Graff, Gerald, "Co-optation," 80, 201n. 3
Gramsci, Antonio, 179, 216n. 56

Habermas, Jürgen, 14, 15; "Modernity versus Postmodernity," 191n. 1; *The Philosophical Discourse of Modernity,* 15, 189–90n. 4, 192n. 3
Hamacher, Werner, et al., *Responses: On Paul de Man's Wartime Journalism,* 193n. 23
Hartman, Geoffrey, 108
Hazlitt, William, 184–86; *Spirit of the Age,* 7
Hegel, Georg Wilhelm, 9, 205n. 32
hegemonic, concept of, 141–42, 213n. 41, 216n. 56
Heidegger, Martin, 24, 148, 149
Heine, Heinrich, 9, 15, 78, 88–89, 122, 142, 183, 194n. 31, 205n. 37, 206n. 44; *Concerning the History of Religion and Philosophy in Germany,* 206n. 42; *Heinrich Heine,* 206n. 45; *Oeuvres complètes,* 96–97, 101; *The Romantic School,* 70,

88–91, 97, 205n. 34, 206n. 42; on Uhland, 91–105
Hellenism, 21; neo-Hellenism, 21, 22, 23, 48, 192n. 11
Hemans, Felicia, 116, 209n. 19
historical revision(ism), 80–81, 203n. 21
history, definitions of, 81, 88, 94, 102–3, 104–5, 141, 158, 203n. 21; collective history, 62 (*see also* collective versus individual; self); *Geistesgeschichte,* 28–29, 194n. 27; historical consciousness, 90, 92, 192n. 11; historical disfigurement, 52, 55; historical identity, 88; historical reflexivity, 95. *See also* Romanticism, revisions of
history of ideas, 28, 32, 34, 70
Hitlerism, 30. *See also* fascism; Nazism
Hodson, Margaret, 116
Hogle, Jerrold E., *Shelley's Process,* 200n. 45
Holmes, Oliver Wendell, *Ralph Waldo Emerson,* 156, 217n. 14
Homans, Margaret, 115, 211n. 27; *Bearing the Word,* 114, 118, 208n. 13, 210n. 25; *Women Writers and Poetic Identity,* 114

idealism, 80, 82–83, 84–85, 86
ideological criticism, 71, 80–81, 84, 93, 102, 146, 208n. 10. *See also* McGann, Jerome
ideology, 86, 102, 106, 150, 155; aesthetic, 43; Romantic, 79, 90, 103, 140. *See also* McGann, Jerome
Industrial Revolution, 85
intellectual genealogies, 80, 149. *See also* feminism
Ireland, 161–63; Great Famine, the, 162; "Irish Problem," 162–63, 218n. 22
Irigaray, Luce, 211n. 30

Jack, Ian, *Keats and the Mirror of Art,* 193n. 14
Jacobin(ism), 39, 56, 80, 183–84; anti-Jacobin, 212n. 33; postmodern Jacobin, 106, 182–84, 187, 188
Jacobin imaginary, 14, 65–66, 88
Jacobus, Mary, 115, 117, 118–19, 140; "Buried Letter," 124, 209n. 13, 211n. 27; "Difference of View," 212n. 36; *Reading Woman,* 114, 211n. 30, 212n. 35; *Romanticism, Writing, and Sexual Difference,* 108–9, 210n. 25, 211nn. 27 and 29
James, William, 149, 216n. 2
Jameson, Fredric, 7, 12, 80, 186; "Periodizing the 60s," 6, 191n. 10; *The Political Unconscious,* 191n. 14, 192n. 10, 200n. 41, 217n. 10, 218n. 23; *Postmodernism, or The Cultural Logic of Late Capitalism,* 16–19, 23, 24, 191n. 10, 192nn. 7–9
*Journal of the History of Ideas,* 33, 195n. 35

Kant, Immanuel, 16, 43, 78
Kaplan, Cora, "Wild Nights: Pleasure/Sexuality/Feminism," 124, 212nn. 35 and 36, 214n. 45
Kaufmann, David, "Thanks for the Memory," 206n. 48
Keats, John, 2, 7, 12–13, 192n. 11, 193n. 14, 198n. 27; "Ode on a Grecian Urn," 16–17, 19–24, 192n. 11; "To Autumn," 84–85, 86–87
Klancher, Jon, 78, 82, 146; "English Romanticism and Cultural Production," 73–75, 190nn. 7 and 8, 194n. 31, 202n. 12, 204n. 23; "Romantic Criticism and the Meanings of the French Revolution," 190n. 7, 195n. 34
Kosellek, Reinhart, *Futures Past,* 190n. 5

Lacan, Jacques, 122, 156, 171, 192n. 10
La Capra, Dominick, *Soundings in Critical Theory,* 191n. 13, 198n. 18
Laclau, Ernesto, and Chantal Mouffe, 19; *Hegemony and Socialist Strategy,* 14, 125–26, 192n. 3, 213n. 41,

Laclau, Ernesto (*continued*) 216n. 56; "Post-Marxism without Apologies," 204n. 24; "Totalitarianism and Moral Indignation," 201n. 51
Langbauer, Laurie, "An Early Romance," 212–13n. 36, 214n. 47
Lanser, Sue, 211n. 30
Left/leftist, 39–40, 77, 87, 104, 105–6, 180, 183; leftist criticism, 65, 66, 81, 104, 147; New Left activism, 67, 201n. 50
Leland, Charles, 97; *The Works of Heinrich Heine* (trans.), 101
Lentricchia, Frank, *After the New Criticism,* 216n. 3, 217n. 7; *Criticism and Social Change,* 196n. 3, 201n. 49
*Le Soir,* 39, 40, 43, 67, 73
Levinson, Marjorie, "Back to the Future," 76, 202n. 12; *Keats's Life of Allegory,* 193n. 14; *Rethinking Historicism,* 191n. 13; *Wordsworth's Great Period Poems,* 204n. 23
Lindenberger, Herbert, 14, 72, 190nn. 7 and 8; *The History in Literature,* 70–71, 189n. 1, 192n. 2, 201n. 1
Liu, Alan, "The Power of Formalism," 202nn. 5, 10, and 12; *Wordsworth: The Sense of History,* 76, 202n. 12
Locke, John, 57
Longfellow, Henry Wadsworth, 219n. 28
Louis XIV, 127
Louis XVI, 60, 62
Lovejoy, A. O., 7, 12, 15, 26, 40, 43, 73, 117, 193n. 23, 194n. 29; "The Meaning of Romanticism for the Historian of Ideas," 26–36, 195n. 34; "On the Discrimination of Romanticisms," 33; "Reply to Professor Spitzer," 27–30
Lukács, George, 17, 218n. 23
Lundberg, Ferdinand, and Marynia Farnham, *Modern Woman,* 211n. 31

Lyotard, François, 17; *The Differend,* 203n. 21; *The Postmodern Condition,* 200n. 43

Macaulay, Catherine, 216n. 52
Marr, David, *American Worlds since Emerson,* 217n. 14
Marx, Karl, 36, 86, 87, 88, 102, 122, 165; *The Eighteenth Brumaire of Louis Bonaparte,* 46, 64–65, 67–68, 81; *The German Ideology,* 81
Marxism/Marxist theory, 6, 13, 19, 71, 72–73, 82, 83, 86, 87–88, 105–6, 122, 142, 147, 180, 183–84, 204n. 22, 207n. 3; British, 81; post-Marxism, 65, 71, 72, 77. *See also* McGann, Jerome
materialism, 32, 75, 82–86, 87–88, 103–4, 147, 173, 180, 204nn. 23 and 24; dialectical, 87, 88, 104; historiography of, 103
materialism theory, 29, 103. *See also* McGann, Jerome
McDowell, Paula, 211n. 30
McFarland, Thomas, "Thoughts on a Twenty-First Anniversary," 185
McGann, Jerome, 6, 8, 9, 15, 17, 108, 122, 140, 141, 142, 146, 147, 183, 203n. 18, 205n. 34, 206n. 44, 207n. 6; *The Beauty of Inflections,* 84, 203n. 23; "The Case of *The Ambassadors* and the Textual Condition," 204n. 23; *A Critique of Modern Textual Criticism,* 204n. 23; "Keats and the Historical Method in Literary Criticism," 84, 86–88; "Poem and Ideology," 204n. 25; "Rethinking Romanticism," 69, 104, 202n. 12, 204n. 23, 205n. 32; *The Romantic Ideology,* 43, 52–53, 71, 75–76, 78, 79, 81–82, 83–84, 88–106, 203n. 21, 204n. 22; *Social Values and Poetic Acts,* 83, 194n. 28, 204nn. 22 and 23. *See also* ideological criticism; ideology; Marxism/Marxist theory; materialism; past-present dialectic
Mellor, Anne, 118, 210n. 23; *Romanticism and Feminism,* 114; *Roman-*

*ticism and Gender,* 117–18, 209nn. 18 and 19
Michaels, Walter Benn, 202n. 13; *The Gold Standard and the Logic of Naturalism,* 201n. 3
migration, 148, 176; reverse trans-Atlantic crossing, 149–50, 160, 161. *See also* Romanticism
Millet, Kate, 122
Milton, John, 4, 148, 153
Mitchell, W. J. T.: *Iconology,* 60, 216n. 55; "Visible Language," 203n. 16
modernism, 4–5, 14, 17, 25, 119, 146; high modernism, 4–5, 16, 75
modernity, 3–7, 10–11, 12, 13–18, 19, 22–25, 35, 38, 39, 70, 73, 76, 79–80, 89, 96, 99, 101, 110, 121–22, 141, 143, 146–47, 148, 150, 156–57, 165, 173, 183–85, 187–88, 189n. 1, 190n. 5, 221n. 6; fantastic modernity, 3–4, 15, 121, 146, 183, 189n. 1
modernization, 166, 169, 170, 172–73, 184, 219n. 23
Montrose, Louis, "Professing the Renaissance," 75
monumentalization, 8, 24, 32, 46, 51–58, 62–66, 122–23, 124, 140, 142. *See also* de Man, Paul
Mouffe, Chantal, 19; *Hegemony and Socialist Strategy,* 14, 125–26; "Radical Modernism: Modern or Postmodern?" 65
Mount Pisgah, 135, 139, 140
museums, 21–22; in France, 192n. 13. *See also* British Museum

Nazism, 29, 30, 31, 32, 34, 35, 39; German National Socialism, 33, 35. *See also* fascism; Hitlerism
New Criticism, 10, 72, 151, 190n. 9
New Historicism, 78–79, 81, 82, 85, 90, 103, 104, 202nn. 5 and 12; Renaissance New Historicism, 71, 73–75, 76–77, 83
Nicoloff, Philip, *Emerson on Race and History,* 157
Nietzsche, Fredrich, 4, 145, 149, 190n. 6; *Twilight of the Idols,* 190n. 6
Norris, Christopher, 44; *Paul de Man,* 43, 77, 196nn. 9 and 10

oppositional criticism, 76, 77, 79–83, 88–89, 91, 102, 105–6, 146–47, 201n. 3

passion and reason, 123, 124–25, 131, 133–35, 136–40, 141, 143
past-present dialectic, 90
patrimony, 112, 113–14
Paine, Thomas, *The Rights of Man,* 133
Pease, Donald: "New Americanists," 202n. 13; *Visionary Compacts,* 217n. 7
Peckham, Morse, 5
Peterloo Massacre, 84, 86, 87
Peters, Rev. Hugh, 60, 62, 200n. 40
phenomenology, 70
Piozzi, Hester Lynch, 127
Pippin, Robert P., *Modernism as a Philosophical Problem,* 190n. 5
Poovey, Mary, *The Proper Lady and the Woman Writer,* 114, 115, 124, 208n. 13, 211n. 27, 212nn. 35 and 36, 216n. 53
Porter, Carolyn, "Are We Being Historical Yet?" 202n. 5
postmodernism, 12–19, 23, 24–25, 71, 74, 80, 106, 182–84, 186–87; historicism, 4; modernity, 7, 18, 19, 24–25, 147; theory, 1–7, 9, 79, 108–9, 191n. 11
poststructuralist theory, 6, 142, 148
Price, Dr. Richard, 59–61, 62, 135, 216n. 55
property, 165–66, 168, 172, 174
psychoanalysis, 142, 147

race/racial theory, 157–59, 163–64, 165, 176, 218n. 18, 220n. 38
Rajan, Tilottama: "Displacing Post-Structuralism," 42, 196n. 6; *The Supplement of Reading,* 196n. 6
rationalization, 165–66, 167, 168–69, 171–72, 174, 176, 218n. 23

real, 35, 84, 192n. 10; the historical real, 17, 18, 36, 175
reception theory, 31
reflexivity, 12, 13, 16–19, 23, 24, 29, 36, 77, 82, 119, 125, 135, 140, 158–59, 162, 164, 175, 176, 180, 185, 186; self-, 12, 22, 27, 36, 80, 91, 111, 119, 121, 158, 172, 183
Reign of Terror, 123
Reiss, Timothy J., "Revolution in Bounds," 213n. 39
Renaissance, 71, 75
Renaissance studies, 72, 73, 76, 77, 83
representative figure(s), 7–9, 78, 79, 142–43, 147, 179
Retamar, Roberto Fernandez, "Caliban: Notes towards a Discussion of Culture," 195n. 38
Richardson, Alan, "Romanticism and the Colonization of the Feminine," 119, 210nn. 24 and 27
Riley, Denise, "Am I That Name?" 213n. 37
Robinson, David M., *Emerson and the Conduct of Life,* 157, 174, 216n. 2, 218n. 16, 219nn. 23 and 24
Robinson, Mary, 116
Rogers, Katharine M., *Female Biography,* 211nn. 31 and 32
Roman Empire, 61–62, 65; Republicanism, 61, 65
Romantic(ism), 1–11, 13–17, 23, 24–25, 27–29, 30–34, 36, 38, 39, 41–45, 47–48, 55, 58, 66, 69–71, 72–73, 75–85, 89–90, 92–93, 101–3, 105, 106, 108–11, 112–22, 141, 142–43, 145, 148, 167, 182–84, 185–88; American, 8, 79, 148–50, 151, 152, 155, 176–77, 178, 180–81, 202n. 7; archival recovery of women writers, 116–20, 189n. 3, 208nn. 12 and 13, 216n. 1; Bloom's migratory narratives of, 217n. 4; English, 2, 39, 41, 47, 70, 73, 78, 89–90, 96, 102, 111, 116, 119, 145–49, 150, 155, 167–68, 176, 190n. 8, 205nn. 32 and 34, 206n. 44; German, 26–27, 31–32, 36, 89, 92–102, 148, 194n. 31; High Romanticism, 210n. 26; and periodization, 48, 116; revisions of, 6, 7, 41, 44–45, 80–82, 102, 105, 118; revolutionary, of the Enlightenment, 14, 81, 91, 120, 183; transmission of, 31–36, 40, 42, 75–76, 77–79, 82–85, 90, 108, 109, 110, 148. *See also* historical revision(ism); history
Romantic historicism, 6, 73, 77–82, 83–85, 89, 183. *See also* Romantic studies
Romantic imagination, 132, 140
Romanticists, 5, 11, 14, 24–25, 90, 146, 203n. 18
Romantic knowledge, 2, 6, 7, 25, 75, 80, 108, 146, 185
Romantic modernity, 25, 190n. 9
Romantic studies, 2, 4, 5, 6, 8, 16, 40, 45, 70, 71, 73, 74–76, 81, 82–83, 85, 103, 107, 109, 111, 113–15, 116, 117, 145, 147, 151, 185, 190n. 7, 191n. 12, 208n. 13, 211n. 27; '80s Romanticist historiography, 8, 43, 71, 77–80, 81, 83, 84, 88, 102, 105, 106, 111, 146, 203n. 21, 207n. 6; post-Vietnam generation of, 6–7, 78, 145, 185; post–World War II, 5, 6, 25, 70, 75–76, 79, 80, 83, 108, 146, 148, 190nn. 8 and 9
Rorty, Richard, 149, 216n. 2
Rosetta Stone, 20
Ross, Marlon, 118; *The Contours of Masculine Desire,* 118, 119, 208n. 7, 209nn. 15 and 19, 210nn. 21, 24, 26, and 27, 216n. 1
Rousseau, Jean-Jacques, 13, 46, 49–50, 52, 54–59, 61, 62, 63–64, 78, 122–27, 131–34, 140, 166, 198n. 20, 199nn. 34, 35, and 38, 200n. 44, 207n. 6, 211n. 32, 215nn. 49 and 51; *Confessions,* 54, 56, 58, 212n. 33, 214–15n. 48; *Dialogues,* 54; *Emile,* 131–32, 211n. 29, 213n. 42; *Essay on the Origin of Languages,* 59, 199n. 37; *Reveries of*

230 Index

*the Solitary Walker,* 54; *Social Contract,* 58
Rusk, Ralph, *The Life of Ralph Waldo Emerson,* 156, 217n. 14

Salisbury Plain, 167–68, 219n. 28
Sammons, Jeffrey L., *Heinrich Heine,* 205n. 34
Schell, Orville, "China Spring," 185–86
Schiller, Friedrich, 189n. 1
Schlegel, Friedrich von, 205n. 34
Schmitt, Carl, *Political Romanticism,* 194n. 31
Scott, Sir Walter, 2, 17, 220n. 39
self, 9, 150, 151, 153, 154–56, 158, 159–60, 177–79, 181, 217n. 4; American, 8, 148, 154, 174, 184; vatic, 8, 149, 151–52, 153, 175, 177, 178–79, 181; versus collective experience, 151–57, 158, 177, 179–80
Shelley, Mary, 47, 114, 208n. 7, 209n. 14; *Frankenstein,* 122
Shelley, Percy Bysshe, 2, 7, 9, 16, 54, 78, 79, 80, 87, 88, 122, 142, 207n. 6; *Prometheus Unbound,* 13; "The Triumph of Life," 8, 37, 40, 46–54, 55, 56–68, 183, 197n. 13, 198n. 27, 200nn. 44 and 45
Sidmouth, Viscount, 87
Siskin, Clifford, 202n. 15; *The Historicity of Romantic Discourse,* 76, 78, 189n. 1, 202n. 12
sixties activism, 38, 39, 42, 66, 67, 78
slavery, U.S., 157, 158
Smith, Charlotte, 116; *The Poems of Charlotte Smith,* 208n. 12
Spitzer, Leo, 7, 12, 26, 40, 43, 73, 193n. 23, 194nn. 27 and 32, 195n. 37; " 'Geistesgeschichte' vs. History of Ideas as Applied to Hitlerism," 26–36; *Leo Spitzer: Representative Essays,* 193n. 23
Spivak, Gayatri, "The Making of Americans, the Teaching of English, and the Future of Culture Studies," 173

Stevens, Wallace, 149; "An Ordinary Evening in New Haven," 177
Stonehenge, 156, 159, 166–68, 169, 173, 176
Strier, Richard, 213n. 44, 214n. 47
Swift, Jonathan, 138–39
symbol, 41–42, 43, 45, 75. *See also* de Man, Paul

Tallyrand-Périgord, M., 125
theory and praxis, 11, 25–27, 29, 30–31, 33, 40, 43, 66, 67, 68, 125, 71, 77, 88, 97, 105, 106, 121, 140, 143, 147, 184. *See also* words (thought) and deeds
Thoreau, Henry David, 176
Tiananmen Square, 186, 187
Tighe, Mary, 209n. 19
totalitarianism, 43, 61–62
Twain, Mark, *Huckleberry Finn,* 176, 220n. 39

Uhland, Ludwig, 89–103, 194n. 31, 205nn. 34 and 37, 206n. 44; "Der Schäfer," 92–94, 100; "Vorwärts," 92, 97, 100, 101–2, 103
United Kingdom: England, 12, 57, 60, 63–64, 79, 84, 119, 126, 127–28, 130, 144, 149–50, 156, 159–74, 176, 184, 194n. 32, 219n. 23; London, 164
United States, 34, 35, 79, 85, 122, 145, 148n. 50, 153, 155, 156n. 57, 159, 162n. 64, 166, 170n. 81, 182, 184, 187, 188, 194n. 32, 218n. 22, 219n. 23; Civil War, 150, 157, 176, 220n. 38; compared with India, 173; war with Iraq, 177, 178n. 79; war with Mexico, 179

Vattimo, Gianni, 15; *The End of Modernity,* 190n. 6
Viereck, Peter, "Reply," 195nn. 34 and 35
Vogler, Thomas A., "Romanticism and Literary Periods," 25, 189n. 1

War of Liberation, 95, 97–98
Wasserman, Earl, 5, 41, 42; "The

Wasserman, Earl (*continued*)
Grounds of Knowledge," 16, 192n. 6
Waters, Lindsay, "Introduction," *Critical Writings,* 41
Weber, Max, 164, 165, 169, 218n.23
Webster, Daniel, 171
Wellek, René, 5, 78, 108, 190n. 9
West, Cornel, *The American Evasion of Philosophy,* 156, 158–59, 179, 216n. 2
Whicher, Stephen, *Freedom and Fate,* 156, 217n. 14
Whitman, Walt, 149, 176
Williams, Helen Maria, 116
Williams, Raymond, 17, 79, 82, 87; *Culture and Society,* 22, 84, 85–86, 193n. 17, 204n. 27; *Marxism and Literature,* 84–85, 86, 193n. 17; "The Romantic Artist," 84, 86
Wilson, Edmund, *Axel's Castle,* 5
Wimsatt, William K., 41, 42
Wollstonecraft, Mary, 9, 109–10, 114, 122, 209n. 14, 211nn. 29, 30, and 32, 212nn. 35 and 36, 213n. 37; *Mary, A Fiction,* 212n. 36; *A Vindication of the Rights of Men,* 120–21, 215nn. 50 and 51; *A Vindication of the Rights of Woman,* 107, 109, 120–43, 183, 211n. 31, 212n. 33, 213nn. 43 and 44, 214nn. 46–48, 216n. 52; *The Wrongs of Woman; or Maria,* 124, 140
Woodring, Carl, *Politics in English Romantic Poetry,* 78
words (thought) and deeds, 40, 44, 64, 65–66, 67. *See also* de Man, Paul; theory and praxis
Wordsworth, Dorothy, 113–14, 115, 208nn. 7 and 8
Wordsworth, William, 2, 16, 70, 78, 80, 90, 108, 111, 112, 113–14, 117, 119, 161, 167, 203n. 20; "Essay upon Epitaths," 197n. 15; "Michael," 111–12, 207n. 5; *The Prelude,* 77, 167–68, 199n. 34, 219n. 28; "Tintern Abbey," 113
Wordsworth studies, 80, 108, 110, 112, 118
Wright, Jay, "The Eye of God, the Soul's First Vision," 177

Yale School, 38, 83, 108, 145. *See also* deconstruction

Zhang Longxi, "Western Theory and Chinese Reality," 221n. 4
Žižek, Slavoj, 80; *The Sublime Object of Ideology,* 26

Library of Congress Cataloging-in-Publication Data

Wang, Orrin Nan Chung, 1957–
Fantastic modernity : dialectical readings in
romanticism and theory / Orrin N. C. Wang.
   p.  cm.
Includes bibliographical references and index.
ISBN 0-8018-5220-X
   1. Romanticism.  2. Criticism.  I. Title.
PN56.R7W36   1996
809'.9145—dc20         95-35731

**OHIO UNIVERSITY LIBRARY**
Please return this book as soon as you have finished with it. In order to avoid a fine it must be returned by the last date stamped below. All books are subject to recall after two